PARTICIPATORY BUDGETING IN BRAZIL

PARTICIPATORY BUDGETING IN BRAZIL

Contestation, Cooperation, and Accountability

BRIAN WAMPLER

THE PENNSYLVANIA STATE UNIVERSITY PRESS
UNIVERSITY PARK, PENNSYLVANIA

Library of Congress
Cataloging-in-Publication Data

Wampler, Brian.
Participatory budgeting in Brazil : contestation, cooperation, and accountability /
Brian Wampler.
p.   cm.
Includes bibliographical references and index.
ISBN 978-0-271-03253-5   (pbk : alk. paper)
1. Municipal budgets—Brazil.
2. Municipal government—Brazil.
3. Political participation—Brazil.
4. Democracy—Brazil.
I. Title.

HJ9386.W35 2007
352.4'82140981—dc22
2007014504

For Paula

CONTENTS

TABLES AND FIGURES

Tables

Figures

Maps

ACRONYMS

ARENA	Aliança Renovadora Nacional National Renewal Alliance Party
CEU	Centros Educativos Unificado Unified Education Center
CJP	Comissão de Justiça e Paz Commission for Justice and Peace
CSO	civil society organization
HDI	Human Development Index
IBGE	Instituto Brasileiro de Geografia e Estadística Brazilian Institute for Geography and Statistics
IDB	Inter-American Development Bank
MDB	Movimento Democrático Brasileiro Brazilian Democratic Movement
NGO	nongovernmental organization
PB	Participatory Budgeting (Orçamento Participativo [OP])
PC do B	Partido Comunista do Brasil Communist Party of Brazil
PCB	Partido Comunista Brasileiro Brazilian Communist Party
PDT	Partido Democrático Trabalhista Democratic Labor Party
PFL	Partido da Frente Liberal Liberal Front Party
PL	Partido Liberal Liberal Party
PMDB	Partido do Movimento Democrático Brasileiro Brazilian Democratic Movement Party

PPB   Partido Progressista Brasileiro
           Brazilian Progressive Party

PREZEIS   Plano de Regularização de Zonas Especiais de Interesse Social
           Special Planning Zones of Recife

PSB   Partido Socialista Brasileiro
           Brazilian Socialist Party

PSDB   Partido da Social-Democracia Brasileira
           Brazilian Social Democracy Party

PSF   Programa de Saúde Familiar
           Family Health Program

PT   Partido dos Trabalhadores
           Workers' Party

PTB   Partido Trabalhista Brasileiro
           Brazilian Labor Party

PV   Partido Verde
           Green Party

UNICAMP   Universidade Estadual de Campinas
           State University of Campinas

UAMPA   União das Associações de Moradores de Porto Alegre
           Union of Neighborhood Associations

ACKNOWLEDGMENTS

This book is the result of three years of living, studying, and conducting research in Brazil. The work could not have been completed without the strong support of friends, family, research institutions, and funding agencies. In Brazil, Marina Kahn, Pedro Jacobi, Ana Claudia Teixeira, Sonia E. Alvarez, Jose Guilherme Andrade, and Leonardo Avritzer deserve special recognition for their friendship and their efforts on my behalf, as well as long discussions that greatly enriched my understanding of Brazilian politics, culture, history, and society. The warmth and inviting arms of many Brazilians made working on this project a memorable and enjoyable experience. Since this research project is comparative in nature, it required a considerable amount of travel and relocation, which was enriched by my friends' broader networks.

In São Paulo, Pedro Jacobi was an invaluable resource, helping me to design and implement the project. At the Getulio Vargas Foundation (FGV), Peter Spink, Marta Farah, George Avelino, Fernando Abrucio, Ilka Camarotti, and Marco Antonio Teixeira gave me tremendous support. Peter Spink helped provide me with office space at the FGV, which allowed me to get some actual work done. Vera Schattan Coelho, of the Brazilian Center for Analysis and Planning (Centro Brasileiro de Análise e Planejamento, or CEBRAP), and Avelino (FGV) both invited me to do presentations in the spring of 2004 as I was wrapping up my postdoctoral year of research. These presentations allowed me to test out my ideas on informed and engaged audiences. Two graduate research assistants, Fernanda Teles and Edi Augusto, did an excellent job of collecting, organizing, and analyzing data on Participatory Budgeting programs. At Instituto Pólis, Ana Cláudia Teixeira, Maria do Carmo Albuquerque, and Pedro Pontual were friends and key contacts who provided much needed insights and observations about participatory politics. Felix Sanchez, coordinator of São Paulo's participatory budgeting, gave me open access to meetings and government documents, which greatly advanced my understanding of their work. Gustavo Venturi provided extensive feedback on the first several drafts of the survey. Jose Guilherme Andrade, whom I first met in 1995 at a Health Council meeting, is a wonderful friend who greatly enriched my understanding of participatory politics from the state's perspective as well as the inner workings of the Workers' Party (Partido dos Trabalhadores, or PT). Finally, the warmth of Marina Kahn and her children, Mariana and Jerônimo, allowed me to think of their apartment in Pinheiros as my Brazilian home.

In Belo Horizonte, Leonardo Avritzer provided intellectual stimulation through the sharing of ideas and data. His graduate assistant, Lillian Gomes, provided invaluable aid. Maria Auxiliadora Gomes, PB's coordinator, opened her office to me in 1999, 2000, and 2004. In Recife, Feranda Costa, Joanildo Burity, Neide Silva, and Marcus Melo were of enormous support during my six-month stay in 1998 to 1999 and my return visits in 2000 and 2003. In Porto Alegre, Sergio Baierle of Cidade welcomed me with open arms, providing a rich sounding board for my ideas. Assis Brasil and Andre Passos were equally welcoming in Porto Alegre's municipal government. In Rio de Janeiro, Athayde Motta, Leonardo Melo, João Sucuripira, Andre Campos, and Liz Leeds were important friends and influences. Finally, in Campinas, while I was in residence at the State University of Campinas (Universidade Estadual de Campinas, or UNICAMP) as a visiting scholar, Evelina Dagnino and Leila Ferreira provided logistical support to make my year enjoyable and profitable. A newly formed study group, O Grupo de Estudos sobre a Construção de Democracia, invited me to participate and was an intellectually stimulating environment. Of all the endeavors I experienced during my first year in Brazil, my participation in this group was by far the most important and had the largest impact on my understanding of Brazilian politics. Carla Almedia, Ana Claudia Teixeira, and Maria do Carmo Albuquerque were especially important in making my yearlong stay in Campinas enjoyable and productive. Sonia E. Alvarez opened many social, academic, research, and academic doors for me, beginning from my time as her undergraduate student. I am grateful for the strong support that she has provided me over the years.

I want to thank several institutions for the generous support that enabled the growth and development of this research project. Each grant provided me the time and resources to increase my knowledge about Brazilian society and politics. I received a Ford Foundation grant (1995), an International Pre-dissertation Fellowship from the Social Science Research Council and the American Council of Learned Society (1996–97), a David Boren NSEP fellowship (1998–99), a Malcolm MacDonald Fellowship at the University of Texas at Austin (1999–2000), several faculty research awards from Boise State University's College of Social Sciences and Public Affairs, and a fellowship from the National Science

Foundation's (NSF's) International Research Fellowship Program (2003–4). At Boise State University, my department chairs, Les Alm and Ross Burkhart, gave me the necessary flexibility to be away from the political science department for an academic year as well as the resources to write the book. I appreciate the support of these organizations and their dedicated personnel. Susan Parris of the NSF was especially helpful during the 2003–4 year. This material is based upon work supported by the NSF under Grant No. INT-0301849. Any opinions, findings, and conclusions or recommendations expressed in this material are those of the author and do not necessarily reflect the views of the NSF.

Various sections of this book, preliminary conference papers, or research proposals were read and commented on by Les Alm, Sonia E. Alvarez, George Avelino, Leonardo Avritzer, Ilona Blanchard, Cathy Boone, Ross Burkhart, Evelina Dagnino, Henry Dietz, Zach Elkins, Charlie Hale, Roger Frahm, Robert Gay, Ben Goldfrank, Lawrence S. Graham, Patrick Heller, Kathy Hochstetler, Wendy Hunter, Margaret Keck, Todd Lochner, Raul Madrid, Nicole Mellow, Gary Moncrief, Dennis Plane, Aaron Schneider, Natasha Sugiyama, and Ana Cláudia Teixeira. I presented versions of the argument that serves as the basis of the book at the University of Arizona, Lewis & Clark College, Boise State University, the University of São Paulo, the FGV, CEBRAP, and several ASPA (American Political Science Association) and LASA (Latin American Studies Association) conferences. My thanks go to these individuals who provided valuable and thoughtful feedback.

This book was also greatly improved through the encouraging feedback of two reviewers. Each made thoughtful suggestions that made the book much better. Sandy Thatcher, director of Penn State Press, has been a constant source of support since I first brought the book project to him. He gave me guidance and feedback when requested, but also provided me with sufficient flexibility that allowed me to refine the book's argument as I saw fit. I greatly appreciate the help Sandy provided. Lisa Burns and Audra Green made valuable and timely contributions to this book, as research assistants while they were undergraduates at Boise State University. Terrina Vail and Romaine Perin did an excellent job copyediting the book during its final stages. Sections of the first chapter previously appeared in an article I published in *Latin American Politics and Society* 4 (2004). A modified version of Chapter 3 was published in *Studies in Comparative International Development* 41 (4) (2007). I also want to thank the Erin Greb and the Gould Center for Geography Education and

Outreach for the work on producing the map of Brazil that appears in Chapter 1.

Finally, my parents, Dave and JoAnn, and immediate family, Lori, Jeff, Kira, Kayla, Carson, and extended family, Bob, Kathy, Ashley, Blair, Laura, Leah, and Antony, were extremely supportive of my comings and goings from Brazil. I also want to thank the wonderful family in Maine that I was fortunate to marry into: Phil and Nancy, Patrick, Antonia, Pam, Pat, and Phil were supportive during the research and writing phases of the project. Friends Driscoll, Tim, Andrea, Mike, and Armando pretended to listen intently while I talked about the project and were, thankfully, able to easily distract me from this narrow focus.

My deepest thanks must be extended to Paula, who was willing to quit her job and move to Brazil for a year to allow me to conduct this research project. Her patience, good humor, and willingness to listen to me work out the argument were instrumental in allowing me to finish. Her willingness to allow me to "steal" writing time during our children's nap time and morning playtime allowed the book to be completed in a timely fashion. Sebastian was born three weeks after we returned from Brazil, and Ginger was born just as the book was being completed. Their arrivals enriched our lives and made the book more enjoyable to write.

Extending Citizenship
and Accountability
Through Participatory Budgeting

> Participatory Budgeting [PB] is the best thing that
> has happened to the poor of Belo Horizonte because
> we can transform our neighborhood from favela into
> city. We can become part of the city.
> —PB DELEGATE IN BELO HORIZONTE

> PB absolves the government of responsibility. In-
> stead of having government officials decide policy
> outcomes, PB pits poor against poor to fight over
> small projects. Instead of working together, we are
> in competition against other poor neighborhoods.
> —PB DELEGATE IN BELO HORIZONTE

Participatory institutions provide citizens with the opportunity to work directly with government officials and their fellow citizens in formal, state-sanctioned public venues, allowing them to exercise *voice* and *vote* in decision-making processes to produce public policy solutions that may resolve intense social problems. Close working relationships among citizens and government officials are frequently forged, allowing for collaborative learning and in-depth negotiations. Citizens use newly won political rights to secure new social rights, thereby improving their communities and lives. Participatory institutions adopted in developing-world countries over the past two decades have often been designed to incorporate low-income and politically marginalized individuals who live in poor and underserviced neighborhoods. And yet, as we will see, the direct incorporation of citizens and community may also allow government officials to dominate the new institution as well as the agendas of civil society organizations (CSOs), which subverts the original intent of many participatory institutions—the expansion of rights, authority, and democratic practices to ordinary citizens.

The widespread adoption of participatory institutions accompanied the establishment of democratic regimes in Latin America during the 1980s and 1990s.[1] In Latin America, many local (subnational) governments have adopted participatory institutions in hopes that the direct incorporation of citizens into state-sanctioned policy-making venues will promote social justice, increase transparency, and engage citizens by giving them *voice* and *vote* over substantive policy issues.[2]

Accountability and citizenship rights are central to political, academic, and policy debates that seek to show how participatory institutions have affected citizens, governments, and state-society relations. The extension of accountability depends on the ability of citizens to be actively involved in monitoring the actions of government officials and requires that government officials be willing to subject their actions to examination by the governed. The establishment of citizenship rights, too, depends on the ability of citizens to actively use the rights legally afforded to them, as well as the willingness of government officials to ensure that these rights are protected in daily life. Participatory institutions are especially well suited to be analyzed using the concepts of accountability and citizenship rights because these institutions require the active participation of citizens and government officials.

Although there has been a proliferation of participatory institutions in the developing world over the past twenty years, we continue to lack a systematic and comparative accounting of how citizens use these institutions. We also do not understand the full range of political and policy outcomes that have been produced. In this book I analyze Brazil's, and Latin America's, best-known and most widely disseminated participatory institution, Participatory Budgeting (PB), in eight Brazilian municipalities. My goal is to develop a generalizable theoretical explanation to more fully account for how and if citizens and government officials use this innovative institution to extend accountability and establish citizenship rights.

PB has the potential to alter the political calculus in municipalities by giving individual citizens the right to express their preferences and interests (*voice*) in public venues along with the right to *vote* on specific policies. PB, as a policy-making institution, delegates specific decision-making authority to citizens, which has the potential to increase tensions among

1. Roberts 1998; Avritzer 2002; Santos 1998; Genro1995a, 1995b; Weffort 1984; Castañeda 1993; Santos 2005; Heller 2001; Barber 1984.
2. Genro 1995a, 1995b; Avritzer 2002; Santos 1998.

elected municipal legislators (*vereadores*), appointed officials, bureaucrats, PB participants, and other interest groups. Because PB operates at the center of key political and policy debates, it has the potential to transform how the state functions and how citizens interact with the state. This type of transformation can help to deepen democracy, promote pluralism, and lay the foundations for social justice.

And yet PB programs can also produce weak outcomes that will not transform basic decision-making processes or allow citizens to be directly involved in policy making. It is possible that poorly performing PB programs will have a negative impact on citizens and CSOs, which should temper calls for the widespread adoption of participatory institutions as a magic bullet that will transform the lives of poor citizens in poor and industrializing nations. In addition, citizens who participate in some PB programs may have little authority delegated to them, thereby limiting their ability to hold government officials accountable and to use PB as a means to activate and exercise their own rights.

The scope of authority exercised by citizens in PB is central to this book for theoretical, policy, and empirical reasons. On the broadest theoretical level, participatory institutions such as PB do have the capability of transforming basic democratic practices. PB has the potential to change basic state-society relations if governments in fact become more responsive to citizens as a result of PB. Citizens may also become more actively involved in political and civil society life, which may directly affect their local communities. PB is a new institutional format in which participatory decision-making processes are grafted onto existing representative democratic institutions. PB does not replace representative democracy, but it allows citizens to be directly involved in crafting public policies. In Brazil's political context, PB has the potential to reshape how government officials produce decisions that directly affect the lives of their constituents.[3] PB also has the potential to reshape how citizens experience democratic politics because citizens can participate in state-sanctioned public debates that result in government officials following the decisions made by these citizens.

How and by whom authority is exercised is central to empirical debates on democratization, which is why it is vital that we establish by whom, when, and where decisions are being made (namely, the legislative branch,

---

3. Ames 2002; Chaui 1989; Ribeiro 1995; Hollanda 1937; Moisés 1995; Diniz 1982; Doimo 1995; Gay 1994.

executive office, and participatory venues). We must verify the scope of decisions that citizens are able to make. From a research perspective, we need to establish—or disavow—that citizens can and do make significant types of decisions within PB. Because PB is being adopted across Latin America and throughout the developing world, it is vital that we understand how citizens affect and are affected by this participatory institution.

Main Argument

The main argument in this book is that the substantial variation in the actual delegation of authority to citizens, which accounts for variations in how accountability and citizenship rights are extended, can best be explained by more closely examining (a) mayoral administrations' incentives to choose to delegate authority, (b) the particular rule structure that is used to delegate authority to citizens, and (c) how csos and citizens respond to the new institutions. Under the most favorable conditions, mayors delegate substantial authority to citizens through PB, which means that citizens are able to exercise a new set of political rights and begin the process of holding governments accountable. This helps to deepen Brazil's democracy because citizens are more active and governments are increasingly transparent and open.[4] However, in several of the PB programs analyzed in this book, there is little to no decision-making authority delegated to citizens, thereby emasculating PB as a decision-making venue. When PB programs are especially weak, there is the potential to increase cynicism about democracy and participation, rather than to help deepen democracy. In these cases, it is not clear that PB has contributed in a positive fashion to either deepening democracy or improving policy outcomes.

To account for the substantial variation in outcomes, there are both institutional and civil society explanations. First, what explains why mayors would be willing to delegate authority to citizens? Mayors, after all, have a broad mandate to govern on behalf of their constituents, so it is not clear why mayors would want to give up the authority they won through an election. Are they responding to their political bases? Are they interested in drumming up support for elections? Are they driven by ideological concerns? Or are they influenced by party politics? Mayors are willing

---

4. Roberts 1998; Mouffe 1992; Santos 2002, 2005; Fischer 2003; Jelin and Hershberg 1996; Sellers 2002; Held 1987; Dryzek 2000.

to delegate authority when they perceive that it is in their electoral, party, government, and ideological interests to do so. I will further detail this argument later in this chapter.

An additional institutional explanation to account for the substantial variation in PB outcomes is based on how PB programs structure the distribution of authority.[5] Do the rules encourage group solidarity? Do the rules fragment neighborhoods and CSOs? Do the rules make it easy for citizens to hold government officials accountable? Variations in rules stem from the timing of an individual PB program's adoption, local political interests of politicians and CSO leaders, location of the municipality, and size of the municipality. My argument will demonstrate that the "rules of the game" matter significantly, which is a logical extension of the reasoning behind the initial adoption of this innovative institution. We must bear in mind that the original rule set, devised in Porto Alegre, was explicitly designed to mobilize low-income residents into public policy–making venues, which would help to legitimize these citizens' demands as well as the policy positions of the government.[6] New rules for participation were written to create PB, so it is quite reasonable to assert that rule variations will affect outcomes.

The civil society explanation, which also helps to account for the substantial variations in PB outcomes, is that citizens and CSOs are choosing a variety of strategies for how they will use this new authority.[7] Comparative research conducted for this project demonstrates that citizens must be able to negotiate among themselves and vis-à-vis the government over the distribution of scarce resources while also being willing to publicly pressure government officials over the government's actions or inactions related to PB. What explains why some CSOs are willing to engage in cooperative and contentious forms of politics? And what explains why some prefer cooperation to the exclusion of contestation? In some cases, CSOs employ both contentious and cooperative political strategies, while in others, they are more likely to employ only cooperation, which is more likely to lead to co-optation. Answering these questions helps explain not only why and how citizens have different levels of authority but also whether PB is contributing to the extension of accountability and citizenship rights.

5. Evans, Rueschemeyer, and Skocpol 1985; Migdal 2001; Dahl 1961, 1971; Eaton 2004a, 2004b; Campbell 2003.
6. Fedozzi 1998; Abers 2000; Fedozzi 2000.
7. Cohen and Arato 1992; Cohen and Rogers 1995; Walzer 1992; Yashar 2005; Fraser 1993; Edwards, Foley, and Diani 2001; Edwards 2004; Escobar and Alvarez 1992.

The Origins of PB

PB was initiated in 1989 in the southern Brazilian state capital city of Porto Alegre by a coalition of civil society activists and Workers' Party (Partido de Trabalhadores, or PT) officials.[8] The rules developed in Porto Alegre spread quickly; more than 250 Brazilian municipal governments adopted PB at some point between 1990 and 2004.[9] Although there has been widespread adoption of PB, its track record is mixed.[10] The majority of the policy and academic literature has not recognized the diversity of PB experiences, because of the absence of comparative research.[11]

This book, the result of two years of field research, is specifically aimed at overcoming this problem by gathering together a broad set of data to better demonstrate and explain PB's outcomes and effects. In the book I analyze PB in eight Brazilian municipalities: São Paulo, Porto Alegre, Recife, Belo Horizonte, Rio Claro, Blumenau, Santo André, and Ipatinga. Porto Alegre's PB is well known internationally and has been a focal point of attention for the Left, for nongovernmental organizations (NGOs), and for international development and lending agencies. The evidence in this book confirms the widespread claim that Porto Alegre's PB has produced strong results, such as an average of fifty thousand participants in PB each year, vibrant debates, fairly transparent governmental processes, and the implementation of U.S.$400 million of PB projects.[12]

However, my argument and evidence also demonstrate that Porto Alegre's PB experience is not representative of the broader set of PB cases. In almost every category I used in analyzing PB, Porto Alegre stands above other cases. This has not only obvious theoretical implications, but also important political and policy ones, because the Porto Alegre–inspired model of PB has been implemented in more than forty countries.[13]

8. Fedozzi 1998; Abers 2000; Avritzer 2002; Goldfrank 2003.

9. Ribeiro and de Grazia 2003; Wampler and Avritzer 2005; Teixeira 2003.

10. Navarro 2003; Nylen 2002; Wampler 2004b; Baiocchi 2003.

11. Abers 2000; Baiocchi 2005; Santos 1998; Guidry 2003; Fedozzi 1998. The political Left has been enamored of PB, leading many to the "Porto Alegre" way as a model to reinvigorate leftist bases across Latin America and the developing world.

12. To determine this figure, I analyzed the yearly *Balanço Geral* of the municipality's direct and indirect expenditures to determine which projects had actually been spent. I used the annual *Plano de Investimentos,* published by the municipal government, to show which PB projects are entered into the annual budget as the basis for analysis. *Diario Oficial de Prefeitura Municipal de Porto Alegre* (1994–2004); *Balanço Geral de Prefeitura Municipal de Porto Alegre* (1994–2004).

13. Cabannes, n.d.

Brazil and cities studied

On the basis of the eight cases examined in this book, I show that PB's track record is actually quite mixed in Brazil. Two PB programs are quite successful (Porto Alegre and Ipatinga), and two are clearly failures (Blumenau and Rio Claro). The successful programs delegate real authority to citizens and implement a range of public policies selected by PB participants. The failed programs are notable for their lack of delegation and the limited number of PB projects implemented by government officials.

In the failed cases, PB did not alter each respective municipality's decision-making processes.

The four middle cases (Recife, Belo Horizonte, Santo André, and São Paulo) have produced the most challenging outcomes to interpret because there are specific advances as well as drawbacks in the areas of accountability and citizenship rights. Governments only partially delegate authority, and CSOs find it difficult to engage in both cooperation and contestation. These experiences demonstrate that it is vital not to universally condemn participatory institutions when they do not work as well as the Porto Alegre experience, but rather to recognize that outcomes may have contradictory elements.

Defining PB programs as "successes" or "failures" is obviously fraught with the dangers of not finding the appropriate time frame for analysis, having methodological biases, and relying on similar but not exactly the same sets of data. I developed the tools to evaluate PB outcomes over a ten-year period while studying Brazilian municipal and participatory institutions and living in Brazil for three of those ten years.[14] I conducted more than one hundred formal interviews, attended countless meetings, held nine focus groups, engaged in dozens and dozens of informal discussions with participants and government officials, and attended graduate courses at the State University of Campinas (Universidade Estadual de Campinas, or UNICAMP), one of Brazil's premier universities.[15] My categorizations of success and failure are drawn from the ideas written and spoken by PB participants, government officials, opposition legislators, and interested observers (NGOs and academics), but they are also situated in the relevant political science literatures.[16]

Participants and government officials commonly assert that participatory processes must allow citizens to decide policy outcomes, monitor government activities, and change how governments act. Therefore, the principal criterion for success is the scope and efficacy of authority that

14. My predissertation work (one year) was supported by the SSRC, my doctoral research was supported by the NSEP David Boren Fellowship program, and my postdoctoral research was supported by the U.S. National Science Foundation (INT-0301849).

15. Formal interviews are listed in the Appendix, in cases in which the individual being interviewed gave his or her both first and last name. Almost all citizen-participants interviewed only provided their first name, so they are not included in the Appendix.

16. Przeworski, Stokes, and Manin 1999; O'Donnell 1998; Weyland 1996; Roberts 1998; Collier and Levitsky 1997; Diamond and Morlino 2004; Domínguez and Shifter 2003; Munck and Verkuilen 2000; Souto, Kayano, de Almeida, and Petrucci 1995; Tendler 1997; Wampler 2002; Boone 2003; Farah 1996.

citizens exercise. Government officials and citizens pervasively argue that the key to P B is allowing ordinary citizens to make decisions that directly affect public policy outcomes. A second criterion for success is based on how the delegation of authority affects the extension of accountability and citizenship rights. This approach allows me to narrow the analysis to a more manageable size. We must not assume that P B will establish accountability or citizenship rights; rather, it is incumbent upon us to show specifically how this new institutional type may help to transform Brazil's illiberal democracy.[17]

P B Vignettes

Five brief vignettes, given below, illustrate the complexity of P B programs in Brazil. P B programs can have decision-making attributes, can promote deliberation, and can help to empower citizens, and their public policy outputs can transform entire neighborhoods. Participants and mayoral administrations can also manipulate P B's rules, producing outcomes significantly different from P B's founding ideals (namely, social justice and deliberation). P B can also act as a signaling device that allows the government to assess the needs and issues that are most important to community leaders and active citizens, which may also allow politicians to use P B as a means for mobilizing a loyal base of supporters. Conducting comparative research allows us to capture a broader range of experiences. By analyzing multiple cases and using multiple sets of data, it is possible to create generalizable theories regarding how P B functions and the outcomes it produces.

Porto Alegre: Cooperation and Contestation (Among Friends) Promotes Accountability and Citizenship

Porto Alegre, as has been well documented, is the birthplace of P B.[18] On June 3, 1999, I attended a P B meeting held at an outdoor basketball court, an unfortunate location given the chilly weather (cold enough that we could see our breath throughout the two-hour meeting). Despite the

17. O'Donnell 1994.
18. Abers 1998, 2000; Fedozzi 1998; Baiocchi 2003, 2005; Avritzer 2002; Wampler and Avritzer 2004.

chill, nearly three hundred people attended. The purpose of that night's meeting was for participants to decide, by majority vote, which specific public works project their region would nominate for inclusion in the final budget. After the government's short presentation, it quickly became clear that there were two groups, each advocating a different policy objective. One group advocated for the construction of a small health care clinic in a poorer part of the region, while the other group wanted a pedestrian bridge to be built over a busy avenue that intersected the region.

The majority of the speakers from both groups were working-class individuals. The fact that low-income, poorly educated individuals dominated a state-sponsored public policy venue—one in which their decision, via majority vote, would directly affect government action—signified a radical change in basic state-society relations in Brazil. Under the meeting rules, each individual had three minutes in which to speak. In PB meetings, generally, ten individuals speak, followed by clarification and comments from government leaders. After ten speakers, there is an informal vote on whether to allow additional speakers or to close the debate. In my experience, debate is allowed to remain open if there is a significant minority that wants to extend the debate. If only a few individuals want to extend the debate, then the debate is generally closed. Interestingly, there are no written rules about this process, but it is a norm of behavior that encourages deliberation.

Individuals representing the group that supported the health care project argued that their region needed a facility that provided preventive care because too many people were getting sick from easily preventable diseases and illnesses. Their explanation for the health problems: financial and time costs associated with traveling by bus to a more distant health care clinic. Public health policy and convenience arguments were made on behalf of pregnant women, mothers with small children, the elderly, and the poor.

Individuals representing the pedestrian overpass group then took the microphone and explained that a pedestrian overpass was absolutely necessary because four pedestrians had been killed by motorists during the previous year while attempting to cross an avenue that bisected their neighborhood. The arguments of many individuals centered on the responsibilities of the state. Should the state not protect the safety of its citizens? Is that not the minimum that a state should provide? The arguments were compelling and spirited, which I attributed to the recent deaths that had resulted from the absence of a pedestrian overpass.

Individuals from the group for health care responded by picking up the threads of the state-responsibility argument. They argued that, yes, the state should protect the health of its citizens, and the best way to provide this service was to establish decent health care services for the poor. Far more benefits would accrue to the community, they stated, if there were high-quality preventive medicine available. Furthermore, as these individuals delicately argued, there was already a pedestrian bridge two hundred meters from the proposed location of the new pedestrian bridge. The problem, they asserted, was not that the state did not provide services but that the community's residents ignored the existing infrastructure. The problem was not the state, one individual argued, but rather the culture of Brazilians who ignore their personal safety for convenience. For this reason, she argued, the pedestrian overpass should not be supported. Individuals from the pedestrian overpass group acknowledged that there was an existing overpass, but argued that an additional overpass was needed because of the increasing population and use of the avenue.

What was particularly fascinating about this discussion was how representatives from each group weaved together the themes of social justice, the public policy outcomes that would be most beneficial to their community, and the role of the state. Deliberations were partly driven by each group's self-interest, but the fact that its members were forced to situate their arguments in a broader debate about the public good and state responsibility produced a stimulating debate. At the end of the night, a vote was taken. A substantial majority selected the health care clinic as the region's policy project.

This example demonstrates one of the strengths of the PB process: deliberation prior to voting serves as a means to influence one's fellow citizens, and it also serves as a means to inform government officials that leaders and residents of the community are concerned about a particular issue. Although the pedestrian overpass group lost, PB allowed this group's members to inform their fellow citizens and government officials about the gravity of their situation. Thus PB helped these citizens communicate their problems to government bureaucrats, who could seek to address the problems through potentially inexpensive means.

*Belo Horizonte: Contestation Promotes Societal Accountability
and Circumvention of Rules*

Twenty minutes by car from downtown, squeezed between fashionable neighborhoods, sits the sprawling Morro de Papagio favela (Parrots' Hill shantytown), in the state capital, Belo Horizonte. On a walking tour of their neighborhood, community leaders who had been involved in PB for nearly a decade pointed out, with obvious pride, various public works projects they had helped to select. A health care clinic, a sewage system, and paving of the hilly streets were the principal projects that had been selected and implemented as a result of their success in PB. Community leaders described how they had constructed alliances within and outside their community to secure a successful vote. They spoke of having nego- tiated a deal with other communities in which they would submit no new projects for two years, to secure the voting support of other communities because their proposed project, a sewage system, was expensive. In return, they would support the other communities' projects during the interven- ing years. The community leaders spoke at length of the solidarity that the process generated, arguing that PB had helped to foster interneigh- borhood solidarity as they gave and received support from other groups.

Yet these community leaders were upset because the government had not begun the implementation of four projects that had been selected through PB during the four previous years. They felt that the government was ignoring the hard work and efforts of the community members. Their community organization had decided to pressure the government through a public demonstration. A Catholic priest working with the community leaders agreed to lead a mock funeral procession in which the entity "Participatory Budgeting" would be buried. Teenagers, dressed as robed monks, had been enlisted to carry a coffin, labeled "Participatory Budget- ing." The "burial site" was alongside a busy avenue that was a main con- duit for car traffic from downtown to middle-class neighborhoods. The funeral procession was conducted in the late afternoon, and there was an explicit threat to block rush-hour traffic on the avenue unless the gov- ernment agreed to immediately begin construction on at least one of the four projects. The fact that this public demonstration tactic was deemed necessary by the community leaders suggests that the Belo Horizonte government was unable to fulfill the pledges it made to citizens who par- ticipated in PB. The community leaders, well versed in the use of direct demonstrations, felt that this tactic would be effective in an election year.

While the "funeral" was being held, a small group of community lead- ers met with the mayor's staff. The government agreed to the demands of the protestors. Construction on all four projects would begin in the near future, and at least one project would be initiated the following week. Prior to ending the funeral, the protestors closed the six-lane avenue for one minute to show the mayor that they had the power to disrupt traffic if the government did not fulfill its promise.

Although this vignette demonstrates the usefulness of contentious politics, it also illustrates that PB is not necessarily a clear and transparent process in Belo Horizonte. Political pressure from well-located and strategically astute groups can influence the implementation of projects, thereby making implementation a politicized process rather than a bureaucratic one defined by PB's rules.

Blumenau: Cooperation Produces "Conceded" Citizenship Rights and Increased Cynicism

Blumenau, a city of 260,000 residents in the prosperous southern state of Santa Catarina, elected a mayor from the Workers' Party (Partido de Trabalhadores, or PT) in 1996, and PB was implemented in 1997. Blumenau had a network of social clubs and self-help groups but lacked contentious social movement activity.[19] When PB began, a politically entrepreneurial young lawyer, Jean Klunderman, from the conservative Liberal Front Party (Partido da Frente Liberal, or PFL), sought to elect as many of his allies as possible. In four of the city's eight regions, Klunderman worked with numerous social clubs to elect nearly 60 percent of the official PB delegates, even though his allies made up less than half of the mobilized population. They were able to accomplish this outcome by carefully analyzing PB's electoral procedures and exploiting the rules for their own benefit.

During the second phase of PB, the selection of projects, Klunderman again carefully studied the rules and developed a plan to secure as many resources as possible for his supporters. Different factions were organized to vote for projects so that no votes were wasted. This enabled Klunderman's group to secure two-thirds of the funding available in the four regions even though it had started the meetings with less than 50 percent of the mobilized population.[20]

Since PB programs depend on the intense involvement of the mayor and the mayoral staff, what was their response? As one might imagine,

19. Pedrini, Andrade, Rolim, and Muller 1999.
20. Jean Klunderman, interview, January 12, 2004. Klunderman's claims were confirmed by the vice mayor on January 22, 2004, and with a PB administrator, Walner Costa, on February 26, 2004.

the mayor downplayed PB as a viable institution for making binding policy decisions because the mayor and the young lawyer were from rival political parties. The mayor was reelected in 2000, but at the time of my interviews in 2003, most interviewees asserted that their PB program was very weak. In many municipalities, the PB staff defended their program and explained the program's "advances," but the Blumenau municipal staff was unique for its harsh criticisms of its own program.

Although Klunderman's success is not the only reason for Blumenau's failed PB program, it is a contributing factor. The vignette helps to illustrate one important feature that single case studies of PB often overlook: it is often the political allies of the mayoral administration who are participating in PB. When the political rivals of the mayor occupy PB, then the mayor does not have a strong political incentive to invest the personnel and resources necessary to allow PB to flourish. Citizens interested in using PB as a means by which to pursue their own agenda therefore find themselves working in a policy-making institution that lacks any meaningful authority. This has the potential to increase distrust and cynicism among participants regarding the appropriate role of citizens in democratic processes.

São Paulo: Weak Delegation of Authority Leads to Signaling

São Paulo implemented PB in 2001 with the lukewarm support of newly elected Mayor Marta Suplicy (PT). A small faction within the PT used its political capital to implement PB as a means to promote transparency, encourage participation, and strengthen the party's connections to CSOs and individual participants.[21] PB's life under Mayor Suplicy's administration was marked by the limited delegation of authority. Suplicy centralized decision making in her office for several reasons: her core set of advisors were not strong advocates of the direct participation of citizens in decision-making venues, she had little practical experience with participatory decision-making processes, and it was her rival's political faction (within the PT) that supported the delegation of authority. Over the course of Suplicy's term in office (2001–4), PB developed into a signaling mechanism, whereby some preferences selected by PB delegates would be incorporated into the government's policy agenda. In turn, Suplicy's main policy agendas were introduced into PB, whereby participants' votes were used to legitimate Suplicy's policies.

21. Wampler 2004c; "90 dias de reconstrução," April 2001.

With regard to the "bottom up" signaling, in 2001 and 2002, citizens selected day care centers and elementary schools in the area of education as the most important priorities to be implemented. These were not part of Suplicy's initial agenda. However, by 2003, Mayor Suplicy's main policy initiative was the construction of large schools that could service the needs of upward of thirty-five hundred elementary school students as well as provide day care facilities. The schools also served as community centers, with a pool, a theater, and playing fields available for use on the weekends. These projects included the most basic demands of the PB delegates, but they transformed the schools from a local project to a major campaign program.

The government sought to enhance the legitimacy of the mayor's policies based on the support of PB participants, which meant that PB delegates competed against one another for where the schools would be located. Since these major policy initiatives were developed and promoted by a small group close to the mayor, it is likely that the policies would have been implemented regardless of the vote outcome. The government's efforts to reach out to PB suggest that government officials were aware that PB could provide important political cover and support to government programs.

São Paulo's PB illustrates the development of a different type of policy-making institution. It was primarily a signaling mechanism through which CSO activists indicated their preferences to the government. The government also used PB as a means to legitimate its policies. Although São Paulo's PB was inspired by the Porto Alegre experience, Mayor Suplicy's inner circle was unwilling to delegate the authority necessary to allow citizens to make meaningful decisions.

Recife: Mayoral Competition Within PB and Contentious Societal Accountability

In Recife, PB has been overseen by three different mayoral administrations. The shifts in leadership resulted in important changes in PB's rules, which meant that CSO activists and individual citizens had to change their political strategy every four years when a new mayor was elected. From 1994 to 1996, PB was overseen by Mayor Jarbas Vasconcelos of the catch-all Brazilian Democratic Movement Party (Partido do Movimento Democrático Brasileiro, or PMDB). Vasconcelos had deep ties to Recife's most active and contentious CSOs. Vasconcelos encouraged debate and sought to incorporate a broad range of individuals and groups into PB. During the initial period, PB was a vibrant decision-making venue; decisions made in PB resulted in specific public polices that resulted, in great measure, from the intense support of Vasconcelos and his closest advisors.

Vasconcelos's chosen successor, Roberto Magalhães, from the conservative PFL, agreed to maintain PB as part of their political alliance. Magalhães was a technocrat and had been appointed governor in the 1970s by the military government. He kept the form of PB, but he took away the content. Meetings were poorly run, participants were not respected by government officials, and policies that were selected were not implemented. PB participants discovered, by 1999 and 2000, that their best strategy was to use the year-end "accountability" meetings to directly confront government officials over PB's basic problems. The contentious politics that Mayor Vasconcelos had nurtured were used against the staff of Mayor Magalhães. Although PB was emasculated by Magalhães, PB participants were able to develop new strategies that permitted them to directly confront their government.

In 2001, João Paulo Lima (PT) was elected mayor in an upset victory over incumbent Mayor Magalhães. The PT government sought to change PB's rules to incorporate CSOs and citizens that were not beholden to the interests of Vasconcelos or Magalhães. In 2003, PB's administrator, João Costa, asserted that "when we took over PB, the delegates supported our political rivals [Vasconcelos]. We needed to create a new process that would break the stranglehold on our participatory institutions."[22] Mayor João Paulo Lima's administration then initiated a series of rule changes that forced participating CSOs to recalculate their strategies and allowed new CSOs to enter the political system.

Recife's PB program illustrates the vital importance of mayoral leadership in how PB rules are established and interpreted. Mayors have varying levels of interests and involvement in PB, which contributes to how legislators, bureaucrats, community leaders, and interested citizens understand and use the process. Each mayor in Recife emphasized rules that complemented that mayor's own political interests and strategies. PB participants reacted to the different emphases by changing their strategies to meet the new opportunities or by pressuring the government to adhere to the previous set of rules.

These five vignettes illustrate substantial variation in how PB programs

---

22. João Costa, Recife's PB administrator, interview, December 9, 2003.

are managed and how they function. It is now time to turn to the account-ability and citizenship debates to gain the maximum theoretical leverage from the vignettes and other evidence.

Theoretical Debates: Accountability and Citizenship

Accountability Debates

The focus within the accountability debates has been on how one agent (the voters, the courts) can control another agent (elected officials, the executive branch). One weakness of the accountability debates is that the conceptual variants—horizontal, vertical, and societal—tend to run on par-allel tracks and are unable to show how citizens, csos, politicians, and institutions may place interlocking checks on the ambitions of other actors. Participatory institutions are excellent case studies that bridge this theo-retical gap because these institutions have the potential to redistribute authority, incorporate citizens directly into decision-making venues, and allow third parties to monitor the implementation of public policies. Par-ticipatory institutions tap into all three dimensions (horizontal, vertical, and societal) of the accountability debates: (1) horizontal: participatory institutions have the *potential* to act as a check on the prerogatives and actions of mayoral administrations; (2) vertical: participatory institutions allow citizens to vote for representatives and specific policies; (3) societal: participatory institutions rely on the mobilization of citizens into a polit-ical process that may legitimize the new policy-making process, but may also foster additional checks placed on governmental action by interested and engaged citizens.

Vertical accountability, generally framed as the control of public officials by citizens primarily through elections, has received significant attention as scholars analyze how citizens can use elections to exercise control over public officials.[23] Horizontal accountability, the distribution of authority among different departments or branches of government, has also received attention as scholars seek to evaluate the consequences of institutional arrangements that were designed to strengthen democratic practices and rights.[24] Societal accountability, the pressures placed on state agencies by

23. Przeworski, Stokes, and Manin 1999.
24. O'Donnell 1998.

csos to encourage elected officials and bureaucrats to abide by the rule of law, has emerged as a counterbalance to the other two approaches because it can directly link ongoing political activity in civil society to formal political institutions.[25]

Przeworski, Stokes, and Manin's volume, *Democracy, Accountability, and Representation*, sets the tone for the debate on vertical accountability. They work within the rational-choice tradition and employ a principal-agent model to explain outcomes. Their book engages a classic theme of democratic politics: how can citizens control their governments? Przeworski, Stokes, and Manin analyze how elections influence the choices of public officials in new democracies, concentrating on the inability of the electoral process to produce binding decisions or guarantee that public officials will remain virtuous. Unfortunately, the authors reduce the range of political roles that citizens can play to one: the voter. "Governments make thousands of decisions that affect individual welfare; citizens have only one instrument to control these decisions: the vote."[26]

Although most citizens may not be actively engaged or interested in policy-making processes, the assertion by Przeworski, Stokes, and Manin is greatly overstated because it ignores the vast range of political strategies and actions employed by activists to influence public officials and policy outcomes. Citizens now have access to a range of legal and political resources, including lawsuits, public demonstrations, public hearings, and participatory institutions, that they can use to pressure public officials. Democratic regimes allow citizens to seek redress in a number of decision-making venues, among them executive, legislative, and judicial branches. In Brazil, groups demanding political reform have used subnational levels of government to challenge traditional mechanisms of control, suggesting that electoral analysis, especially of national elections, is not a sufficient indicator of how csos affect policy making.[27] The approach used by Przeworski, Stokes, and Manin assumes the absence of political and social organizing outside of elections. Elections, however, are but one avenue through which citizens may encourage increased accountability and improvements in public policies. The citizen as activist, the citizen as community organizer, and the *active* citizen do not appear on the radar screen in their analysis. And this analytical focus also ignores the role that csos play in democratic politics.

25. Smulovitz and Peruzzotti 2000.
26. Przeworski, Stokes, and Manin 1999, 50.
27. Dagnino 1994b; Jacobi 2000; Hochstetler 2000.

Smulovitz and Peruzzotti recognize the drawbacks of relying on elections to show how citizens might influence elected officials. They introduce the concept of "societal accountability" to complement vertical accountability, and they demonstrate how csos can act as watchdogs by monitoring the actions of elected officials and bureaucrats. "Societal accountability is a nonelectoral yet vertical mechanism of control that rests on the actions of a multiple array of citizens' associations and movements and on the media, actions that aim at exposing governmental wrongdoing, bringing new issues onto the public agenda, or activating the operation of horizontal agencies."[28] This concept moves us beyond a narrow conceptualization of citizen participation to show how some citizens and csos are engaged in continual efforts to influence the actions and behaviors of state actors.

Smulovitz and Peruzzotti demonstrate how csos have taken advantage of the partial extension of civil and political liberties to develop new strategies with which to pressure elected officials. The authors' approach greatly expands the analytical box because it recognizes that the extension of civil and political rights has emboldened citizens to enlarge the terrain on which they make claims on the state. Yet their approach is also limited because it depends on csos putting sufficient pressure on elected officials rather than showing how new actors can contribute to policy outcomes. csos are transformed into interest groups rather than active agents that participate in policy-making venues where binding decisions are made. The authors' empirical examples show that csos in their model do not have the authority or ability to make binding decisions, but can influence powerholders. pb introduces a new principal to municipal decision making: citizens are not limited to roles as either "voters" or "watchdogs," but they become meaningful actors in the policy-making process.

O'Donnell's work on horizontal accountability focuses on a classic dilemma of politics: how can state agencies act as effective checks on the actions and ambitions of other state agencies? Horizontal accountability "depends on the existence of state agencies that are legally empowered— and factually willing and able—to take actions ranging from routine oversight to criminal sanctions or impeachment in relation to possibly unlawful actions or omissions by other agents or agents of the state."[29] State agents must be able to exert effective oversight to ensure that other state agents— elected and appointed officials or bureaucrats—can be held accountable

28. Smulovitz and Peruzzotti 2000, 150.
29. O'Donnell 1998, 117.

for the violation of rules and laws. The system of checks and balances requires that third parties can make binding decisions. Beyond the authority to make binding decisions, there must be the ability to carry out and enforce them. "Effective horizontal accountability is not the product of isolated agencies, but of networks of agencies (up to and including high courts) committed to upholding the rule of law."[30] This is an important advance to the work of Przeworski, Stokes, and Manin and of Smulovitz and Peruzzotti because O'Donnell includes formal binding decisions, which are indicative of the distribution of authority as well as the degree to which the rule of law has been extended.

Although O'Donnell's approach highlights the importance of the judicial branch and legislature acting as checks on the potential misuse of authority by executives, this approach too is limited because it fails to address how different interests are represented within state agencies. O'Donnell argues that contemporary polyarchies include "various oversight agencies, ombudsmen, accounting offices, *fiscalías*, and the like," but he does not sufficiently theorize how these institutions incorporate new actors that seek to use their authority to promote alternative institutional formats or alternative policies.[31] These new institutions have the potential to place the political ambitions of different actors into direct competition with one another, thereby promoting interlocking sets of authority. Horizontal accountability, as framed by O'Donnell, does not sufficiently treat the ways that the ambitions of different actors may be pitted against one another to produce different outcomes; institutions seemingly float above political and civil society rather than being occupied by specific actors with particular interests.

The concept of accountability is central to this book because it captures how PB depends on government officials and citizens sharing responsibility in the deliberation, selection, and implementation of public policies. Without citizens using institutional and extrainstitutional means to pressure government officials to respect the law and fulfill their promises, accountability is a concept void of meaning. Without government officials seeking to promote increased transparency, openness, and public involvement, accountability is virtually impossible to extend. Accountability, thus, depends on multiple actors, all working to promote their own interests while simultaneously working to block other actors' trampling on their rights.

30. O'Donnell 1998, 119.
31. O'Donnell 1998, 119.

Citizenship Debates

The ability of citizens to exercise rights guaranteed under a constitutional framework and the capacity of citizens to work for the expansion of those existing rights is at the heart of citizenship debates. T. H. Marshall's work on the political, social, and economic variants of citizenship set the tone for the modern citizenship debates. Marshall's analysis of the extension of citizenship rights to English citizens shows that the extension of rights to citizens was partial, uneven, and contested and occurred over several centuries.[32] Civil rights were established during the eighteenth and nineteenth centuries, political rights were extended during the nineteenth and twentieth, and social rights were primarily established after the end of World War II. Marshall argues that rights are won over time, under different conditions, and as a result of protracted struggle and conflict, suggesting that we look for currents of change as political movements devise new strategies and objectives.[33] Although he set the tone for the citizenship debates, scholars working in Latin America have made important contributions to exploring how rights were extended in this famously unequal and unjust society.[34]

Since the 1980s, Brazilian intellectual and political debates on the course that democracy should take have focused on the role of citizens in this process.[35] Brazil is a country with limited citizenship—high levels of poverty, intense political and social exclusion, and the state's inability to, or lack of interest in, protecting basic civil liberties have contributed to a public sphere notable for the absence of citizenship. Brazil's political history is marked by the systematic exclusion of lower-income and poorly educated individuals from policy- and decision-making venues.

Rights were established unevenly in the country over the nineteenth and twentieth centuries. Citizenship rights were restricted when the republic was founded in 1889. Former slaves and lower-class individuals were formally included in the national community at this time, but state elites did little to guarantee that individuals who were excluded from

32. Marshall 1950.
33. Marshall's case study is England. He argues that rights were won and implemented over the eighteenth, nineteenth, and twentieth centuries; civil rights were won in the eighteenth century, political rights in the nineteenth, and social (welfare-state) rights in the twentieth. He never asserts that this was the necessary order, but tries to show how different kinds of rights affected the struggles for new rights. Tarrow 1998.
34. Somers 1993; Oxhorn 2003; Yashar 2005.
35. Dagnino 1998; Avritzer 2002; Santos 1979; Carvalho 1987.

networks of power and patronage would have access to these rights. José Murilo de Carvalho argues that the foundation of the republic "did little in terms of the expansion of civil and political rights. What was done had already been demanded by imperial liberalism. You can say that there was even recession of what we refer to as social rights."[36] The lower classes, especially former slaves, were unable to seek redress for the violations of individual rights. There were strict literacy qualifications for voting, which greatly reduced the number of individuals who could actually make use of basic political rights.

Teresa Sales conceptualizes citizenship rights in Brazil as "conceded citizenship" (*cidadania concedida*), showing how the extension of citizenship rights has largely been contradictory.[37] Rights, as T. H. Marshall, E. P. Thompson, and others have demonstrated, are generally established on the basis of the demands of politically marginalized groups. When rights are won through political struggle, the newly established set of rights is not easily co-opted or withdrawn by state officials. In the Brazilian case, Sales argues, rights have been "conceded" or "given" by elites to the masses, which means that the new rights can be easily withdrawn or not enforced.[38] Sales's work demonstrates that most rights in Brazil have been established by the state, which makes these rights easier to withdraw. The difficulties faced by csos (for example, the collective action problem, repression, and castelike social system) mean that most citizens are unable to draw upon the basic rights formally guaranteed by the constitution.

A key part of Sales's argument is that Brazilian political bosses, the infamous local *coreneis,* "gave" rights to the masses, thereby extending a "culture of donation" into the realm of liberal rights. "This culture of donation outlived the private domination of the colonial estates and sugar plantations, it outlived the abolition of slavery, and it expressed itself in a particular way in the commitment of the colonel, and has even survived up to the present day."[39] The culture of donation is an intrinsic part of the patronage system, but it is linked not only to material goods. Specific rights, too, can be distributed by elites when it is in their interests to do so. The Brazilian state and political elites extended rights to individuals based on the workers' employment in industrial production or in a state bureaucracy.

36. Carvalho 1987, 45.
37. Sales 1994.
38. Marshall 1950; Thompson 1996; Tarrow 1998.
39. Sales 1994, 26.

Regulated citizenship (*cidadania regulada*), as conceptualized by Guilherme Wanderly de Santos, extended social and economic rights to specific categories of workers while simultaneously denying any new rights to the vast majority. "By regulated citizenship, I refer to its roots found not in the 'code' of political values but in the system of occupational stratification, which, by the way, is a system of stratification defined by legal norms."[40] The rights extended to workers privileged a specific class of workers. These workers enjoyed access to state services (housing, education, and health care) that were beyond the reach of most Brazilians. When democracy returned to Brazil in the mid-1980s, small groups of unionized workers had social rights, but the vast majority of the population had limited social rights and few political rights that could be activated to allow them to expand their social and civil rights.

During the political struggle against the military regime (1964–85), opposition groups united around the principle of citizenship (*cidadania*).[41] *Cidadania* represents the capacity of all Brazilians to exercise political rights, the protection of basic civil liberties, and the guarantee of social rights. Dagnino argues that the promotion of "the right to have rights" has helped to inculcate a belief among lower-class Brazilians that they have the right and responsibility to engage in public life.[42] There was a deliberate effort led by political reformers and political outsiders to work with low-income individuals to educate them on their rights.[43] Local CSOs, often neighborhood associations, partnered with reformist politicians, NGOs, and international funding agencies to work with ordinary Brazilians to broaden their expectations of what the government should provide and how the government should provide access to decision-making venues.[44]

The right to have rights directly challenges clientelistic relationships, which are a fundamental axis of Brazilian elite-mass political relationships.[45] The internalizing of the right to have rights might mean that these individuals are less likely to enter into patron-client relationships. Citizenship has come to embody the efforts of individuals seeking to deepen Brazil's democracy and promote social justice. To create a new Brazil,

40. Santos 1979, 75.
41. Dagnino 1998; Baierle 1998.
42. Dagnino 1998.
43. Weffort 1984; Villas Boas 1994;Villas Boas and Telles 1995.
44. Wampler and Avritzer 2004.
45. Fox 1994; Roniger 1994; Avelino 1994.

it is deemed necessary to limit clientelism, which was understood to be limiting the capacity of citizens, undermining the efficacy of the state, and allowing for the entrenchment of traditional political groups in the state. The concept of the right to have rights spawned the development of policy-making institutions that were specifically concerned with transparency, participation, and social justice, leading to the establishment of PB. Therefore, PB is the institutional expression of a decades-long effort to extend rights, whereby citizens increased their control over their lives by increasing their authority over their government.

One key aspect of citizenship is the demand for the "publicization" of the state. Paoli and Telles argue that "the conquest and recognition of rights signifies the invention of *rules of public coexistence* and of *regulating principles of a democratic sociability*."[46] This process is based on the opening and expansion of the decision-making process and on the ability of citizens to hold governments accountable for policies they do or do not implement. The proliferation of rights is the first step to empowering citizens and making elected officials accountable for their public policies. PB is illustrative of an institutional structure that attempts to incubate the incipient culture of rights and to open up the state.

The concept of citizenship is central to this book for two reasons. First, PB's innovative set of rules was partially derived from the citizenship debates, since the rules were explicitly designed to increase the authority of citizens. PB's advocates believed that citizens had to be directly involved in using rights if Brazil's democracy was going to be deepened. Second, PB allows for contestation and competition between citizens, which means that citizens must work to secure their interests in PB. This has the potential to overcome the problem of "conceded" citizenship, because citizens are not being given a set of rights but rather must work to secure their new rights. Citizens seeking to expand their rights often engage in contentious forms of politics to place their demands on political elites.[47] McAdam, Tarrow, and Tilly define contentious politics as "episodic, collective interaction among makers of claims and their objects when (a) at least one government is a claimant, an object of claims, or a party to the claims, and (b) the claims would, if realized, affect the interests of at least one of the claimants."[48] PB allows for cooperation and contestation, thereby enabling citizens to use PB as an institutional venue to expand their

46. Paoli and Telles 1998, 67 (emphasis in original).
47. Tarrow 1998.
48. McAdam, Tarrow, and Tilly 2001, 5.

citizenship rights. Contentious politics can be used inside and parallel to
PB to allow citizens to present their demands and arguments to fellow
citizens as well as to government officials.

Examination of PB Programs

The Spread of PB Programs Across Brazil

PB programs were first established in 1989 and 1990, just after the prom-
ulgation of Brazil's new constitution (1988), which decentralized resources
and authority over the provision of basic social services.[49] Municipalities
are responsible for 15 to 18 percent of all public spending, which translates to roughly 7 percent of Brazil's GDP.[50] The level of resources available to municipal governments now means that policies created at the
local level can significantly affect citizens' lives. The financial impact of
PB can be substantial. A conservative estimate of the eight municipalities included in this study suggests that at least U.S.$600 million was
spent by governments during the 1997–2004 period on projects that
were debated and voted on by citizens.[51]

The Workers' Party (Partido de Trabalhadores, or PT) has been the principal advocate of PB. As the PT grew in electoral strength between 1982
and 2006, so too did the number of PB programs. At the municipal level,
the PT governed 36 municipalities in the 1989–92 period, 53 in 1993–
96, 115 in 1997–2000, 187 in 2001–4, and 411 in 2005–8.[52] The political
strategy of the PT at the municipal level is inextricably linked to PB.
Through 2004, all PT governments in municipalities with at least one
hundred thousand residents had adopted PB.[53] Most PT governments in

49. Weyland 1996; Montero and Samuels, 2004; Montero 2000; Willis, Garman, and Haggard 2001.
50. Montero 2000.
51. I calculated this figure on the basis of the proposed cost of a project and whether the project was completed. For example, if X project had a proposed value of U.S.$50,000 and it was completed, I counted this as U.S.$50,000 that was spent on a PB project. I recognize that the value of projects often changes from the proposal stage to implementation, but generally the cost is higher, rather than lower. This is a conservative estimate. I also recognize that some PB projects may never be implemented, so I do not use the value of the proposed project but only include the value of those projects that had actually been completed.
52. Singer 1999.
53. One possible exception is the second administration of the PT in Belém (2001–4). During its first administration (1997–2000), PB was adopted. During the second period, the government moved away from the PB format and created an alternative participatory format.

smaller municipalities also adopted PB, but I am not able to verify the number that actually adopted PB. The PT invests heavily, ideologically and politically, in the "PT way of governing," which is a strategy based on transparency, the direct participation of citizens in decision-making venues, public deliberation, and a "co-administration" process.[54]

PB has also spread to municipalities that are not governed by the PT. During the 1989–92 period, 13 municipalities had PB (92 percent were PT). This increased to 57 (62 percent were PT) in 1993–96 and to 103 (42 percent were PT) in 1997–2000.[55] By 2004, 170 municipalities had active PB programs, but fewer than half (47 percent) were governed by the PT.[56] Most of the non-PT cases had been initiated during the 2001–4 administrations, which means that the close association between the PT and PB that is often cited in the literature is no longer empirically valid.

What Do We Know About Existing PB Programs?

There is an extensive body of literature on PB that this book builds upon to better account for PB's impact over a broader range of cases. The majority of published studies are of single cases, most of which target the successful example of Porto Alegre.[57] These accounts are richly detailed, providing excellent records of how PB developed; how it works; who participates; and its political, social, and policy impacts. I will summarize the main findings below to demonstrate what researchers have established as the principal processes and outcomes associated with the most successful cases.

There are also a number of works that analyze two or three cases and offer somewhat less optimistic accounts of the PB process.[58] The use of multiple cases, especially outside Porto Alegre, allows researchers to gather additional data to better evaluate whether the findings in Porto Alegre are replicable outside that pioneering experience. Of the authors cited above, Nylen is the only scholar not to use Porto Alegre as one of his case studies. He is also one of the few scholars to develop starkly different accounts of PB's impact, which may be a result of his case selection.

The academic literature on PB has focused on four main areas: (1) PB's

54. Guidry 2003; Hunter 2004.
55. Ribeiro and de Grazia 2003.
56. Wampler and Avritzer 2005, 41.
57. Abers 2000; Baiocchi 2003, 2005; Goldfrank 2003; Navarro 2003; Marquetti 2003; Santos 1998; Fedozzi 1998.
58. Nylen 2002, 2003; Wampler and Avritzer 2004; Goldfrank, 2007.

origins; (2) the enabling social and political environment that encourages successful outcomes; (3) who participates; and (4) the substantive effects of PB on citizens, public policies, state-society relations, and deliberation. I will refer throughout the course of the book to the principal findings of these authors to verify whether the main set of findings from the single- and dual-case-study approaches has been replicated in other cases.

PB's Beginnings

There is a general consensus in the literature that PB was developed in 1989–90 by the PT, which was then a leftist and socialist party, in conjunction with its CSO allies in the southern city of Porto Alegre. PB was initiated because of the shared set of interests of the newly elected PT municipal government and its political allies. The shared interests included using the state to promote social justice, opening the decision-making process to ordinary citizens, using the local state to empower individuals to exercise the rights they had won under the 1988 Constitution, and subverting the clientelistic relations that have long characterized the distribution of scarce resources.[59]

Although PB's particular rule set was developed in Porto Alegre, there were similar participatory experiences occurring across Brazil. For example, Recife, in Brazil's poor northeast, had two pioneering experiences— the Special Planning Zones of Recife (Plano de Regularização de Zonas Especiais de Interesse Social, or PREZEIS) and the "Mayor in the Neighborhood" program (see Chapter 6). The latter was an ad hoc program through which Recife's mayor held hundreds of meetings in the 1980s in low-income neighborhoods. The former program was legally constituted in 1989. It has a complex rule structure and focuses on the urban development of low-income neighborhoods. In São Paulo, to cite another example, community organizations working in the area of health care reform initiated citizens' councils, elected bodies of citizens who were responsible for negotiating with municipal, state, and federal administrations over heath-related issues. Porto Alegre's PB, therefore, was not an isolated development, but it is noteworthy because its particular rule set has proved to be quite successful in drawing large numbers of participants, producing identifiable policy outcomes, and being replicable in a variety of different settings.

59. Genro 1995b; Fedozzi 1998; Avritzer 2002.

Although there is a general consensus that PB was initiated in Porto Alegre on the basis of the shared set of interests among the PT and its civil society allies, there is different weight given to the importance of these actors in this process. Avritzer, for example, argues that Brazil experienced a political awakening in the 1980s and early 1990s, based on the development of "participatory publics" in civil society. He demonstrates that there was not only growth in the numbers of CSOs, but also a change in how these groups conducted business. There was an emphasis on public deliberation, public votes, and rotation of leadership. In other words, citizens re-created their own CSOs in hopes of avoiding clientelism. According to Avritzer's argument, these ideas traveled from civil society into political society and the state. When leftist politicians who were allied with these new CSOs were elected to the mayor's office, they helped to institutionalize the participatory practices that were initially experimented with by local and community organizations. According to this argument, PB was initiated by a government that drew from the ideas and interests of CSOs. The government and citizens created a new rule set that followed the spirit of the "participatory publics" but also reflected an interest in producing specific public policies.

The second line of argumentation about PB's origins is that it was principally initiated by the PT government.[60] This argument focuses on the PT's narrow 1988 electoral victory. The PT won the election with just over a third of the votes and needed to reach out into the community to build a stronger base of support. The PT, thus, initiated PB as a means to reorder how the local state functioned, while simultaneously mobilizing large numbers of citizens. The PT began a series of internal administrative reforms that allowed the government to promote good governance and social justice.[61] In other words, the PT worked with CSOs to establish PB, but the principal agent behind the necessary administrative, legal, and political changes that supported PB was the PT.

Even though these accounts place different emphases on the relative weight of the government and CSOs, there is general consensus that PB was founded through their shared interests. As this book will demonstrate, especially in the cases of São Paulo, Rio Claro, and Blumenau, PB can also be adopted by government officials who have not been strongly pressured by CSOs to adopt this form of participatory democracy. This,

60. Abers 1998, 2000; Baiocchi 2003; Fedozzi 1998.
61. Fedozzi 1998.

as we shall see in Chapters 5 and 6, helps to produce significantly different outcomes from those of the original cases that were largely based on government-cso cooperation.

Political and Social Environment

Municipalities that elect leftist mayors tend to have higher-than-average standard of living (measured by the Human Development Index [HDI] score) and have denser networks of csos.[62] PB therefore is more likely to be adopted when there is a higher HDI score, dense networks of csos, and the presence of a leftist mayor. PB has been adopted almost exclusively at the municipal level of government in Brazil (for a more extensive analysis of federalism and the distribution of authority, see Chapter 2). The state government of Rio Grande do Sul, of which Porto Alegre is the capital, adopted a statewide PB program between 1998 and 2002 under the leadership of a PT governor, but this remains the only substantive attempt to adopt PB at the state level.[63]

During the first phase of PB, from 1989 to 1996, the overwhelming majority of governments that adopted PB were from the PT or other leftist parties.[64] Between 1997 and 2004, the PT and other leftist parties adopted just under half of all PB cases in Brazil, with centrist parties adopting an additional third, and conservative parties adopting the remainder.[65] In Brazil, the political Left was the primary opposition to the military government, which had centralized authority and closed access to most decision-making venues. The political Left, the PT in particular, was a strong proponent of the decentralization of authority as a means to overhaul the Brazilian state and society. The late adoption of PB by non-leftist governments reflects the mainstreaming of PB as it began to be considered a good government program as opposed to an experiment in radical democracy that would reorder the Brazilian state and society.[66]

Why is it that wealthier municipalities were among the first to adopt PB? One reason is that wealthier cities are more likely to have a broad base of unions, NGOs, and middle-class activists who are interested in promoting

62. Ribeiro and de Grazia 2003; Wampler and Avritzer 2005.
63. Goldfrank and Schneider 2003; Faria 2002.
64. Wampler and Avritzer 2005.
65. Ribeiro and de Grazia 2003; Wampler and Avritzer 2005.
66. Wampler and Avritzer 2005.

good government and direct citizen involvement in decision-making venues.[67] Likewise, this broad base is also more likely to support left-of-center political parties in Brazil, which have been the primary political society agents that support participatory institutions. An additional reason that wealthier cities are more likely to adopt PB is that their municipal budgets are larger, which makes it easier for both politicians and CSO activists to envision how the budgetary process may become the center of political disputes.[68] A final reason is that wealthier municipalities in Brazil have larger middle classes that no longer rely on the state for health care, education, or private services. Simply put, the middle class has exited the municipal service-provision system, which leaves greater resources for the lower classes. Although this explanation has not been substantiated empirically, this book introduces anecdotal information.

Goldfrank's work on participatory programs in Porto Alegre, Montevideo, and Caracas emphasizes two additional factors that strongly condition how participatory democracy will function.[69] Goldfrank compares participatory experiences in Venezuela, Uruguay, and Brazil and demonstrates that participatory programs are more likely to be successful when authority has been decentralized to local governments from national and state governments. In the eight cases under review in the present volume, the level of decentralized authority is largely constant, which means that this institutional explanation cannot account for the differences in outcomes. Goldfrank also argues that strong party institutionalization precludes the development of a strong participatory program because entrenched politicians and interest groups block the reformers' efforts.

Who Participates?

PB programs were initiated to allow citizens who had previously been excluded from policy-making venues to be directly involved in shaping state policies. PB's rules, as we will see in Chapter 2, are geared toward the redistribution of state resources to low-income neighborhoods. Most PB programs' rules are crafted in such a way that the results will likely favor low-income residents over those of the middle and upper class. Even though PB is formally open to all residents of a municipality, we should not expect that all inhabitants will have equal incentives to participate.

67. Wampler and Avritzer 2005.
68. Teixeira and Albuquerque 2006.
69. Goldfrank, 2007.

Research in Porto Alegre, Betim, and Belo Horizonte demonstrates that the majority of participants in PB are, in fact, from low-income households and neighborhoods.[70] Women participate in equal numbers to those of men, numbers far above their participation rates in other political institutions.[71] However, the participants do not reflect the "average" individual, because most participants belong to CSOs. Nylen, for example, finds that PB does not mobilize or empower the unorganized.[72] Rather, he notes that PB provides new political opportunities that allow civil society activists to be directly involved in policy decision-making venues. Abers, by contrast, finds that Porto Alegre's PB encourages the growth of new CSOs, which gives voice to the previously unorganized. She explicitly argues that the previously unorganized find their way to PB, which then helps them to build CSOs in their communities.[73]

In Chapter 3, I will lay out the basic demographic results of a survey, the PB Comparative Survey, that I conducted among elected representatives in all eight PB programs. The survey participants are from Brazil's lower classes, although they are not among the poorest. The chief characteristic that differentiates PB participants from their fellow Brazilians is that the PB participants had high levels of participation in CSOs.

Outcomes

PB programs have been analyzed from a variety of approaches, which has helped to produce a rich tapestry of verifiable outcomes. In this section, I present an overall but clearly not exhaustive list of the changes that PB has been identified as having produced.

The effect of PB on CSOs and civil society receives the lion's share of attention, since scholars have sought to demonstrate how this new participatory democracy institution reshapes civil society. Abers, for example, argues that Porto Alegre's PB has helped to reinforce existing CSOs and to contribute to the development of new CSOs. PB, therefore, has the capacity to generate a denser civil society, which helps to spread social capital. Abers's key insight is that state-sanctioned institutions, in this case PB, can help produce the types of social capital that Putnam has long argued

70. Baiocchi 2001; Goldfrank 2003; *Quem é o Público do Orçamento Participativo*, 1999; Nylen 2003.
71. Baiocchi 2001.
72. Nylen 2003.
73. Abers 1998, 2000.

are crucial to producing effective democratic institutions.[74] Abers argues that a state-society "synergy" developed in Porto Alegre, thereby allowing PB to promote the interests of citizens and government officials. The principal drawback to this analysis is that the government's political interests in supporting the delegation of authority to citizens are not clearly spelled out. We are left to believe that it is the "political will" of the government that is largely responsible for creating this "synergy," but we do not know why the government would want to engage in this form of governance.

Baiocchi's 2005 book, *Militants and Citizens*, does an excellent job of showing how PB affects CSOS in very different ways.[75] For example, in neighborhoods with CSOS that want to participate in PB, PB can have the effect of reinforcing existing CSOS (similar to Abers's and Nylen's argument). In neighborhoods with few CSOS, PB can have the effect of stimulating the growth of new CSOS (again, similar to Abers's argument). However, in neighborhoods that have existing networks of CSOS that are not interested in participating in PB, the effects of this new participatory-democracy experience can be divisive. CSOS that are not interested in working within a participatory-democracy format may resist the institutionalization of PB at the local level and may actively work to undermine the experience. For example, a CSO hostile to PB could question the legitimacy of the institution as a means to discourage community residents from attending PB meetings. New CSOS might find it difficult to use the new institutional structure because of the older CSOS' resistance.

Baiocchi's work also focuses on the deliberative processes that occur within PB meetings. There are two different findings of importance. First, Baiocchi finds that education or gender differences do not "pose insurmountable barriers to effective participation."[76] PB provides an opportunity for individuals to learn how to use the rules to more effectively pursue their own interests. Individuals who participate for many years learn how to navigate the complex process and devise strategies that mitigate the stark social differences that mark Brazilian societies.

Baiocchi also finds that PB is helping to foster a deliberative public space that allows for contestation and group solidarity. The deliberative public space does not assume consensus, nor does it assume that individuals should be able to avoid conflict. Rather, Baiocchi demonstrates how social and political conflicts are brought into PB by citizens and CSO leaders,

74. Abers 2000; Putnam 1993.
75. Baiocchi 2005.
76. Baiocchi 2001, 51.

thereby allowing extended discussions of divisive issues. Beyond conflict, PB also has the potential to generate intra- and intergroup solidarity. Intragroup solidarity is promoted when groups specifically work to generate and defend proposals for public works that they would like to have the government implement. Intergroup solidarity is promoted when groups must reach out to other groups to build broad coalitions to have their public works included in the budget, as illustrated in the vignette about Belo Horizonte presented earlier in this chapter.

The redistributive effect that PB is supposed to have on social policies is one of the reasons that PB was initiated and is another line of research that has been undertaken. Researchers have found it very difficult to measure the redistributive impact of PB for methodological and data reasons. The most successful attempt to illustrate a connection between PB and social spending was undertaken by Aldemir Marquetti, an economist living and working in Porto Alegre. Marquetti demonstrates that lower-income neighborhoods in Porto Alegre received a greater share of investment spending than did middle- or upper-income neighborhoods.[77] Marquetti's argument and data set are the strongest evidence to date that a PB program has had a redistributive effect. Porto Alegre's municipal government spent a greater per capita share of its "new capital spending" over a ten-year period in poorer neighborhoods than in wealthier neighborhoods. But two caveats are in order. First, the evidence presented in the present volume suggests that the experiences of Porto Alegre are not representative of most PB programs, which means that Marquetti's findings are not generalizable. Second, we do not, of course, have any way to know whether the redistribution effects are a result of PB or of the presence of a leftist government that held municipal power for sixteen years and was committed to social justice.

Nylen's comparative work on Betim and Belo Horizonte (also one of the case studies in the present volume) is the foundation for his argument that PB is helping to "democratize democracy."[78] He finds that PB provides political opportunities for already active members of CSOs, which gives interested citizens the ability to have their voices heard. PB therefore marks a shift in how decisions about state resources and power are made in Brazil because citizens are directly involved in policy making. There is extensive literature that has shown that traditional policy-making

77. Marquetti 2003.
78. Nylen 2003.

venues in Brazil are primarily open to small numbers of elected and appointed government officials.[79] If Nylen's arguments can be substantiated, then it will be plausible to assert that PB is helping to transform political life in Brazil.

Avritzer and I argue that one of the primary effects of PB is that it is helping to change the basic processes through which citizens gain access to resources. Clientelism is less likely to exist in PB than in Brazil's traditional resource-distribution system, in which citizens must negotiate directly with legislators or members of the executive branch. Avritzer and I used a survey conducted in Porto Alegre and Belo Horizonte to show that prior to PB's adoption, most respondents negotiated directly with government officials over policy outcomes (such as clientelistic exchanges). According to Wampler and Avritzer:

> *Prior* to PB, 60 percent of survey respondents in Belo Horizonte and 41 percent in Porto Alegre relied on the direct intervention of politicians to secure public goods.[80]

> After [PB's] implementation, 90 percent of respondents in Porto Alegre and 60 percent of respondents in Belo Horizonte responded that they were able to gain access to resources by working within the new institutional format. When asked if the intervention of politicians was needed in order to secure the implementation of a public project, 74 percent in Porto Alegre and 67 percent in Belo Horizonte responded negatively.[81]

This overview of scholarship on PB helps to confirm that PB has helped transform state-society relations in Brazil. Most significant, low-income citizens who have traditionally been excluded from public decision-making venues are now at the center of this new institution. Low-income citizens are making decisions that change how their governments function as well as the policies that are implemented. Even though the majority of the works cited above are largely supportive of PB, the analysis in this book will demonstrate that PB programs have produced both negative and positive outcomes. It is my hope that an analysis of these eight cases will shed light on the generalizability of the aforementioned works.

79. Hagopian 1996; Weyland 1996; Abrucio 1998.
80. Wampler and Avritzer 2004, 305.
81. Wampler and Avritzer 2004, 305–6.

The Argument: Explaining Outcomes

To account for the wide variation in PB outcomes, three factors have strong explanatory power and two additional factors have a secondary level of importance. The three most important factors are (1) level of mayoral support for the delegation of authority through PB, (2) type of civil society activity, and (3) PB's rules. The two secondary factors that affect PB outcomes are mayoral-legislative relations and available new capital investment spending. To produce a strong PB program, it is necessary to have high levels of mayoral support, a civil society that can engage in both cooperation and contestation, and rules that delegate specific types of direct authority to citizens. As mayoral support drops, as CSOs are unable to engage in both forms of political behavior, and as the rules fail to delegate authority, PB outcomes will weaken. There is clearly interaction between mayoral support for delegation and the presence of contentious politics, since an increase in contentious politics by CSOs can lead governments to delegate additional authority and resources. PB's rules can fragment, centralize, promote deliberation, or encourage co-optation. Although most PB programs largely replicate the rules that were created in Porto Alegre, there are some significant differences that help to explain outcomes.

Strong results in the final two areas, mayoral-legislative relations and available investment spending, are necessary but not sufficient to produce positive PB outcomes. These factors are included in the analysis because they often help limit PB's impact, but a positive result in either area is insufficient by itself to produce a positive outcome.

Mayoral Support

Mayoral support for the delegation of authority is vital because mayoral administrations initiate and administrator PB. Mayors make calculated decisions regarding the degree of authority they are willing to delegate. Mayoral administrations are responsible for deciding which projects selected by the PB participants will be implemented.[82] In Brazil, the implementation of new capital investment spending, which is the principal focus of PB programs, is at the complete discretion of the mayor's office.

---

82. According to Brazilian law, no "new capital investment" projects (focus of most PB programs) included in the budget have to be implemented; they are legally classified as discretionary funding. Federal law 4.320, April 3, 1964.

Decision makers within the mayoral administration must be willing to spend scarce resources on projects selected by citizens.

Although PB is a form of participatory democracy with direct and representative elements, it also falls within Brazil's historical legacy of mayoral domination of municipal agenda-setting.[83] Ironically, mayors must first centralize authority in their own hands before they can hand that authority back to citizens through PB. For PB to work well, mayors need to decentralize the administration to bring PB processes "closer" to the people; create internal procedures for preparing and presenting information through workshops and seminars that allows citizens to make sense of complex policy issues; retrain staff and bureaucrats to work directly with citizens; and, perhaps most important, transform the process through which projects are "green-lighted" toward implementation.[84] If a mayor is unable to gain control over the bureaucracy or his or her own political appointees, then it is not likely that the mayor would be able to delegate authority directly to citizens.

What accounts for strong mayoral support? What explains why some mayors are more willing to delegate authority than are others? Several factors help account for delegation. First, mayors delegate authority through PB as a means to reach out to their municipality's most active CSO participants. PB gives mayors direct access to community leaders, which means that PB serves as a potential recruitment site as well as a forum through which government officials can discover a community's most pressing problems. PB allows the mayoral administration to reach out to citizens and CSO activists who are not necessarily part of the mayor's political party. Second, mayors delegate authority to reward their most loyal base of supporters. CSO activists who work on behalf of political parties have demanded, since the late 1980s, that they have direct access to decision-making venues. PB provides a means for government officials to give their political base a direct role in governmental decision making.

Elections are held every two years in Brazil. Presidential, gubernatorial, and state and federal legislative elections are held in the same years (for example, 1994, 1998, 2002, 2006), and mayoral and municipal legislative contests are held in the "midterm" years (1996, 2000, 2004). Federal senatorial elections may occur in either election cycle. Therefore,

83. Leal 1997.
84. Abers 2000; Baiocchi 2005; Fedozzi 1998.

mayors and their parties face important elections every two years. PB not only provides mayors with an opportunity to have constant access to the most active CSO leaders; it also allows the mayors to identify which CSO leaders do the best job at turning out their supporters, which is crucial information for elections.

The third factor that helps explain mayoral delegation is party politics. PB has helped the PT to brand itself as participatory, democratic, and concerned with social justice. The political party that has most strongly advocated PB is the leftist (sometime socialist) Workers' Party (Partido de Trabalhadores, or PT). Within the universe of the PT governments in large municipalities (more than one hundred thousand residents), all but one implemented PB between 1989 and 2004. PB became part of the "PT way of governing."[85] As we will see in Chapters 4 through 7, there are significant differences within the PT, which means that not all PT mayors demonstrated a similar commitment to PB.

Finally, mayors are also willing to delegate authority because of an ideological commitment to deepening democracy through the direct involvement of citizens in public life. The political opposition that came of age during the resistance to the military government in the 1980s strongly supported the direct incorporation of citizens in order to "empower" citizens and to transform how the Brazilian state functioned.[86] Mayors who are connected to the "participatory publics" that Avritzer and I have written about elsewhere are also more likely to increase the degree of authority that they are willing to delegate.[87]

This factor, mayoral support, demonstrates the vital importance of analyzing PB through an institutional lens. PB is a new institutional format that is housed within the mayoral administration. The role that PB will occupy within a municipality is largely conditioned by decisions made by the mayor and his or her inner circle regarding the degree of authority that should be given to citizens.

Type of Civil Society Activity: Cooperation and Contestation

How do CSOs and individual citizens act inside and outside PB? What strategies do they pursue vis-à-vis government officials and their fellow

---

85. Hunter 2004; Guidry 2003; Wampler and Avritzer 2005.
86. Dirceu and Palmeria 1998; Genro 1997; Villas Boas and Telles 1995.
87. Wampler and Avritzer 2004.

participants? csos and individual citizens must be willing to cooperate in a government-sponsored program while also being able, when necessary, to engage in contentious behavior.[88] Cooperation and contestation are both needed, since there are deliberative and competitive decision-making components to PB. Participants must be willing to cooperate with the government and their fellow participants in order to facilitate meetings and negotiation. If groups are bitter rivals and unable to agree on seemingly simple matters such as a meeting format, then PB begins to weaken because it is no longer a deliberative space focused on a broader set of problems, but instead becomes a political space that rival groups try to occupy and control.

Cooperation is necessary but can easily breed co-optation, which means that contentious politics is a necessary component to allow PB programs to flourish. Citizens must vigorously defend their projects in the face of governmental and other participants' doubts and potential indifference. Since PB is a decision-making body, there are multiple groups (government officials, neighborhood associations, bureaucrats, contractors) pursuing their own interests, and participants need to contest the information and interests of other groups and government officials. If groups are unwilling or unable to vigorously defend their interests against those of other groups and government officials, then PB will weaken because the participants will likely be steamrolled by the government or other groups.

Explaining the variation among municipalities with regard to contestation and cooperation requires that we examine the history of civil society activity prior to PB, the relationship between csos and political parties, the deliberative and accountability spaces that have been created within PB, and the reaction of the mayoral administrations to contestation. In each case study chapter, I will show how these factors led to the degree of cooperation and contestation present in and around PB.

The capacity of csos to engage in cooperative and contentious forms of politics demonstrates the importance of csos' choices as they design the strategies they will use to pursue their interests. The density of civil society, which can be conceptualized as the number of csos per capita or as the percentage of individuals who participate in a cso, is a contributing factor, but it is less important than the ability of csos to simultaneously engage in cooperative and contentious politics, which should give pause to scholars who advocate that a dense civil society will help strengthen

88. Tarrow 1998.

democracy. Deepening democracy through PB necessitates both cooperative and contentious politics.

PB's Rules

PB's rules, which will be explained in greater detail in Chapter 2, provide a series of incentives intended to produce specific types of behavior. Although the rules are largely similar across the eight municipalities studied, there is sufficient variation in rules to produce different outcomes. Rule variations stem from the timing of PB's initiation, local political and social factors, the location of the municipality, and the size of the municipality. One of the benefits of a cross-municipal study is the ability to show how different rules produce different outcomes.

Rule changes that directly pertain to participants' authority are of particular importance to the argument presented in this book. *The rules do matter,* which suggests that PB has emerged as a significant political institution capable of inducing different types of attitudes and behaviors. For PB programs to be successful, citizens must have decision-making authority independent of the mayor's office. Citizens must be granted the right to make significant policy decisions that affect their communities. As the level of authority weakens, PB's outcomes become weaker and shallower. If citizens participate in meetings but do not make any meaningful decisions, PB programs will be emasculated as an institutional space that can help deepen democracy.

In the most telling example, the municipality of Santo André created a "PB council" in 1989 whose membership consisted of twenty-six citizens and twenty-six government officials. This effort to create a "co-administration" led to extensive negotiations between "PB delegates" and government officials but not to the delegation of authority to citizens, because the government held a virtual veto over all decisions. Rules matter because they are intended to help delegate authority and because the unintended consequence of unclear rules is a limited delegation of authority.

PB's rules provide incentives that reward low-income individuals who live in communities that can mobilize large groups. Individuals living in smaller communities, or in unorganized communities, have few direct incentives to continue to participate in PB programs. PB's rules encourage public deliberative processes, both in formal meetings and in local community meetings. Finally, PB's rules encourage public and private negotiations among citizens and vis-à-vis government officials, both within PB and in parallel meeting spaces.

Mayoral-Legislative Relations

An electoral and political environment that is generally supportive of the delegation of authority directly to citizens increases the likelihood of producing positive results through PB. PB redistributes authority at the instigation of the mayor and cso allies, meaning that members of the legislative branches, particularly opposition municipal legislators, are the most likely to resist changes. After all, citizens in PB are principally negotiating over small and medium-sized public works projects, which have long been the "bread and butter" of local politicians. An electoral and political environment favorable to the mayor helps to dampen the prospect of opposition legislators' derailing the PB process. PB is more likely to succeed if the government has a broad base of support in the municipal legislature. Legislators often claim that they have a higher degree of legitimacy than PB delegates because the legislators were elected from a broader pool of citizens and received a greater number of votes. This issue will be explored in greater depth in Chapter 2.

Mayors who must spend considerable political capital shoring up support in the municipal legislature may have to redirect scarce resources to provide small pork barrel projects to satiate the legislators' thirst for campaign resources. São Paulo is an extreme case where the municipal legislature was extremely combative, successfully derailing the efforts of PT Mayor Erundina (1989–92) to implement a viable PB program. PB can be systematically undermined if there are enough municipal legislators opposed to it. Moderate support for the mayor in the municipal legislature increases the mayor's flexibility, should he or she choose to delegate authority, but it does not guarantee that he or she will do so.

Strong support from legislators for the PB process may also free up funds that might otherwise be earmarked for building legislators' support. These legislators are willing to subsume their short-term political interests to a broader strategy of building a new institution, which may ultimately give the mayor's party a solid base of mobilized supporters. Some legislators may support PB because of the dividends that may be gained at the ballot box. Overall, positive mayoral-legislative relations are necessary for producing successful PB programs because they increase the mayor's flexibility, while acrimonious mayoral-legislative relations can put a halt to the mayor's efforts to delegate authority.

Available New Capital Investment Spending

Finally, an adequate level of financial resources is necessary because PB programs allow citizens to make decisions regarding the distribution of public works. If governments have limited resources, the decision-making power of the participants will also be limited. As the level of resources increases, there is an increasing probability that citizens will have greater opportunities to select policies that have the potential to reshape their communities. The amount of available new capital investment spending must be analyzed in absolute and relative terms. In absolute terms, we can compare the amount of resources that each municipality dedicates to PB with the amount of non-PB new capital investment spending. It is also important to compare the spending among the eight municipalities. For this, I will use per capita new capital investment spending. Some municipalities are constrained by low resources and high demand. In other municipalities, the mayoral administrations choose not to fully fund PB, which is again best demonstrated through comparative research design. Differentiating between structural barriers and mayoral choice will be unraveled in each case study chapter.

In Chapters 3–7, I demonstrate how these factors, when analyzed together, provide the most compelling explanation for outcomes. It is necessary for a PB program to have positive results in each area to produce a successful PB program. When PB administrators face difficult conditions in any one area, there is a drop-off in the overall results produced.

Comparative Research Design and Methodological Advances

PB programs have been widely studied. What, then, does this book add to the debate that no other book has been able to offer? This book offers the first systematic comparison of multiple cases to generate better explanations for PB's origins, internal processes, and outcomes. There are wide variations in the outcomes that PB has generated, ranging from the delegation of authority to citizens and the implementation of PB-selected public policy works to the inability, unwillingness, or both, of mayoral administrations to spend much time on PB projects.

Of the eight municipalities included in this study (see the map included at the beginning of this chapter for a visual reference), two are in Brazil's southernmost region: Porto Alegre (Rio Grande do Sul) and Blumenau (Santa Catarina). Three municipalities are in the state of São Paulo: Rio Claro, Santo André, and São Paulo. Two municipalities are in the state of Minas Gerais: Belo Horizonte and Ipatinga. And one municipality is located in the northeast: Recife, the state capital of Pernambuco.

These eight municipalities have been selected to allow for variation in the composition of each respective municipality's political history, economic development, and civil society. The aim is to include municipalities that are similar enough to allow for rigorous comparison without selecting only the best-known cases, which should help to avoid "selecting on the dependent variable" problem. To select specific municipalities, I considered their population size, PB's length of time in operation, regional location, and political party in control of the government in 2003.

First, only municipalities with more than one hundred thousand residents have been included. Of Brazil's 5,500 municipalities, 225 have at least one hundred thousand residents; of the 225, a total of 103 (45 percent) had PB in 2003. Only municipalities with more than one hundred thousand residents have been included, because there are fewer financial and economic differences among this group of 225 than among Brazil's other 5,275 municipalities. By excluding smaller municipalities, it is possible to better control the impact of wealth on PB outcomes. The drawback to this approach is that it does not compare large to small or wealthier to poorer. However, as shown in Chapters 3–7, there are enough substantial differences among the eight municipalities to indicate that this was a viable research strategy.

Second, I only considered PB programs that had functioned for at least seven years in a municipality, because there is a sharp learning curve associated with PB that only begins to level off after three or four years.[89] This reduced the range of possible cases to thirty-five in 2003, which means that 31 percent of eligible municipalities are included in the study.

I also have sought regional diversity, which was harder to establish. Of the eight municipalities, two are in the south, three are in the southeastern state of São Paulo, two are in the southeastern state of Minas

89. Ribeiro and de Grazia 2003; Wampler 2004a.

Gerais, and one is in the northeast. Recife was the only large municipality in the northeast that had been using PB for the seven-year minimum. There were no municipalities in the north that fit the criteria for inclusion.

The second addition that this book makes to the ongoing theoretical and empirical debates is the collection of a broad set of evidence and data. To successfully compare the selected municipalities, I draw from several different sources of data, including a survey among PB participants, interviews with government officials and PB participants, budgetary analysis, focus groups, legislative analysis, and participant observation in more that one hundred meetings over a ten-year period. As I reviewed the literature on PB, I was struck by two recurring shortcomings: the absence of data to demonstrate the effect of PB on spending and public policy outcomes, and the use of government-produced data that has not been independently verified. Governments that adopt PB seek to promote transparency in the policy-making process, but we must remember that these same governments are run by politicians engaged in extremely competitive electoral environments. In Porto Alegre's successful case of PB, I was given documents by a government official five months prior to the municipal election. I was asked, "Please, do not to share these documents [until after the election] because the information might be manipulated."[90] Governments have a tendency to inflate their good works and downplay their problems, but this, unfortunately, has been overlooked by many scholars and policy makers publishing work on PB.

The third methodological advantage of this book is the collection of similar data over a ten-year period. I first studied participatory institutions in Brazil in 1995, with the support of a University of Texas and Ford Foundation summer grant after my first year in graduate school. This was followed by a yearlong predissertation grant that provided me the opportunity to take graduate courses at one of Brazil's premier universities (the State University of Campinas [Universidade Estadual de Campinas, or UNICAMP]) and conduct preliminary research. I then spent one year in Brazil conducting my dissertation research (1998–99). This was followed by a ten-month U.S. National Science Foundation postdoctoral fellowship (2003–4).

These methodological advantages hopefully will help situate the reader in the most important theoretical and political debates in Brazil and in

90. Andre Passos, interview, April 26, 2004.

comparative politics. The purpose is to create generalizable theories about participatory institutions, decentralization of authority, governance, and civil and political societies.

Book Outline

Chapter 2 begins with a detailed description of PB rules. I explain the complex process with an eye toward those readers unfamiliar with PB. Six of the seven other municipalities designed or revised their PB programs based on the Porto Alegre experience, so that experience will serve as the basis for describing PB. Santo André is the exception, because its PB program was initiated in 1989, the same year as Porto Alegre's PB. For those familiar with PB, the second part of Chapter 2 might be an appropriate place to begin because I highlight the unintended consequences generated by PB's rules.

The focus of Chapter 3 is a survey applied to 695 PB delegates in the eight municipalities. In the first half of the chapter I use descriptive statistics to show that most PB delegates are members of Brazil's lower classes (along education and income lines) but are extremely active in civil society (75 percent are active in civil society organizations). In the second half, I use ordinary least squared (OLS) and logistic regression to establish which factors explain the respondents' attitudes concerning their level of authority and their preferred strategies for securing public policies. I apply three models: individual level, municipal level, and aggregate level (each municipality). The broad collection of data provides us with the most comprehensive understanding of PB to date.

Chapters 4–7 are substantive, with each centered around a pair of municipalities that have similar outcomes. By focusing on two similar cases, I hope that the explanation for the outcomes will be more easily digestible for the reader. These chapters are rich in detail but are written with the intent of explaining the different outcomes. PB is now at a crossroads. It is being implemented across the world on the basis of a limited number of studies of the most successful cases. This book corrects that basic methodological error as I clearly explain what factors effect the successful, mediocre, and weak outcomes.

Participatory Budgeting:
Rules of the Game

> I participate in PB because before we didn't have
> access to the mayor's office, to the different parts
> of the bureaucracy. Today, in PB, we have the right
> to openly discuss our issues, our problems, our
> criticisms.
>
> —PB DELEGATE IN BELO HORIZONTE

> I did not participate in the previous PB programs
> because it always seemed too difficult and too far
> away from me. . . . But in João Paulo's administra-
> tion, PB came to us and I dove in to try something
> new.
>
> —PB DELEGATE IN RECIFE

When PB was being designed in Porto Alegre during the late 1980s, Brazil was experiencing a moment of political renewal. There was considerable change, reform, and upheaval in Brazil's political, institutional, and civil society environments.[1] The military government returned power to civilians in 1985 (via indirect elections), a new constitution was written over a two-year period and promulgated in October 1988, and direct presidential elections were held in 1989. There were widespread mobilizations of civil society actors in conjunction with each of these events, all of which contributed to a vibrant political atmosphere that provided an opportunity for reform and renovations.[2]

At the municipal level of government, the late 1980s and early 1990s were marked by political renewal as reformers and political entrepreneurs sought to devise new policies and institutions that would solve basic

1. Weffort 1984; Alvarez 1990; Keck 1992.
2. Villas Boas 1994; Fedozzi 1998; Wampler and Avritzer 2004; Avritzer 2002; Jacobi 1989.

problems and appeal to voters.[3] In Porto Alegre, citizens affiliated with an umbrella civil society organization (cso), the Union of Neighborhood Associations (União das Associações de Moradores de Porto Alegre, or uampa), began to demand direct participation in decision-making venues. Not willing to accept an electoral democracy in which citizens are required to vote every two years, uampa's leadership demanded that they exercise voice in public venues and have a vote on significant policy issues. These demands were not unique to Porto Alegre; cso activists in São Paulo, Belo Horizonte, Recife, and Santo André also demanded to be directly involved in the political institutions that would be established after Brazil's military government returned power to civilians and allowed for direct elections.[4]

The 1988 Constitution greatly increased municipal and state governments' authority and resources. Municipal governments find themselves responsible for providing public health care, educating larger numbers of elementary students, and being responsible for more infrastructure projects. And even though there has been devolution of authority to municipalities from the federal government, there has *not* been a corresponding deconcentration of authority between the mayoral and legislative chambers.[5] Mayors, for example, continue to be in firm control of the budgetary process, although legislators do have some basic checks that are intended to limit mayors' authority. Importantly, mayors continue to have complete discretion over the spending of new capital investments.

The most significant constitutional effort to redistribute authority within Brazilian municipalities was the introduction of issue-oriented councils (*conselhos*), which were designed to give csos, labor groups, and government officials a voice in policy making. The impact of these councils on policy making, however, has been limited because the institutional rules allow government officials to easily dominate them.[6] Nevertheless, the councils have served as an important instrument for agenda setting and influencing the debate.[7] Since the councils have had limited policy-making successes, pb is the principal institution in Brazil that gives

3. Dagnino 1994a.
4. Goldfrank, 2007. Goldfrank shows that uampa's early documents highlight eight previous experiences in which local governments had experimented with budgetary issues.
5. Couto and Abrucio 1995; Abrucio and Couto 1996; Figueiredo and Limongi 1999, 2000.
6. Dagnino 2002; Wampler 1997; Carvalho and Teixeira 2000, 37; Barban 2003; Tatagiba 2002; Santos, Ribiero, and de Azevedo 2004.
7. Coelho and Nobre 2004; Tatagiba 2002.

participants meaningful decision-making authority. Ironically, PB's most significant innovations have been made possible because of the continued concentration of authority in the mayor's office.

During the 1980s, many CSOs worked to increase their access to decision-making venues, often through the establishment of public forums at which citizens and government officials would directly interact. Many CSOs also sought to reorganize themselves internally, to create more transparent and democratic processes so that their leaders would not be able to negotiate private clientelistic deals with traditional politicians.[8] Thus, PB was developed in a context of increased municipal authority and resources, a continuation of the concentration of authority in the mayor's hand, and a willingness among CSOs and reformist politicians to experiment with new institutional types.

The purpose of this chapter is to situate PB in its broader institutional and political environment as well as to explain how PB functions. The first section places PB within Brazil's federal and municipal institutional environment to show the types of authority that are given to mayors, legislatures, and PB participants. The focus of the second is PB as an institution. Here I lay out a yearlong process of meetings and decision-making points to show when, where, and how citizens and governments officials affect policy outcomes. I make a specific effort to show how PB's rules are crafted to produce certain types of behaviors among citizens, participants, and government officials. The chapter concludes by looking at the limitations and unintended consequences of PB's rules.

Intragovernmental Relations and Mayoral Authority

Brazil's 1988 Constitution devolves considerable authority and resources to municipal governments. Municipalities now control between 15 and 20 percent of all government spending.[9] Brazilian municipalities are now responsible for education, public health care, and urban development; as a result, there are substantial resources and jobs available for distribution to voters. Municipal governments receive the majority of their resources through transfers from federal and state governments. They also have access to local property and sales taxes, although this resource largely

8. Wampler and Avritzer 2004.
9. Couto and Abrucio 1995; Montero 2000.

benefits larger and wealthier municipalities. During the two-year-long drafting of the constitution (1986–88), support to devolve authority came from the political Left as well as the Right. The Left supported the devolution of authority as a political strategy to gain control of the state from the bottom up; leftist politicians believed that they had the greatest chance of victory in elections.[10] The Left also supported the devolution of authority because they believed that the government should be as close as possible to the people to allow citizens to be involved in government, which they believed would help create a new and broader sense of citizenship.

The Right, especially entrenched conservative politicians, supported the devolution of authority because their base of support was in the thousands of small towns that dot Brazil. Many conservative politicians successfully made the transition from elected office under the military regime to holding elected office in the democratic regime.[11] During the military regime, Brazil's military government maintained elections for mayors in municipalities of fewer than one hundred thousand residents and for all municipal legislative offices. Candidates had to be in the government-sponsored ARENA party or the opposition, the MDB. The devolution of resources and authority greatly increased the staying power of conservative politicians.[12] Conservative groups also supported devolution for ideological reasons, most important among them the belief that local government can provide better solutions and services than the federal government.

Even though there has been the devolution of authority to municipalities, most legislative and budgetary authority still remains concentrated in the hands of the mayor, which is best conceptualized through the concept of "executivismo."[13] The institutional rules encourage mayors to initiate reform efforts and policies that reflect their interests; the rules concentrate legislative, budgetary, and administrative authority in the mayor's office, which gives the mayor great flexibility to govern. The broader set of laws (municipal, state, federal) discourage legislators from assuming active roles in the policy-making process and limit their access to important decision-making venues. Instead, the rules encourage municipal legislators to act as brokers between citizens and mayors.[14] Conflicts

10. Villas Boas 1994; Genro 1995a.
11. Power 2000; Hagopian 1996.
12. Hagopian 1996; Power 2000.
13. Couto and Abrucio, 1995; Wampler 2000b.
14. Wampler 2000b, 1999.

among municipal legislators and PB participants are driven by ideological, institutional, and public resources interests.

Municipal legislators, elected by citizens via an open-list proportional representation system, claim that they are more representative than local community leaders.[15] Municipal legislators often claim that they are the legitimate representatives of the people and therefore should be the ones responsible for making public policy. Municipal legislators back up their claim by highlighting that most PB programs mobilize between 1 percent and 3 percent of the adult population. PB delegates often counter these arguments by contending that they are more closely aligned with their communities, making them more qualified representatives. Community leaders back up their claim by pointing out that most municipal legislators receive a very small fraction of the vote. For example, the 247 municipal legislators elected in 1996 in the eight municipalities included in this book received an average of less than 1 percent of the total valid votes casts.[16] This low percentage indicates that the municipal legislators' claims about the degree to which they represent the voters should be viewed rather cautiously. Municipal legislators receive such a small percentage of the vote that their claims to be the "legitimate" representatives of the people appear to be quite questionable.

Materially, municipal legislators and CSO/PB participants are in direct competition over the distribution of scarce resources and public works. The majority of PB-approved projects are small and medium-sized public works, which are the lifeblood of local politicians. CSOs often focus on these local issues and local projects as a way to motivate their supporters to participate and because these projects fit within their range of policy experiences. Therefore, a successful PB program will likely diminish the informal and formal powers of municipal legislators, which is why those legislators outside the mayor's governing coalition will be hostile to this new institutional space.

The charters that govern these eight municipalities are virtually identical, which provides for a "natural experiment."[17] Brazil's electoral system

---

15. For an extensive discussion of these issues, see Nylen 2003, chaps. 6, 7.

16. Tribunal Supremo Eleitoral de São Paulo.

17. After the 1988 Constitution was promulgated, each municipality debated and passed its own charter. A recent study, based on forty of the largest municipalities, suggests that the differences between each municipality's respective charter are minimal. See Ribeiro 1994. A close reading of the charters of Recife, São Paulo, and Porto Alegre confirms the lack of substantial differences between their respective charters. One difference is the language surrounding how direct participation occurs within decision-making venues.

for city council members is open-list, municipal-wide, proportional representation, which means that seats are allocated first to each electoral
coalition based on the number of votes that the electoral coalition receives.
Within that electoral coalition, the number of votes that individual candidates receive determines who gets those seats. Therefore, candidates
are in competition with members of their own party as well as with candidates from other parties.[18] Municipal legislators are charged with the
responsibility of approving the annual budget, giving them a formal role
in budgetary processes.

Federal legislation dating back to March 1964 (prior to the military
coup) gives the mayor virtually all power over budgetary and allocation
decisions.[19] This legislation diminished the legislators' role in producing
public policy and stifled their voices in key decision-making venues.

The budgetary and legislative powers of municipal legislators are sum-
marized below.

(a) Legislators have no legislative authority to order the mayor to spend
resources. Municipal council members *cannot* introduce legislation that
would require the mayoral administration to spend resources.

(b) Authority to amend the mayor's proposed budget requires municipal council members to transfer a spending allocation from one budget
line to another. It does not allow council members to "zero-out" any budget
allocation, nor does it allow them to increase or decrease the mayor's proposed budget.

(c) The mayor has a line-item veto, allowing vetoes of any specific
amendments. The mayor does not have to implement any budgetary
amendment.

(d) The budget, proposed by the mayor and approved by the council,
indicates the limit of what the mayor may spend but *does not require* the
mayor to spend any discretionary resources (for example, new capital
investment spending).

(e) The mayor may increase spending on any item in the budget between 5 percent and 40 percent without seeking the prior approval of the
council.[20]

18. Ames 1995a; Samuels 2002.
19. Federal legislation 4.320, March 1964.
20. Porto Alegre's council members reduced this percentage over a number of years and
reached a low figure of 5 percent in 1998. Recife's council members reduced this percentage
over the course of a number of years and reached a low figure of 20 percent in 1998. São

(f) If the municipal council fails to approve an annual budget, the previous year's budget is legally reissued. This avoids a shutdown of government, but it also diminishes legislators' negotiating power.

Most important, municipal legislators do not have the "power of the purse."

The legislative branch does have some authority it can use to pressure mayors to respond to its demands. Municipal legislators have oversight functions that can be applied to investigate allegations of mayoral, legislative, and administrative misconduct. These investigative functions require legislators to establish majority support, which is often difficult to do in the face of overwhelming mayoral authority. There are few incentives for municipal legislators to work on a complicated policy proposal because legislation initiated by a municipal council member may not have any resources tied to it, and the "liberation" of resources is at the discretion of the mayor's office.

Legislators do have the right to pass budget amendments. They cannot increase the size of the mayor's proposed budget, but must transfer resources from another budget line to fund their proposed amendment. Budget amendments approved by the municipal legislative branch and included in the annual budget do *not* have to be spent by the mayor. This offers little incentive for legislators to pass budget amendments. Evidence from Recife, Porto Alegre, and São Paulo illustrates this point. Between 1994 and 1998, municipal legislators in Recife approved 290 budget amendments that altered less than 1 percent of the overall budget.[21] In Porto Alegre, 53 budget amendments were approved, which altered just 0.54 percent of the overall budget.[22] In São Paulo, no budget amendments were approved during this period.[23]

What this tells us is that mayors have been given increased authority and resources by the 1988 Constitution that they can implement with few checks from municipal legislators. Although the checks-and-balances system at Brazil's municipal level does provide municipal legislators with a few institutional checks on a mayor's policies, these checks require majority support. And since mayors have wide latitude over spending decisions,

---

Paulo's council members reduced this figure to 5 percent under Luiza Erundina but increased it to 40 percent under the Maluf and Pitta administrations.

21. Câmara Municipal de Recife 1994–98.

22. *Diario Official de Prefeitura Municipal de Porto Alegre* (1994–98).

23. *Diário Oficial do Prefeitura Municipal de São Paulo* (1994–98).

they can use these resources to parcel out small infrastructure or "constituency service" projects to draw the support of centrist legislators and create a stable voting majority.

Rules of the Game

The rules of PB are similar but not identical in the majority of PB programs. The rules covered in this section are largely based on Porto Alegre's PB. In Chapters 4–7, where I analyze each of the eight municipalities in greater detail, I will cover the principal deviations from the rules. In Porto Alegre, government officials and cso leaders designed the rules. In the other municipalities, there was a lesser degree of direct involvement by cso leaders. Participants generally, but not always, approve the initial set of rules and any subsequent changes in the rules. Although the rules do vary from city to city and state to state, it is possible to identify the typical guiding tenets of PB programs. The basic components of PB are as follows:

(a) There is a division of the municipality into regions to facilitate meetings and the distribution of resources. Citizens are elected as "PB delegates" within their region. Municipalities are decentralized to the local, district level.

(b) Government-sponsored meetings are held throughout the year, covering different aspects of the budgeting and policy-making cycles: distribution of information, policy proposals, debates on proposals, selection of policies, election of delegates, and oversight.

(c) A "Quality-of-Life Index" is created by the government to serve as the basis for the distribution of resources. Regions with higher poverty rates, denser populations, and less infrastructure (for example, government services) receive a higher proportion of resources than better-off and wealthier neighborhoods.

(d) There is public deliberation and negotiation among participants and vis-à-vis the government over resources and policies at the regional level.

(d) The "Bus Caravan of Priorities" allows PB's elected representatives to visit all preapproved project sites before the final vote. This allows delegates to evaluate the social needs of a proposed project.

(e) Citizens vote for elected representatives, PB delegates, who represent their interests during negotiations with other delegates and government officials.

(f) Elected representatives vote on all final projects. Voting can be done by secret ballot or though a public show of hands. The results become part of the public record.

(g) A municipal-wide council (PB council) is elected to make final decisions and to exercise oversight committees. All regions elect two representatives to this council, which oversees PB and makes final budget recommendations. This council meets regularly with the municipal government to monitor the program.

(h) After the final approval of the annual budget by PB delegates, the mayor sends it to the municipal legislative chambers to be approved. The legislative branch can block specific projects.

(i) There is the publication of a year-end report that details the implementation of public works and programs.

(j) The establishment of regional or neighborhood committees serves as a mechanism to monitor the elaboration and execution of policy projects.

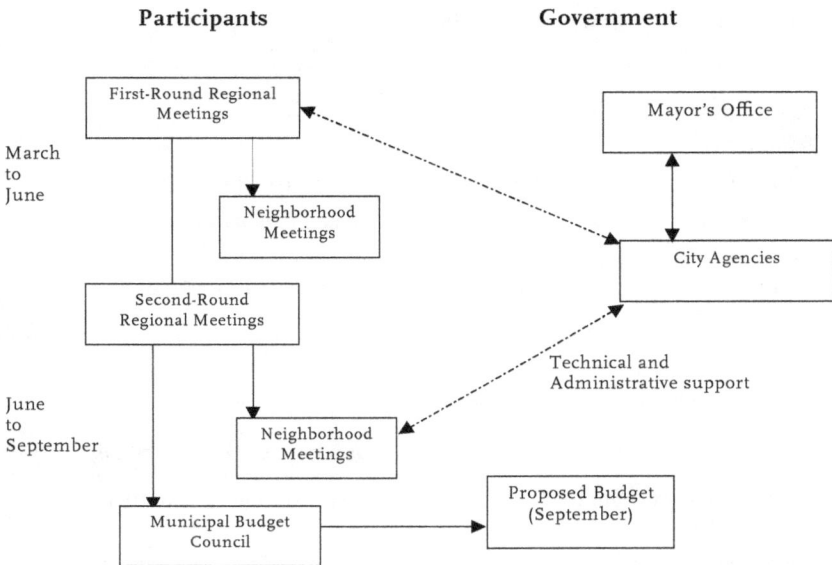

Source: Wampler 2000a.

Fig. 1. Responsibilities in Yearly PB Cycle

First Round

Table 1 lists the principal roles of the government and the responsibilities of participants during the first round of PB. The first round, which typically runs from March to June, involves the distribution of information, the initial discussions on policies, and the establishment of the number of elected representatives. Mobilization in neighborhood meetings is high because turnout determines the number of elected representatives from each neighborhood to the regional meetings. Since final votes are held at the regional level, a greater number of elected representatives (citizen-delegates) from a particular neighborhood increases the likelihood of having a project selected.

Meetings, at the both regional and neighborhood levels, tend to be roughly two hours long. The first part of the meetings is often dedicated to allowing participants to update their colleagues on upcoming events or issues of concern, the second part entails the formal presentation of information by government officials, and the last part is question-and-answer period. Participants are generally limited to three minutes to speak

Table 1. Regional Meetings, March–June

Government's Role	Participants' Responsibilities
• Draws district and subdistrict boundaries	• Mobilize citizens
• Prepares Quality-of-Life Index	• Build capacity through meetings
• Distributes financial information	• Analyze financial information
• Presents its own projects that it wants participants to approve for implementation	• Have preliminary discussions on available resources

Table 2. Neighborhood Meetings, March–June

Government's Role	Participants' Responsibilities
• Provide detailed technical information	• Discuss priorities for municipalities
• Give bureaucrat support to participants (i.e., photocopies, access to telephones)	• Discuss specific public works
• Establish meeting places and times	• Preselect public works

or ask questions. A three-minute time limit helps to keep the pace of the meeting moving along. Deliberation over priorities and projects occurs informally as participants analyze the probable level of resources for their region and begin negotiating with one another over proposed projects.

Government officials and participants must work closely together. Without strong levels of cooperation, this part of PB does not work well.[24] For example, citizens must be willing to agree to the basic agenda and meeting format that has been laid out by the government. Citizens must also be willing to abide by the three-minute time limit. And citizens must be willing to listen to their fellow citizens as well as government officials. When citizens refuse to abide by the basic rules, then there is an increased likelihood that PB will not function. In a telling example from Recife in 1998, I attended one meeting where some citizens refused to abide by the three-minute time limit, which infuriated their fellow citizens and government officials. Nearly one hour of precious meeting time was spent trying to resolve this dispute, precluding the participants from engaging in substantial policy-making discussions.

Second Round

The second round defines the policies and projects that will be implemented by the government for the coming fiscal year (in some cases, two or three years). During this stage, participants should have acquired sufficient information to promote the priorities of their communities and to make decisions at the regional meetings. Final decisions on specific public works or the definition of general social priorities are made at the regional meetings. Between the first and second rounds, it is common for csos to hold meetings at the neighborhood level to plan their strategies.

Distribution of resources is based largely on two criteria, the first being the Quality-of-Life Index. Each region receives a portion of the budget, the specific percentage depending on the region's overall need. Wealthier regions with more advanced infrastructure receive a lower percentage than that of poorer regions with little formal infrastructure. The purpose is twofold. First, this is an attempt to ensure that the limited resources will be spent in the poorest neighborhoods and on the most vulnerable sections of the population. However, PB's rules are based on the recognition that democracies tend to favor organized groups, with middle- and

24. Abers 2000.

Table 3. Regional Meetings, July–November

Government's Role	Participants' Responsibilities
• Provides initial estimates of cost for proposed projects	• Debate proposed policies or public works
• Distributes information and arranges "priority trip" in each district	• "Priority trip"—site visits to proposed public works projects
• Monitors vote	• Vote on policies or public works to be implemented
• Oversees Municipal Budget Council	• Elect two representatives from each region to Municipal Budget Council

Table 4. Neighborhood Meetings, July–November

Government's Role	Participants' Responsibilities
• Technical staff works closely with oversight committees	• Continue mobilization on behalf of projects and policies
• Drafts technical plans	• Elect oversight committee members
	• Approve technical plans

upper-income groups having the greatest advantages. PB therefore marks an attempt to level the playing field by having individuals and groups compete against others that have similar means and resources. PB does not necessarily overcome basic income differences but it does make an attempt to do so.

The second criterion for the distribution of resources is the mobilization and deliberation processes within the region. Organized groups compete, mobilize, negotiate, and deliberate within their own regions over available resources. Obviously, not all projects can be supported, so groups form alliances to promote particular projects. The "priority trip" is a key part of this process, because participants may visit the site of proposed projects so they can personally evaluate the level of need. The more individuals who support a project, the more likely is it be selected for implementation. This gives CSOs a strong incentive to turn out as many supporters, neighbors, and colleagues as possible. In Porto Alegre, for example, attending PB meetings is now an integral part of the political and social agendas of some communities. People attend the meetings with their neighbors, helping to foster group solidarity and encourage public learning. However, CSO leaders may also "pack" PB meetings with their neighbors to increase their group's vote share, thereby contributing little to group solidarity or public learning. As we shall see in the case of Blumenau (Chapter 5), politicians may also pack the meetings with their allies, thereby helping to circumvent the spirit of PB's rules. The Blumenau case demonstrates that the mayoral administration is not likely to support PB when the rules are being manipulated to help particular politicians.

Yearlong Implementation

Although most of the attention is on the selection of policies, an important aspect of PB is the implementation of the selected projects, which may occur for many years after a project is selected (see Table 5, page 66). Some projects can be implemented during the subsequent year, but larger projects may take several years to complete. Governments must overhaul their bureaucratic procedures to encourage implementation. If the government does not initiate internal changes in the implementation process, it is not likely that PB will transform basic decision-making processes. Government officials need to transform how projects are "green-lighted."

Participants have a reduced role in this process, although they participate in oversight meetings to ensure that the policies are being implemented according to previously established criteria. In Belo Horizonte, for example, regional committees must approve the technical plans of all PB projects. These committees also oversee that the public works are implemented according to the already approved technical plans. Neighborhood committees are formed to monitor the construction project on site, which helps to guarantee that the public works are implemented according to the established criteria. This is a crucial part of the process because it diminishes the likelihood of overt corruption. It is telling that in the city of Recife, where PB has worked moderately well (see Chapter 7), the oversight committees are weak. In Recife, effective, independent monitoring committees have not been supported by the government, which restricts the ability of citizens to monitor the quality of the work. Finally, in São Paulo, there were few, if any, internal administrative changes that might have helped to more readily green-light PB projects. One reason for PB's problems in São Paulo (see Chapter 6) was the inability of the government to initiate any internal reforms.

Forms of Representation

PB programs generally have two forms of political representation. First, citizens vote for "PB delegates" within their region. There is no set number of delegates per region, since the numbers will increase as participation increases. In Porto Alegre, which is the standard model that most other PB programs have followed, as the number of citizens mobilized for a PB meeting increases, a larger number of participants are required to create a new PB delegate seat. For example, for every ten participants, one PB delegate can be elected. One hundred participants results in the election of ten delegates. For between 101 and 250 participants, an additional delegate seat is created for every twenty participants. For between 251 and 400 delegates, an additional delegate seat is created for every thirty participants.[25] This sliding scale continues through 1,000 participants, at which point PB moves to a proportional scale. The primary purpose of this sliding scale is to allow for an adequate number of representatives (PB delegates) to be elected without creating too many, which would limit the quality of debates and diminish the effectiveness of local representation.

This formula also helps protect the interests of smaller communities, because larger communities cannot simply mobilize hundreds of their residents in an effort to capture the majority of resources. Even though the sliding-upward scale of mobilization dampens the effect that large communities have on the process, it does not eliminate it. Small and poor communities face the same difficulties in PB that they face in representative democracy: low numbers of voters/participants make it more difficult to have policy projects—which would directly affect their communities—included in the budget.

The second form of representation is the establishment of a municipal-wide council. Each region and thematic area elects two representatives, who serve one-year terms on the council. The council is charged with the responsibility of overseeing PB and making decisions on behalf of its region or thematic area. The PB councils must endorse rule changes, approve the final budget that is sent to the municipal council, negotiate the distribution of resources if there is a shortage or surplus, and monitor how the government administers PB. The PB council is the highest level of representation within PB, most closely mirroring the responsibility of municipal legislators.

Of the eight municipalities analyzed in this book, five have adopted a form of representation that is, by and large, similar to Porto Alegre's method. Santo André and Belo Horizonte are the exceptions. As will be

---

25. "Orçamento Participativo: Regimento interno, critérios gerias, técnicos e regionais," 2003, 8.

demonstrated in Chapter 6 (Santo André) and 7 (Belo Horizonte), deviations from this basic rule format had significant repercussions.

Social Policies and Public Works Projects

PB programs have two general tracks. One track, PB *public works*, focuses
on specific public works projects, which range from the paving of specific
streets to building day care centers. This track garners the lion's share
of citizens' interests because it involves the distribution of specific projects. The second track, PB *thematics*, focuses on general spending policies (for instance, education and health care). These policies focus on
more general spending trends, such as allocating increased spending to
a particular type of health care program. These meetings tend to draw
better-informed activists, who are more likely to be part of an issue-
oriented social movement.

PB Public Works: A Focus on Local, Territory-Based Issues

Most PB programs initially focus on specific public works, but over time,
discussions broaden to include general social policies. There are several
pragmatic reasons why governments initially choose to dedicate their time
and energy to specific projects. First, the focus on specific public works
establishes a direct connection between participation and outcomes.
When PB participants select a specific project, an expectation is obviously
created that the government will implement the project. When the government successfully implements selected projects, it reinforces the notion
that participation in PB is a valuable tool for promoting change.[26] For
example, the government of Porto Alegre has an established track record
of implementing PB projects in a two- to three-year period. This means
that PB participants know that decisions they make will result in government action. The efforts of the government have helped to stimulate
accountability in Porto Alegre because participants believe that the government will fulfill its promise in a timely manner.

Second, the focus on specific public works represents an effort to allow
communities to define their own development. The underlying assumption is that citizens understand their own problems better than government officials and therefore will be able to match proposed public works

---

26. Wampler and Avritzer 2004; Wampler 2004b.

to their needs. By giving citizens the power to select public works, PB programs contribute to the decentralization of the decision-making process. This is an empowerment tool because many neighborhood groups first propose small projects but expand the range of their demands over time. For example, a neighborhood association might initially work for street paving but may expand its demands to include housing projects or the establishment of health posts. Public learning occurs, especially when the government successfully implements PB projects, as delegates begin to strategize about how to receive additional (and often larger) projects.

The third reason that PB programs focus on specific, targeted public works is that local governments are often responsible for small infrastructure projects. Public works have long been a key source of patronage exchange between governments and community leaders. By placing public works at the center of PB, it has been hoped that the cycle of patronage politics can be broken. Breaking the cycle of patronage entails public discussions of the public works, access to technical information, and the eventual implementation of the public work. By removing public works from the clientelistic exchange, governments and community leaders hope to generate a new type of politics at the local level. However, municipal legislators also focus on small infrastructure projects, which is why PB can become such a hotly contested decision-making venue. PB delegates make meaningful decisions that have long been the bread and butter of municipal legislators. One sign of the importance of PB is that municipal legislators, who are not part of the governing coalition, will actively work against PB because it is emerging as a parallel power.

PB Thematics: Broader Social and Public Policies

The purpose of PB thematics is to further democratize the policy-making process by letting citizens establish the general priorities of the municipal government. This encourages participants to analyze and understand the city as a whole rather than concentrating on the problems specific to their neighborhoods. This is part of the larger empowerment or "citizenship school" component of PB: citizens are encouraged to envision and work for broader social change.

PB thematic meetings allow participants to set broad priorities for public policies. The first stage of this process requires that the government provide detailed information on the current policies and spending priorities. The second stage is a series of discussions in which the participants evaluate the government's priorities. The final stage is the ordering of priorities by the participants. For example, participants prioritize the level of spending that should be dedicated to prenatal care or to the eradication of infectious diseases. In this way, PB participants work closely with government officials to determine how best to spend resources. Governments bring their expertise and participants signal their policy preferences. When government officials strongly believe in a policy program (such as prenatal care), they will strongly argue on behalf of the program, thereby trying to convince participants to support a particular program. There is a fine line between providing information and co-opting participants that is treaded very carefully by most governments. Government officials do, of course, overstep this line, which helps explain how government officials may use PB as a means to co-opt some leaders. If there is complicity between government officials and citizens (especially leaders), PB runs the risk of having participants rubber-stamp the government's policy positions. As will be highlighted in Chapter 6, this line was frequently crossed in São Paulo and Santo André as the government's interests began to supplant the interests of participants.

The quality of the meetings and debates varies significantly. Some participants are longtime advocates on behalf of a particular issue (for example, health care, housing, or education). Their knowledge about other policy issues may be low. One of the most complicated parts of PB as a policy-making process is that citizen-participants have low levels of information and knowledge about most policy arenas. Broad policy decisions may be largely acts of rubber-stamping if the majority of participants follow the lead of the most experienced policy advocates or the positions of the government. This is a clear drawback to PB programs. Citizens with low levels of information and expertise are involved in making important public policy decisions.

Most governments that administer PB programs conduct workshops and seminars intended to inform and educate participants. Attendance at these meetings is voluntary, so attendees, typically the retired, the unemployed, or full-time stay-at-home mothers, often are the most active leaders. Government or NGO officials lead the training sessions, during which they provide information about budgetary and administrative processes, the state's responsibility, citizenship rights, and negotiation tactics. Most workshops have a technical focus, although there is often an effort to encourage attendees to mobilize more of their neighborhoods to participate.

A key tension within PB thematics is whether the most well informed political activists try to lead political discussions or whether they really dominate such discussions. This tension is most acute during the initial years of any PB program. As a program is consolidated, it is expected that the average participants' political knowledge will expand. Is public learning occurring? This question lies at the heart of the controversies over PB programs. It is not clear whether participants are gaining the information and knowledge necessary to become full-fledged policy advocates in the future or whether their participation is being used to legitimize the policy choices of the government. In the best cases, Porto Alegre and Ipatinga, it was clear to me, from interviews and observation of participants, that there was a high level of information about PB and budgetary issues in general. Information was shared and participants knew how to use this information. However, one sobering piece of data comes from the survey used in this book (see Chapter 3 for an in-depth analysis). In the survey, respondents were asked, "What percentage of the yearly budget is negotiated within PB?" Government officials most commonly talk about available resources in percentage terms. Among the survey respondents, just 2 percent of PB delegates (already an elite within PB) were *able* to identify the amount of resources that PB delegates negotiated on a yearly basis in their municipality's respective PB program. In other words, almost all the elected representatives, the elite within the PB programs, did not know the amount of resources that they would be negotiating. From a public-learning standpoint, this is a very sobering finding because it suggests that few participants are sufficiently well informed to be involved in complex policy debates.

A parallel problem is that uninformed citizens may select policies that do not conform to the constraints placed on the government (participants vote to spend far more resources than are available). There is a danger that uninformed citizens will make decisions that derail the program (such as demand spending far beyond the capacity of the government). This problem was most acute in Recife during the 2001–4 period, because the PB process was overhauled to allow many more demands to be selected than there were available resources.

PB's Limitations

There are several limitations to PB programs that reduce the overall level of authority that can be delegated. Although there are important differences in how PB programs function in different municipalities and states, the limitations discussed below appear to be present in most cases. The limitations outlined in what follows suggest that PB programs have a moderate capacity to challenge social and political exclusion while promoting social justice. PB programs are an important step toward political inclusion and greater social justice, but they are by no means a magic bullet.

The first limitation stems from the focus on specific public works. Many communities mobilize to secure a specific paving or drainage project. The emphasis on specific goods diminishes the impact of the public learning or empowerment sessions. Many participants are less interested in learning about rights, the fiscal responsibility of the government, or broader social policies than in obtaining a small infrastructure project. This is the principal Catch-22 of the program. PB programs flourish when citizens discover that the specific decisions they make in regional meetings will be implemented. The message is clear: when the government values participants' time and energy by implementing specific projects, participation rates will increase and public debates will flourish.[27]

Although this seems to be a necessary first step in encouraging participation, it associates PB programs with the distribution of specific goods. After the improvements have been made, the community organizations may stop participating. The community has received its desired public good, satisfying the need motivating the citizens' original organizing effort. The downside, from the perspective of strengthening the PB program, is that the participants may immediately exit the program and demonstrate little interest in working with the program once their goal is obtained. Thus, the narrow focus on public works has the potential to also dampen participation rates, although many individuals may also continue to participate to secure additional projects. It is also quite likely that individuals who are not able to have their preferred policy projects approved will also stop participating because they may not see the usefulness of committing their time and energy to a program that does not provide benefits.

A second limitation in the PB process is the dependence of the participants on the mayor's office. Even though PB programs directly incorporate civil society actors in the policy-making process, the government remains the principal actor. Why? The government organizes meetings, provides information, ensures that bureaucrats meet with the population, and guarantees that selected policies will be implemented. The influence

27. Baiocchi 2005; Avritzer 2002.

of the mayor and the governing coalition is substantial. Without their strong political commitment to the program, it is less likely that the program will succeed. For example, in Recife, the mayor began to use PB as a means to distribute public monies for the yearly carnival. Instead of holding open, transparent meetings, the mayor manipulated the release of funds so that "friendly" PB participants would benefit. Nonparticipating citizens and "unfriendly" citizen-delegates did not have access to the public resources. PB participants expressed concern that they had to act a certain way or they would be "boycotted" by the government. This does little to empower citizens and may just be a new form of clientelism.

A third limitation is that long-term planning has a rather ambiguous place within PB, which means that new capital investment projects are geared toward more immediate-need projects. Many of the PB participants are interested in securing short- to medium-term public works. The focus on specific public works makes it more difficult to generate discussions on planning for the future of the city. Although several municipal governments have made concerted efforts to stimulate discussions and develop long-term plans, these processes have been limited. The complexity of the issues involved requires that citizens have substantial technical and analytical skills to weigh the relevancy of different arguments. PB programs slowly build these skills, but it may take years for participants to develop a decent grasp of the complexities of the proposed solutions.

A fourth limitation is the emphasis on local issues and local public policies. Many participants, including longtime political and social activists, spend their time and energy on the intricacies of local public policies. This reduces the amount of time that activists are able to dedicate to regional, national, or global problems. Although PB participants dedicate their efforts to securing changes in local public policies, the principal problems their communities face are often related to unemployment, violence, or the lack of educational opportunities. This should be considered a limitation because the PB program does not provide the opportunity for participants to challenge the underlying reasons for their social and economic exclusion. For example, in Recife, I interviewed many active PB participants, many of whom dedicated five to ten hours of work a week on PB. When I asked them what the major demand of the neighborhood was, the nearly unanimous response was unemployment. The participants, mainly women, worked in PB in the hope that they could improve the day-to-day conditions of their neighborhoods, but their largest concerns focused on broader socioeconomic changes that were far beyond the scope of PB.

Participants and governments hope that the PB program will foster increased awareness of the broader global social problems faced by Brazil's urban poor.[28] There are, however, no guarantees that the participants will make the leap from the lack of basic infrastructure to the broader socio-economic forces that shape their lives. Although this is obviously a lot to ask of PB participants, it is clearly the goal of the governments and the most active participants. Empowering citizens is a key reason behind why many government officials, citizens, and CSOs are involved in PB.

Finally, PB programs can be manipulated because of the central role played by the mayor's office. Municipal agencies, bureaucrats, or elected officials may try to use PB programs to advance their own agendas. Non-disclosure of key information, the lack of implementation of selected public policies, and the weakening of citizen oversight committees are all potential ways that the program can be manipulated. It is important to note that some PB programs in Brazil, at municipal and state levels, have been rejected by social movements and NGOs because of the government's interference.

Unintended Consequences

Table 6 lists PB's rules, the desired outcomes, and unintended consequences. One downside to PB is that CSO activists now spend a considerable amount of their limited time, energy, and resources involved in discussions focused on the provision of small infrastructure projects. "Think globally, act locally" is taken to the extreme as PB participants spend countless hours focused on where a storm drain or streetlight should be located. In a related development, PB helps to absolve government officials of having to decide where small infrastructure will be located. Municipal governments can now assert that they have no authority to make spending decisions, because decisions are made by citizens within the PB. This can pit poor neighborhood against poor neighborhood as citizens struggle to obtain basic services.

PB rewards mobilization. Individuals living in communities with a history of community organizing and larger numbers are more likely to benefit than are individuals living in smaller communities. Voting outcomes within PB are decided through the use of a majoritarian voting system in which public policy projects are awarded to the groups who can

28. Genro 1995a; Avritzer and Navarro 2003; Teixeira and Albuquerque 2006.

turn out the highest numbers of citizens. Individuals living in smaller communities or in communities where mobilization is weak are not likely to be able to secure resources. Although PB was intended to promote social justice by granting greater levels of resources to poor neighborhoods, the poorest of the poor have not necessarily been well served, because they face the greatest hurdles as they try to organize. PB rewards those who can mobilize, and there are few mechanisms in place that recognize that certain groups face even greater challenges as they attempt to organize.

Citizens may use PB as a means to gain access to government officials to lobby those officials for other types of goods and resources. Participation in PB is not simply about PB. Rather, it fits into citizens' and CSOs' broader political strategies of trying to secure their preferences from not just municipal officials but also from state officials. For example, CSO activists who regularly mobilize high numbers of their neighbors to attend PB meetings are a hotly sought-after commodity by candidates during municipal, state, and federal elections. These activists may become paid campaign workers, receive the benefits of constituency service, or help to shape public policies. Participation in PB is therefore not just about PB, but also about giving the most active participants access to politicians and government bureaucrats.

The Quality-of-Life Index helps promote social justice between regions but not necessarily within a region. Poorer regions receive greater resources (on a per capita basis) than wealthier regions. However, there are few rules or formal mechanisms to ensure that social justice is established at the regional level. Belo Horizonte is the one exception. In 2002, it enacted a new category of "at risk" neighborhoods that were guaranteed funding because of the high levels of poverty and problems in these specific neighborhoods.

Table 5. Yearlong Implementation

Government's Role	Participants' Responsibilities
• Prepares technical plans, contacts, etc.	• Approve technical plans
• Integrates among administrative agencies	• Monitor order of project implementation
• Technical staff works closely with oversight committees	• On-site monitoring of project implementation
• Oversees Municipal Budget Council	• Municipal Budget Council delegates meet once a week

Table 6. Desired Outcomes and Unintended Consequences

Rule	Desired Outcomes	Unintended Consequences
• Establish district boundaries.	• Improve efficiency, accountability, and decentralization.	• Meetings at district level may limit the formation of citywide CSO networks.
	• Create intradistrict competition over resources.	• Small groups within district may be unable to mobilize sufficient numbers to secure projects.
• Use yearlong series of meetings.	• Higher participation produces greater deliberation and potential for empowering citizens.	• Mobilization becomes an end in itself to secure resources; "inattentive" participation if people attend meetings with the sole purpose of voting for their specific policy proposal.
• Use Quality-of Life Index.	• Promote social justice by allocating increased resources to dense, low-income districts.	• Poor neighborhoods are not uniformly distributed, so small, marginalized populations may not receive benefits.
	• Encourage participation by having citizens compete within their regions.	• Well-organized groups benefit at the expense of the poorly organized and small groups; discourages participation among unlikely recipients.
• Use Bus Caravan of Priorities.	• Promote solidarity and greater information by allowing delegates to see site of proposed project.	• Delegates lack basic skills to be able to evaluate need and are more likely to be swayed by passionate appeals.
• Elected representatives vote on final projects.	• A more limited number of participants are better able to make final policy decisions.	• Process may be dominated by community leaders; instead of a citizen-oriented process, community leaders dominate PB.
• Elect a municipal-wide council.	• A small body of citizens negotiates directly with government and legislative officials to reduce inefficiencies, enhance quality of debate, and make difficult decisions.	• A small group of community leaders may use their access to government officials to promote their own interests; creates a new type of political actor who may not be accountable to the base of support.

A final, and potentially debilitating, unintended consequence is the reliance of PB delegates on government officials for information. PB delegates and participants are often sympathetic to government officials and trust that the information given to them is correct. Delegates have low levels of information; make policy decisions based on these low levels; and, even worse, make these decisions largely based on the information provided to them by government officials without any independent verification. Low levels of knowledge suggest that there has not been a successful effort to educate and inform delegates about budgetary issues. Low levels of knowledge about basic participatory processes allow government officials to manipulate PB if they feel so inclined.

Conclusions

PB is a decision-making process through which citizens deliberate and negotiate over the distribution of public resources. PB programs are implemented at the behest of governments, citizens, NGOs, and CSOs to allow citizens to have a direct role in deciding how and where resources should be spent. These programs create opportunities for engaging, educating, and empowering citizens, which can foster a more vibrant civil society. PB also helps to promote transparency, which has the potential to reduce government inefficiencies and corruption. Since most citizens who participate are low income and have low levels of formal education, PB offers access for citizens from historically excluded groups to make choices that will affect how their government acts. Quite simply, PB programs provide poor and historically excluded citizens with access to important decision-making venues.

PB opens up obscure budgetary procedures to ordinary citizens and helps to generate a broader public forum through which citizens and governments discuss spending, taxation, and implementation. PB is simultaneously a policy process that focuses on the distribution of resources *and* a democratic institution that enhances accountability, transfers decision-making authority to citizens, and empowers citizens.

PB programs confront social and political legacies of clientelism, social exclusion, and corruption by making the budgetary process transparent, open, and public. Social and political exclusion are challenged as low-income and traditionally excluded political actors are given the opportunity to make policy decisions. By moving the locus of decision making from the private offices of politicians and technocrats to public forums, PB's public meetings help to foster transparency. PB programs also serve as "citizenship schools" because engagement empowers citizens to better understand their rights and duties as citizens as well as the responsibilities of government. Citizens learn to negotiate among themselves and vis-à-vis the government over the distribution of scarce resources and public policy priorities. It is important to keep in mind that there is no precise or exact model for PB programs. Although there are similar tenets and institutional mechanisms, PB programs are structured in response to the particular political, social, and economic environment of each city or state.

PB programs may also generate a series of unintended consequences. Citizens have low levels of information and generally rely on government officials, which undermines efforts to promote PB as an institutional venue that promotes transparency. When citizens assume passive positions, they are less likely to be able to extend accountability and make use of the rights that have been afforded them. Co-optation of CSO leaders becomes a viable strategy for government officials because some PB participants begin to rely extensively on the information and organizational skills of government officials. The ability of CSO leaders to avoid this dependence, as will be argued in Chapters 4–7, is based on the ability of CSOs to use different forms of pressure, or contentious politics, against government officials.

The full extension of citizenship rights guaranteed under Brazil's 1988 Constitution requires that government officials abide by the rules and that citizens work to exercise their rights. PB's emphasis on small and medium-sized public works projects is a first step toward helping citizens learn how to exercise their rights, but it is vital not to lose sight of the fact that CSOs' and community leaders' involvement in PB is directly linked to their ability to secure public works. The question that will be examined in Chapter 3 is whether the involvement of citizens in PB is helping to shift their attitudes and behaviors. If PB is helping to modify participants' attitudes and behaviors, it may be possible to claim that PB is contributing to a basic shift in state-society relations.

3

Authority, Negotiation, and Solidarity: PB Delegates' Attitudes and Behaviors

> My neighborhood is a poor, needy neighborhood.
> I participate in PB because I want to improve the
> basic conditions. I want to feel proud and be able to
> say, "That plaza was constructed with my help; I
> helped to bring sewage pipes to the neighborhood."
> This is not just for me, but for my children and my
> grandchildren.
> —PB DELEGATE IN BELO HORIZONTE

> We work with other associations to secure projects.
> The association of São Bento gave up one of their
> projects to secure the passage of our project. The fol-
> lowing year, we supported one of their projects and
> didn't elect one of our own projects. There is an on-
> going exchange between community associations.
> —PB DELEGATE IN BELO HORIZONTE

> We live in a small shantytown. We can't mobilize
> many people. Won't you please support us? We have
> many needs but there is no one to help us.
> —PB DELEGATE IN PORTO ALEGRE DURING PUBLIC
> MEETING

PB participants invest considerable amounts of time and energy in attending government-sponsored meetings. They also hold their own pre- and
post-PB community meetings to analyze the current political environment,
map out strategies, and solidify their intra-CSO alliances. PB delegates are
often fiercely loyal to the overall intent of PB programs, but can also be
extremely critical of how these programs are managed, often because of
their perception that the government is not investing as much time and
as many resources into PB as the delegates believe is necessary to create
a successful institution. Elected by their fellow citizens, PB delegates are

crucial links between government officials and citizens. They are privileged actors in the process because they have been elected as representatives of their communities. A better understanding of PB delegates' attitudes toward authority, negotiation, and monitoring will greatly increase our knowledge about how PB affects accountability and citizenship rights. The purpose of this chapter is to lay out the demographic profile of PB delegates as well as to explain whether and how PB affects the delegates' strategies, attitudes, and behaviors.

Although PB programs are designed to directly incorporate citizens into decision-making venues, it remains unclear whether PB participants *believe* that they exercise authority. We draw from four different survey questions to answer this question. Do PB delegates believe that they exercise authority that directs governmental outputs? It also remains unclear *how* citizens secure their preferred policy outcomes. Do PB delegates engage in partisan political activity? Do they use intra- and intergroup alliances to engage in pressure politics? Or are individual connections used?

To begin answering these questions, in this chapter I draw from a survey, the PB Comparative Survey, which was applied to 695 elected PB delegates in the eight Brazilian municipalities included in this book.[1] The principal purpose of the survey was to assess the respondents' attitudes on issues pertaining to their degree of authority within PB.

The distribution of decision-making authority links the concepts of accountability and citizenship rights. Accountability depends on citizens' capacity and willingness to pressure government officials to follow their campaign promises and adhere to the policy and budgetary processes. It also depends on government officials' willingness to fulfill their public commitments and follow existing legislation. Accountability, a concept for which Portuguese vocabulary does not have a word, can be established over time as citizens use formal institutional venues to pressure public officials. Through PB, citizens have the opportunity to make specific decisions and monitor how the government implements the citizens' policy choices. The survey data reveal that delegates in Rio Claro and Blumenau hold very negative attitudes about their degree of decision-making authority and their ability to monitor their municipal government. In Porto Alegre and Ipatinga, citizens believe that they do, in fact, have decision-making authority and that they can monitor their government. The wide

---

1. The PB Comparative Survey was field-tested and redesigned with the help of Gustavo Venturi. I want to thank Ilka Camarotti for her input at an early stage. See the Appendix for further information about research methodology.

differences among the eight municipalities indicate that accountability and citizenship rights are being extended in an uneven manner among and within the municipalities that have adopted PB.

The extension of citizenship rights is partially dependent on the standardization of rules and procedures establishing how participants may use the authority afforded to them. Circumventing rules and laws through informal exchanges, a long-standing hallmark of Brazilian politics, is officially, publicly, and consistently repudiated by government officials and the most active PB participants. PB is often described by its strongest proponents as an institution that has the potential to inculcate respect for the rule of law. These bold claims have not been empirically verified, and yet they are an indication of the impact that PB's proponents believe their participatory institution may have on Brazilian politics. PB provides citizens, at least on paper, with a series of rights that allows them to decide specific policy outcomes. This chapter establishes that the most active PB delegates do, in fact, believe that they have the right to make decisions and monitor government officials via PB. Individuals elected multiple times as PB delegates and those who perceive that their community has directly benefited from PB believe that they exercise authority. Yet some PB delegates also believe that they do not exercise much authority, indicating that the extension of decision making has only been partially extended.

I begin this chapter by laying out the demographic profile of PB delegates included in the survey to illuminate the basic characteristics of activists. PB delegates are elected at the district/regional level by PB participants. PB delegates are charged with representing the interests of their local community during negotiations with other PB delegates and government officials. The basic social, political, and economic characteristics of the PB delegates included in the survey are similar to what has been found elsewhere.[2] The vast majority of participants are low income, and most have less than a high school education.[3] The PB delegates included in the survey are representative of the poor, although they are not from the poorest and most marginalized sectors of the population. What distinguishes PB delegates from the general population is their level of activity in CSOs: 85 percent of the delegates are active in a CSO, a far cry from the 5–20 percent that has been reported elsewhere for the general public.[4]

2. Nylen 2003, 2002; *Quem é o Público do Orçamento Participativo*, 1999; Avritzer, Recamán, and Venturi 2004; Avritzer 2002.

3. Goldfrank 2003; Baiocchi 2003.

4. Avritzer, Recamán, and Venturi 2004; for similar findings, see Nylen 2003.

In this chapter, three models (individual level, municipal level, and aggregate level) are developed to explain the variation in respondents' attitudes. These models are tested using ordinary least squared (OLS) and logistic regression. The survey was conducted to provide a research "check" on the other types of data collected, namely, elite interviews and participant observation. One common methodological weakness of political anthropology approaches is the lack of a systematic method of selecting individuals to be interviewed or of choosing which meetings should be observed. The survey, in which PB delegates were randomly selected within each municipality, provides an opportunity to confirm or contradict the data gathered through elite interviews and participant-observation methods.

Demographic Data on PB Delegates

The data shown in Table 7 demonstrate that the population included in the survey comprises Brazil's lower classes. Overall, 63 percent of the survey respondents live in households that earn less that U.S.$400 per month. In Recife, 90 percent of the respondents fall into this category. Since PB's rules (see Chapter 2) are structured to reward residents of low-income districts, this evidence confirms that PB programs successfully mobilize low-income residents.

Half of all respondents, 51 percent, did not complete high school. In Porto Alegre, 75 percent of the delegates have less than a high school diploma, which is the highest percentage in this category. This is surprising because Porto Alegre has the highest Human Development Index (HDI) score of the eight municipalities. Therefore, Porto Alegre, the municipality with the highest standard of living among the eight municipalities, has been the most successful at drawing low-income residents into PB. This provides some preliminary evidence that one reason for PB's success in Porto Alegre is nonparticipation by Porto Alegre's middle class. Porto Alegre has a larger and wealthier middle class than most other cities included in this study. This suggests that a larger middle class, which does not rely on municipal services, may not occupy political space in PB, thereby creating additional opportunities for low-income citizens.

Overall, the data confirm that the vast majority of survey respondents are low income and poorly educated, which means that when authority is transferred to PB, it is transferred to lower-class individuals, who have long been marginalized from policy-making venues. Thus when PB programs successfully delegate authority, they are directly confronting state-society

Table 7. Demographic Profile of PB Delegates by Municipality (%)

	Porto Alegre	Ipatinga	Belo Horizonte	Recife	São Paulo	Santo André	Blumenau	Rio Claro	Average
Monthly household income of less than U.S.$400	78	62	61	90	63	63	58	46	63
Less than high school diploma	75	60	51	53	46	37	62	40	51
Percentage of women respondents	71	30	48	55	61	52	33	35	52
Currently active in association life	80	70	89	72	78	72	61	36	75
Current leadership position in community association	57	45	63	55	55	77	28	43	53
Current union membership	7	17	18	10	12	28	12	20	14
Participation in *conselhos*	29	28	51	18	27	80	27	13	13
Partisan political identification	94	77	79	46	81	95	34	70	75

Source: Comparative PB Survey.

relations in Brazil, which have long been based on the exclusion of low-income citizens from key decision-making venues.

PB delegates are extremely active in civil society, with 85 percent of the respondents declaring that they are currently active in a CSO. A 2003 study in São Paulo found that although 20 percent of the general public belong to a CSO, just less than 5 percent participate in civic-oriented CSOs.[5] The vast majority of individuals who do participate in a CSO mainly attend religious services. The 85 percent participation rate in CSOs by PB delegates in the survey conducted for this book suggests that elected positions in PB are dominated by organized groups; PB's rules reward organized groups and provide few benefits for individuals or small groups who face difficulties when organizing. Even though PB is open to all municipal residents, it is not necessarily the case that all individuals will be able to compete on equal footing. The 15 percent of PB delegates who declare that they are not active in a CSO are clearly at a competitive disadvantage.

Furthermore, 46 percent of those active in CSOs declare that they hold some type of leadership position in their CSO, which indicates that PB delegates are community leaders. What distinguishes PB delegates from the rest of Brazilian society is their high levels of involvement in CSOs. Although the income and education data place the survey respondents within Brazil's lower classes, the extremely high rates of participation in CSOs and leadership in those CSOs mean that they are community and CSO leaders. This finding confirms the results of Nylen's work in Betim and Belo Horizonte.[6] PB is now providing a political space in which the most organized and active members of civil society can be directly engaged in policy-making processes.

Union membership is low, just 14 percent. It was my expectation that the percentage of union members would be higher, since one of the Workers' Party's (PT's) key bases of support is unions. There is, however, high partisan political identification. In the survey, several questions are asked that seek to establish whether an individual has an identifiable partisan political affiliation: "Do you belong to a political party? If so, which one?" and the follow-up questions "Do you remember who you voted for city council in 2000? If so, who?" Fifty-eight percent of the respondents have an identifiable political identification. Of these, 73 percent are from the same political party as the mayor or remember voting for a candidate from

5. Avritzer, Recamán, and Venturi 2004.
6. Nylen 2002, 2003.

the mayor's political party. The results show that PB delegates are over-whelming leftists (with the exception of those in Blumenau and Recife), suggesting that leftist governments adopting PB have created a policy-making space that is occupied and controlled by their political allies.

Finally, just 33 percent of the respondents participate in parallel partic-ipatory institutions (*conselhos*). Respondents in Santo André (80 percent) and Belo Horizonte (51 percent) have higher results in this category, indi-cating that PB delegates in these municipalities are using multiple par-ticipatory institutions to achieve their preferred policy outcomes. In the other six municipalities, it is a small minority of PB delegates who are active in complementary participatory institutions. Since PB is the pri-mary municipal-level political institution that PB delegates use to pursue their interests, how the program works will have the largest effect on how PB delegates engage with formal policy-making institutions. If PB programs do not work well, it is likely that there will be an increase in cynicism about the role that participatory decision making can play in "deepening" Brazil's democracy.

Eighty-five percent of survey respondents are active members of civil society, but 68 percent had been elected for the first time as a PB dele-gate in 2003. This confirms a process that has been described to me in multiple cases: CSOs rotate their support for different individuals to be elected as PB delegates. Support is rotated among members of CSOs to lessen the burden (time, energy, bus fare) on any one individual and to ensure that no single individual becomes the "owner" of the CSOs or of PB. This stems from an interest in eliminating the role of the political boss within CSOs.[7] Even though the rotation of leaders may limit the likeli-hood that particular leaders will capture PB, it is also the case that the new delegates must learn the complex intricacies of policy making in a short period. The renewal of delegates may mean that PB's institutional memory rests with government officials and PB delegates who choose to participate each and every year. Leadership rotation is intended to limit individual leaders' control over their CSOs, but this renewal may actually strengthen the power of activists who dedicate the greatest amount of time and energy to PB. PB, like other representative democratic institutions, favors indi-viduals who are willing to spend countless hours, over a number of years, crafting majority coalitions to support their positions. CSOs that renew their leadership as a means of avoiding authoritarian practices, such as

7. Wampler and Avritzer 2004.

the "ownership" of the cso, may actually be disadvantaged because their new leaders may have a harder time competing for resources against csos that do not engage in this type of leadership renewal.

An overwhelming majority of respondents state that they or their communities have received a material benefit from the PB process. Since the majority are first-time PB delegates, this means that the benefits were initially negotiated when they were a participant (unelected) or a bystander. The survey respondents thus perceive that PB is a decision-making venue that distributes resources to their community. An important issue is whether PB is one decision-making venue among many or if it is the primary decision-making venue for citizens. In Porto Alegre, 77 percent of respondents assert that they have been unable to secure a public resource outside PB, which means that the most active cso leaders are using PB as their primary means to secure public goods. This is a remarkable shift, because it signifies that a public venue, in which decisions are made by majority vote, is now the primary institution used by low-income activists to secure their policy preferences. This is clear evidence that PB, at least in Porto Alegre, is transforming basic state-society relations. In Rio Claro, just 29 percent say that their only means of securing resources is PB, suggesting that they continue to use informal and backdoor channels to secure resources. This evidence provides a counterweight to the Porto Alegre case, because the Rio Claro example demonstrates that PB delegates may use PB as one of many channels to secure their policy preferences.

Most survey respondents hold a favorable view of the activities and actions of government officials within PB. Porto Alegre has the highest positive ratings, 87 percent, while Blumenau has the weakest, at just 50 percent. The decrease in the percentage of support for the government largely mirrors this book's argument for the success, partial success, or failures of the PB programs. This finding is significant because it suggests that the respondents believe that government officials are largely respectful of PB's rules. The open manipulation of rules and institutional procedures so prevalent in other Brazilian institutions appears to be less present in PB, which means that PB may be helping to establish trust among citizens in Brazilian institutions. Most respondents also believe that their fellow delegates are largely respectful of the process. The robust level of responses suggests that delegates do not believe that their fellow delegates are trying to manipulate or bend PB's rules for their own gain.

This section has provided an overview of the demographic characteristics associated with PB delegates. They are clearly an active and engaged

Table 8. PB Delegates' Participation Characeristics and Attitudes (%)

	Porto Alegre	Ipatinga	Belo Horizonte	Recife	São Paulo	Santo André	Blumenau	Rio Claro	Average
Delegates elected 3 or more times	39	35	47	13	5	25	10	17	16
Delegates received a government benefit from PB	91	92	79	79	54	89	68	71	70
Delegates received a benefit outside of PB	23	57	43	38	43	43	37	71	43
Favorable view of government's actions within PB	87	82	59	61	57	70	50	78	65
Favorable view of fellow delegates' actions within PB	80	92	83	71	77	81	73	79	79

Source: Comparative PB Survey.

part of the population, which distinguishes them from the majority of their fellow citizens. The vast majority have received some sort of a benefit from PB. They also hold favorable views of the actions of government officials and their fellow participants in PB. Yet it is crucial to move beyond descriptive analysis to identify which factors best account for delegates' attitudes.

Explaining PB Delegates' Attitudes and Behaviors

Research on participatory institutions typically focuses on the citizens who choose to participate in the policy-making process. Empowerment, deliberation, mobilization, and group solidarity are the conceptual anchors of this debate, focusing on the role of citizens and CSOs.[8] There are four types of explanations that are most likely to strongly influence citizen-participants' attitudes and behaviors in the context of a participatory institution: institutional rules and strength, participation in a CSO, social context (individual and municipal level), and partisan political affiliation.

First, we need to establish whether these participatory institutions are strong enough to alter the attitudes of participants. As institutions grow stronger and are consolidated, we would expect that there would be an accompanying increase in the effect that the institutional rules have on individuals' attitudes and behaviors.[9] As individuals increase their levels of participation in PB, it is likely that they have more positive attitudes than first-time participants, because of a basic selection bias. Individuals who perceive that PB is a positive institutional venue in which to address their demands are more likely to continue to participate. We would also expect that disaffected participants will drop out of PB, which means that the participants who remain are likely to be gaining something from the process. Since the survey cannot account for participants who have come and gone from the process, we will have to assume that the survey respondents are likely to be generally more supportive of the PB process than would the average participant.

Abers finds that PB fosters an increase in associational activity and that there is an increase in the numbers of associations as well as in individuals' intensity of participation in their local associations. Her explanation

8. Abers 2000; Avritzer 2002; Baiocchi 2003, 2005; Heller 2001; Santos 2005.
9. Abers 1998, 2000; Baiocchi 2005; Wampler and Avritzer 2004.

is that PB decentralizes decision-making venues to the neighborhood level, which decreases the costs of participating, thereby increasing the ability of ordinary citizens to participate.[10] Abers also finds that individuals who are returning PB participants do, in fact, change their voting behavior, moving from a focus on local and immediate interests to an interest in broader public policy issues.[11] Baiocchi argues that PB encourages public learning and new forms of deliberation. In his 2005 book, *Militants and Citizens,* which focuses on three regional districts in Porto Alegre, he substantiates these claims as he demonstrates how participants altered their strategies and practices to work more effectively within PB's rules.[12]

Second, we would expect individuals who participate in CSOs to be more likely than non-CSO participants to hold positive attitudes about their ability to exercise authority and their willingness to work with other CSOs rather than the government during negotiations over the distribution and implementation of public works. Nylen's survey findings from Betim and Belo Horizonte demonstrate that most PB participants were already active members in civil society, which means that PB is not empowering the unorganized. To the contrary, Nylen finds that PB increases the participation of CSO activists in political society, thereby helping to empower individuals who were already active in civil society prior to the adoption of PB.[13] According to Nylen, PB creates an institutionalized venue for debate and negotiation; he argues that PB has contributed to the "pluralization of democratic activism" and, therefore, the "democratization of democracy."[14] PB changes the political landscape, allowing the previously excluded to be directly involved in decision-making venues.

Baiocchi finds that PB supports civil society in myriad ways, such as through "networks of conversations" and workshops and training seminars and through facilitating the management of neighborhood associations.[15] Thus, the participatory institution encourages the formation and strengthening of CSOs, which in turn support the complex participatory processes. If CSO participants have more positive assessments of their authority and exhibit new forms of behavior in comparison with non-CSO participants, we will be able to confirm that CSO participation is positively

---

10. Abers 1998, 531–32.
11. Abers 1998, 526–27.
12. Baiocchi 2005.
13. Nylen 2002, 2003.
14. Nylen 2003, 90.
15. Baiocchi 2001, 64.

associated with PB. However, if civil society participation is not associated with more positive attitudes, it will be necessary to conclude that individuals' activity in civil society does not affect their attitudes and behaviors.

Third, the social context, at individual and municipal levels, is also likely to affect participants' attitudes and behaviors. At the individual level, factors such as age, gender, income, and education may shape participants' attitudes and behaviors. We would expect, for example, that higher-income and male respondents would have more positive attitudes about their ability to exercise authority because of the broader public role played by higher-income individuals and men in Brazil. However, there is some evidence that PB programs dampen basic socioeconomic effects. Baiocchi, for example, finds that the lack of education or gender differences does not "pose insurmountable barriers to effective participation."[16] We will be able to confirm Baiocchi's argument if the two socioeconomic variables included in the argument are not statistically significant.

At the municipal level, it is reasonable to propose that wealthier and less populated municipalities would produce more robust results because wealthier cities have greater resources to dedicate to the basic problems of the poor. However, there is conflicting evidence in the broader literature regarding this claim. Heller finds that participatory processes worked well in Kerala, India, as a result of class-based political organizing and of an emphasis on education by the local Communist Party.[17] Kerala is one of India's poorer states, which is why the successful outcomes are particularly surprising. Porto Alegre, the site of Abers's and Baiocchi's research, and Belo Horizonte, the site of Nylen's, are wealthy cities in the contexts of Brazil, Latin America, and the developing world. Of course, within Porto Alegre and Belo Horizonte, there are stark disparities in income, infrastructure, and access to services, but the cities have higher-than-average standards of living. Given that the experiences of Kerala, Porto Alegre, and Belo Horizonte are considered to be successful experiences, there is no consensus in the literature regarding the relationship between a community's standard of living and the outcomes produced by participatory institutions.

Finally, partisan political activity is often cited as a reason that people choose to be involved in participatory institutions.[18] Political opponents of governments that adopt participatory institutions often allege that these new policy-making venues are principally ways to distribute resources to

16. Baiocchi 2001, 51.
17. Heller 2001.
18. Nylen 2003.

the governments' allies. If this is true, we should expect that partisan political activity will be strongly associated with positive evaluations of participants' authority. However, if partisan identification is not strong, it would be reasonable to conclude that participatory institutions can be used in a manner that promotes group competition that is buffered from partisan government intervention.

Multiple and Logistical Regression Analysis

I have developed three models to better identify which factors might be more closely associated with the respondents' attitudes. The first is the *individual-level* model, derived entirely from the survey data. It assesses how individuals' social, political, and civil society characteristics might help to explain their attitudes. The second model is based on *aggregate-level* data from each municipality, designed to assess how electoral results, economic factors, population, and PB-specific characteristics might influence respondents' attitudes. The third is a *municipal-level* model. I created a dummy variable for each municipality to assess whether differences among the programs might explain respondents' attitudes.

Survey Questions: Authority

The first group of questions taps into the level of authority that PB delegates believe that they and their fellow delegates exercise in PB. Citizen-participants are often assumed to exercise authority in participatory institutions, but my previous research and fieldwork in Brazil had demonstrated that participants did not share this rosy view. The respondents were read the following statements: "Delegates have the power to establish the rules that regulate the functioning of PB"; "delegates have the power to decide general priorities for the city"; "delegates have the power to stop government-sponsored projects"; and "delegates have the power to monitor the implementation of PB projects." The survey respondents were asked to assess whether they believed that PB delegates "always," "almost always," "at times," or "never" exercised that particular type of authority with PB. Ordinary least squared (OLS) regression analysis was used to test the power of the different independent variables to explain outcomes.[19]

19. I also estimated this model using ordered logit and probit. Since the results are substantively the same, and OLS results are more widely used and understood, I have continued to report my results using OLS.

Survey Questions: Negotiation and Implementation

Logistic regression is used to analyze the responses to two questions that pertain to how PB delegates negotiate during the policy formation and implementation stages. We first asked, "To have a public work or service included in PB, in your opinion, the support of which of the following groups is the most important?" This question focuses on negotiations within PB *prior* to having a specific public work or service project included in the annual budget. Delegates were also asked, "After your public work or service is included in the PB budget, in your opinion, the support of which of the following groups is the most important?" This question focuses on the actual process of implementation. In Brazilian municipalities, many projects included in the budget are never implemented (and do not legally have to be). This question taps into whether PB has generated a pressure process in which csos and PB delegates organize themselves to make sure the government adheres to its PB commitments or whether the delegates believe that they must work more closely with government officials to secure the "liberation" of funds to implement their projects.

The respondents were provided with a list of six groups that they could select as being their most important allies. These groups include a variety of csos and governmental offices (such as legislators, bureaucrats, and the mayor's staff). A dummy variable was created to recode the responses into two groups: political society officials and csos. Political society officials include elected legislators, the mayoral staff, and the bureaucracy. csos include social movements, community organizations, and neighborhood associations. If PB delegates believe that they need to negotiate with their fellow delegates and csos more than with government officials, then PB may be significantly changing the state-society relationship in municipalities with PB. If, by contrast, PB delegates believe that they must work more closely with government officials than with other PB delegates, the PB programs are not achieving their objectives of creating a political institution that allows citizens to negotiate with one another to decide policy outcomes.

Explaining Delegates' Attitudes

Model 1: Individual-Level Data

These variables capture the four likely explanations, as discussed above: institutions, civil society, socioeconomic status, and partisan political identification. Gender (coded here as *male*) and income level are included to assess the extent to which an individual's social position affects his or her perceptions. We propose that higher income and male individuals will have more positive attitudes regarding their authority because they are more accustomed to exercising authority. *Times elected* and *PB benefits* are included in the model to test how PB as an institution is shaping attitudes. Individuals who have been elected more times or live in communities that have secured public works and social services from PB will be more likely to believe that they have authority. If PB is functioning as designed, these individuals will also alter their strategies for securing public goods.

cso participation, participatory council attendance, and *union membership* test for the activity of an individual in civil society. *Union membership* identifies a link between employment and participation, while *cso participation* is based on an individual's participation in a social movement or a community-based association. Participatory council attendance is based on an individual's involvement in a parallel participatory institution, such as the municipal health care councils. Of these three variables, we would expect that cso participation will have the strongest influence on an individual's attitudes. Finally, *partisan political affiliation* is included to assess whether an individual's partisan identification strongly shapes attitudes. We propose that if partisan political affiliation is a strong predictor of attitudes, then PB has developed into a policy-making institution that rewards the most loyal supporters of the government and does not allow for groups to pursue their interests outside narrow partisan agendas.

Model 2: Aggregate-Level Data

The second model includes data on each municipality and its respective PB programs. These data were collected separately from the survey. The independent variables are the *Human Development Index* (*HDI*), the municipality's *population*, the *total number of years* that the municipality has had PB, whether PB was continuously governed by the same political party since its inception (*continuous*), the *per capita spending* on new capital investments for 2001–2, the *percentage of leftist city council members* in the municipal legislative chambers for 2001–4, and the percentage difference between elected mayors' first-round votes and the second-place candidates in the 2000 election (*mayor's vote*).

There are two municipal-context variables: *HDI* and *population*. HDI measures the municipality's overall standard of living. The earliest and most successful cases of PB have been in wealthier municipalities.[20] We propose that as a municipality's wealth increases, there should be a positive increase in respondents' attitudes toward authority and negotiation. As the *population* of the municipality *increases*, we would expect that the respondents' perceptions of their authority would *decrease* because of the increasing complexity of implementing a participatory program in a larger setting as well as the decreasing importance of any single individual in a context of more participants.

There are three institutional variables: *total number of years, continuous*, and *per capita spending*. We would expect that the total number of years a PB program has functioned will be strongly associated with the increase in delegation of authority and cso-centric negotiations because of institutional consolidation. When the same political coalition has governed the PB program since its inception, we expect that there will be an increase in positive associations with authority and negotiation because the government leadership would learn how and when to turn authority over to its allies (citizen participants). We would expect that an increase in *per capita spending* will be strongly associated with increasingly positive attitudes on authority. It is reasonable to assume that as the available resources increase, there will also be an increase in the perception that individuals wield authority.

Finally, the political characteristics of the government are assessed through *percentage of leftist city council members* and *mayors' vote*. We would expect that a higher winning percentage by a mayor would give him or her increased flexibility to delegate authority, which will directly lead to an increasing perception that delegates are able to exercise authority. Furthermore, we would expect that as the *percentage of leftist city council members* increases, there will be a corresponding increase in the respondents' belief that they hold authority.[21] In Brazil, the strongest support for the direct delegation of authority to citizens has come from leftist politicians and csos operating at the local level.[22]

---

20. Ribeiro and de Grazia 2003; Wampler and Avritzer 2005.
21. The Workers' Party (PT), the Socialist Party of Brazil (PSB), and the Communist Party of Brazil (PC do B) were identified as leftist political parties in all eight municipalities.
22. Keck 1992; Wampler and Avritzer 2005.

Model 3: Municipal-Level Data

The final model includes seven of the eight municipalities in the survey. São Paulo was removed from the model because of high degrees of multicollinearity with the other seven municipalities. The inclusion of these seven municipalities allows us to analyze whether there is general agreement among the delegates within a given municipality and whether there are substantial differences among the eight municipalities. This research project is predicated on the assumption that there will be significant differences among the different municipalities in how PB programs were created, how they function, and what types of outcomes they generate. Significant differences among the municipalities will validate the research strategy because it is an indication of substantive differences in PB delegates' attitudes on PB. It also assumes that the attitudes of respondents will be significantly different as a result of the particular processes in each municipality.

Results: Exercising Authority and Negotiation Strategies

Individual-Level Data

As shown in Table 9, the institutional variables, followed by civil society variables, offer the strongest and most consistent statistically significant explanations for citizens' attitudes. Specifically, *times elected, PB benefits,* and *CSO participation* variables offer the strongest explanatory power. When delegates perceive that their community received a direct policy benefit from PB, then they believe that they have decision-making authority. Delegates elected multiple times and those who participate in CSOs also believe that they have the authority to make decisions.

These explanatory factors are intertwined. Seventy-five percent of survey respondents participate in CSOs, which helps them to be elected as PB delegates and to secure PB projects, because they can mobilize their fellow CSO activists to attend the appropriate meetings in order to vote. Delegates who help their communities secure projects are then interested in continuing their participation because their community receives direct benefits based on their participation in PB. Delegates who are elected multiple times have an advantage over first-time delegates because they know what strategic steps must be taken to secure resources. PB's rules

Table 9. Authority and Negotiation: Individual-Level Data

	OLS Regression				Logistic Regression	
	Authority to make rules	Authority to establish budget priorities	Authority to stop government's own projects	Authority to monitor government	CSO support is needed more than government's support during negotiation phase	CSO support is needed more than government's support during implementation phase
Income	−.006	−.68**	−.058#	.019	−.025	.069
	(.028)	(.029)	(.030)	(.030)	(.056)	(.055)
Union	.127	.217#	.100	.143	.213	−.001
	(.121)	(.124)	(.131)	(.0130)	(.128)	(.118)
CSO participation	.054	.235#	.063	.136	.082	.213#
	(.125)	(.127)	(.133)	(.133)	(.120)	(.119)
Partisan political affiliation	.076	.049	.014	.173#	.112	−.022
	(.086)	(.087)	(.092)	(.092)	(.086)	(.083)
Policy council participation	−.078	−.075	.144	−.040	−.076	.081
	(.091)	(.093)	(.098)	(.098)	(.125)	(1.65)
Times elected as delegate	.130***	.066#	.106**	.060	.195	.201**
	(.039)	(.040)	(.042)	(.042)	(.086)	(.079)
PB benefits	.170#	.257**	.042	.234**	.254*	.164#
	(.092)	(.094)	(.099)	(.099)	(.090)	(.090)
Men					.023**	.254**
					(.085)	(.081)

Table 9. (*continued*)

	OLS Regression				Logistic Regression	
	Authority to make rules	Authority to establish budget priorities	Authority to stop government's own projects	Authority to monitor government	cso support is needed more than government's support during negotiation phase	cso support is needed more than government's support during implementation phase
Constant	2.34*** (.158)	2.33*** (.162)	1.63*** (.170)	2.30*** (.170)	.387* (.275)	−.254* (.264)
F	2.813**	3.951***	2.43**	2.378**		
ADJ R2	.019	.030	.015	.014		
Log likelihood					−1030	−1037
N	667	694	694	694	672	675

≤ .1.
* p≤ .05; ≤.
** ≤.01.
*** ≤.001.

VIF tests reveal no significant multicollinearity.

Figures in parentheses are absolute T-ratios.

Note: In OLS estimates of the logistic regression models (two right columns), the tolerances for each predictor are greater than .10, indicating that multicollinearity is not a problem.

reward intra- and intergroup coalition-building, because the groups that can mobilize the greatest number of supporters will receive the greatest level of resources. This confirms the findings in Porto Alegre by Abers, Baiocchi, and Avritzer, who found that PB reinforces existing CSOs and encourages the establishment of new ones.[23]

It is possible, of course, that survey respondents enter PB predisposed to hold the attitude that they exercise authority. Many CSOs have long advocated that individuals from historically excluded groups should have direct access to decision-making venues, which may encourage people to believe that they are exercising authority merely because they are involved in a state-sanctioned participatory institution. We lack longitudinal studies that might directly and conclusively answer this question. However, *times elected* and *PB benefits* are statistically significant, indicating that respondents' involvement within PB has had a stronger influence on shaping their attitudes than their previous or current civil society activity.

With regard to negotiation, *times elected, PB benefits,* and *CSO participation* are again statistically significant. The most active and successful participants have a common understanding of the importance of forming groups to negotiate with other groups and with government officials. Although PB formally allows citizens to participate as individuals, the rules are structured to reward group behavior, which accounts for why *CSO participation* is statistically significant. This finding confirms the works of Avritzer, Nylen, and Baiocchi.[24] The *times elected* variable also suggests that negotiations with their fellow delegates and with CSOs are more important than negotiations with government leaders. This implies that PB is altering long-standing state-society relationships, because governments that administer PB can no longer use public resources in a clientelistic fashion. Delegates are beginning to engage in group-oriented behavior in which they pressure their fellow delegates and CSOs to secure the passage of their preferred public policies. Delegates are declaring that their successes are based on working with their fellow citizens rather than establishing private political deals with the government. This is solid evidence that PB is helping to establish accountability and citizen rights. PB appears to be permitting citizens to avoid the intense dependence on government officials that has long marked the interactions between CSOs leaders and government officials.

---

23. Abers 2000; Baiocchi 2005; Avritzer 2002.
24. Avritzer 2002; Nylen 2003; Baiocchi 2005.

In addition, the implementation of policy projects continues to require pressure from CSOs to induce the government to comply with the directives established by PB. Those who benefit directly from PB (*PB benefits*) and CSO activists share the attitude that they must work with other CSOs to pressure government officials to secure the implementation of projects. Therefore, clientelism, long a hallmark of Brazilian politics, has a smaller role in PB programs than in other policy and service-delivery institutions. This finding confirms the work of Wampler and Avritzer.[25]

The delegates were also asked if they were able to secure benefits from their municipal government outside PB. Fifty-seven percent asserted that PB was the *only* format through which they were able to secure resources. Therefore, the presence of PB in a municipality encourages most delegates to use institutionalized mechanisms to secure scarce policy outputs. Taken in conjunction with the finding that most delegates focus their negotiation efforts on creating intra- and intergroup alliances, this is further evidence that PB acts as an institutionalized space that is helping to erode clientelistic exchanges.

With regard to individuals' social positions, *income* and *male* are both statistically significant. *Income* is statistically significant in a counterintuitive way. First, as income *increases,* there is a corresponding *decrease* in the perception that the delegates wield authority on the two questions directly focused on specific budgetary authority. There are two likely explanations for this finding. The first possible explanation is that middle- and upper-income respondents have more difficulties in mobilizing allies and supporters because PB's rules are geared toward creating "social justice" by providing more resources to lower-income communities. Middle- and upper-class individuals are less likely to secure resources for their communities, which means they do not perceive that they have authority because they are not directly affected by PB-related policy outputs. A second possible explanation is that middle- and upper-income respondents are used to exercising authority (namely, in the workplace) and they do not believe that this new institutional space is really allowing for much decision-making authority.

Interestingly, men were more likely to believe that it is necessary to negotiate with government officials rather than with CSOs.[26] This suggests that male respondents were more likely than women to engage in

25. Wampler and Avritzer 2004.
26. Gender was not statistically significant on any of the "authority" models and was excluded from the model.

traditional government-citizen exchanges (for example, clientelism). We can infer from this data that women are more likely to work with other csos as they pursue their interests. Women became more politically active in csos during the 1970s and 1980s, a time of political renewal in Brazil geared toward challenging political exclusion and clientelism.[27] It is quite possible that women PB delegates are more likely to work with csos because they had participated in early efforts to transform Brazil's civil and political societies. Additionally, it is possible that this political renewal has taken place in larger urban areas, where women represent 60 percent of the PB delegates.

Finally, since the results confirm that the most active, long-serving members of PB believe that they have the authority to affect policy outcomes (*times elected*), it could also mean that PB is captured by csos affiliated with the government. Of the survey participants with an identifiable political identification (58 percent), 70 percent shared a *partisan political affiliation* with the incumbent mayor, which gives credence to the warnings of both Nylen and Navarro that PB provides a venue for activists affiliated with the government to gain access to policy-making venues.[28] However, *partisan political affiliation* is only statistically significant on the question of whether the respondents believe that they have the ability to monitor the government. Participation in PB, rather than a *partisan political affiliation,* is a better indicator for whether delegates believe that they exercise authority and whether they should negotiate with other csos rather than government officials. This finding provides evidence that as an institution, PB, rather than partisan politics, has a significant effect on shaping the attitudes of PB participants.

Aggregate-Level Data

Table 10 presents the results from the municipal-level data analysis. The institutional and the municipality context variables are consistently statistically significant. On the institutional level, the *total number of years, continuous PB,* and *per capita spending* are statistically significant. With regard to the context variables, *population* and *HDI* offer strong explanatory power to account for respondents' attitudes. Counterintuitively, as the city's population *increases,* so too does the likelihood that delegates believe that they exercise authority.

27. Alvarez 1990.
28. Nylen 2003; Navarro 2002.

First, the institutional variables: as the number of years that a municipality has PB increases, so too does the respondents' belief that they exercise authority. PB is a complex process that takes government officials and citizens many years to effectively use because the process requires participants to shift their strategies about how to get resources. It may not be apparent for several years which strategies the participants should pursue to produce their preferred outcome, so it is only over time that PB delegates can exercise authority. Governments that are reelected multiple times may delegate increasingly broader levels of authority because government officials perceive that part of their electoral success is based on "participatory democracy." Municipalities that adopted PB in the early 1990s (Porto Alegre, Ipatinga) have governments that were dedicated to delegating authority for ideological and political reasons. This also indicates that long-standing PB programs are beginning the process of institutionalization. This confirms Abers's and Fedozzi's observations that PB is a complex learning process that requires time for institutions to consolidate.[29]

Second, *continuous PB* is also statistically significant, which means that single-party/coalition rule over the process is strongly associated with the belief of survey respondents that they exercise authority. There are several possible interpretations. One possible explanation is that the party that initiated PB is more committed to PB than its successors. This strong level of commitment helps ensure that PB programs will successfully delegate authority. A second possible explanation is that PB's rules may be largely consistent in municipalities that have had PB administered by a single party (when a new government assumes control of PB, they often modify the rules, which then forces PB delegates and participants to alter their strategies and behaviors). A stable rule set may help PB delegates learn how to maximize their authority under PB's rules. A final explanation is that PB is a complex process, which means that consistency among PB's administrators may increase institutional memory and, in turn, promote greater efficiencies.

Third, as the level of per capita investment spending *increases,* the respondents' attitudes on their authority *decreases,* a surprising finding. There are two possible explanations for this counterintuitive finding. There may not be a direct relationship between per capita investment spending by the municipal government and the actual level of resources that PB

29. Abers 2000; Fedozzi 1998.

Table 10. Authority and Negotiation: Aggregate-Level Data

	OLS Regression				Logistic Regression	
	Authority to make rules	Authority to establish budget priorities	Authority to stop government's own projects	Authority to monitor government	cso support is needed more than government's support during negotiation phase	cso support is needed more than government's support during implementation phase
HDI-2000	22.45** (8.01)	28.96*** (7.60)	4.03 (8.00)	14.66# (8.16)	8.73 (16.73)	2.874 (14.89)
Population	.000*** (.00000027)	.000*** (.00000027)	.000*** (.00000028)	.000*** (.00000028)	.000*** (.000000044)	.000# (.000000053)
Total number of years	.051# (.031)	.087** (.031)	.179*** (.033)	.110*** (.034)	.035 (.068)	–.012 (.060)
Continuous PB	–1.68*** (.514)	–2.46*** (.460)	–1.04* (.485)	–.703 (.495)	–.040 (.982)	.032 (.438)
Investment per capita	.011*** (.003)	.014*** (.003)	.004 (.003)	.002 (.003)	–.003* (.006)	–.003 (.005)
% mayor's victory	.365 (.919)	1.264 (.926)	3.61*** (.975)	.107 (.994)	–1.69 (2.141)	–2.36 (1.88)
% leftist in legislature	–.858 (2.05)	–8.892*** (1.93)	3.61 (.975)	–2.196 (2.08	2.51 (4.43)	5.61 (3.76)

Table 10. (*continued*)

	ols Regression				Logistic Regression	
	Authority to make rules	Authority to establish budget priorities	Authority to stop government's own projects	Authority to monitor government	cso support is needed more than government's support during negotiation phase	cso support is needed more than government's support during implementation phase
Constant	−15.24** (6.26)	−20.23*** (5.96)	−1.38 (6.27)	−9.84 (6.41)	−6.56 (13.18)	−2.92 (12.04)
F	7.969***	14.294***	10.521***	6.434***		
ADJ R2	.068	.118	.088	.051		
Log likelihood					−839.41	−1008.58
N	667	694	694	694	672	675

\# ≤ .1.

* p≤ .05; ≤.

** .01.

*** ≤.001.

VIF tests reveal no significant multicollinearity.

Figures in parentheses are absolute T-ratios.

Note: In ols estimates of the logistic regression models (two right columns), the tolerances for each predictor are greater than .10, indicating that multicollinearity is not a problem.

delegates negotiate over. Government officials may allow delegates to negotiate more than 100 percent of investment spending, as in Porto Alegre,
but they may also allow the delegates to negotiate just 10 percent, as in
Rio Claro.[30] A second possible explanation is that increases in per capita
investment spending help reinforce the perception that delegates are only
negotiating a small fraction of the budget. An increase in resources therefore increases delegates' demands, which, if unfulfilled, may lead to the
perception that the authority wielded by delegates is actually quite limited. However, additional research on this issue is necessary for establishing a clearer explanation.

The size of the *population* presents surprising results from the perspective of participatory democracy. As the population of the municipality
increases, so too does the belief that delegates exercise authority. This is
counterintuitive because typically when we think about participatory programs, "smaller is better." Direct democracy in the form of New England
town halls is commonly thought to have a better chance of success in
smaller locales than in larger ones because the localized focus allows individuals to make informed decisions about local issues and a smaller number of delegates makes it easier to reach collective decisions.[31]

Brazilian civil society offers answers to this puzzle. It is weak in comparison with its European and North American counterparts but robust
in comparison with other countries in Latin America and the developing
world.[32] Within Brazil the most prevalent types of organizations include
labor unions (state bureaucracies and private sector), social movements,
neighborhood organizations, and NGOs, which have a greater chance of
establishing a strong voice in larger urban centers. These data suggest
that CSOs in larger municipalities might be better able to handle the difficult task of simultaneously cooperating with and confronting the municipal government within and outside PB. It is not just the density of CSOs
that affects PB outcomes, but also what strategies these CSOs use to pursue their political preferences.

Furthermore, an increase in a municipality's population is associated
with an increase in the belief that CSOs are more important than government officials in the negotiation and implementation phase. In larger
municipalities, CSOs are more willing and able to engage in contentious
behavior against, and cooperation with, municipal governments in larger

---

30. Wampler and Avritzer 2004; Teixeira and Albuquerque 2006.
31. Barber 1984; Bryan 2004.
32. Alvarez, Dagnino, and Escobar 1998; Dagnino, Olvera, and Panfichi 2006b.

urban settings.[33] csos in smaller urban areas are likely to have less auton-
omy, less capacity to form alliances with other csos, and less competition for their support from rival political parties.

Municipal-Level Data

The results from the municipal cases, as shown in Table 11, demonstrate
that in five municipalities (Porto Alegre, Ipatinga, Blumenau, Rio Claro,
and Santo André) there was general agreement among the survey respondents regarding the level of authority that they believe they are able to
exercise.[34] These five municipalities are consistently statistically significant, which indicates a grouping of delegates within each municipality
around particular attitudes and positions. Two municipalities, Porto Alegre and Ipatinga, are notable because there was broad agreement among
their respondents that PB delegates exercise a substantial degree of authority. PB programs that delegate authority have strong and positive effects
on their citizens, which indicates that PB programs can have a transformative impact on a broad number of citizens when governments delegate decision-making authority. Of the eight municipalities included in
the survey, only Porto Alegre's delegates believe that they have the capacity to stop government projects and monitor governmental action on PB
projects. This evidence supports the general set of claims about Porto
Alegre's PB by Abers, Avritzer, Baiocchi, and Goldfrank, all of whom
indicate that citizens are directly influencing a broad segment of Porto
Alegre's public policies.[35]

In three municipalities, Blumenau, Rio Claro, and Santo André, respondents share the attitude that they and their fellow delegates do not
exercise much authority, although Santo André's delegates believe that
they have the authority to monitor the government. These respondents are
clearly claiming that their PB programs are not functioning the way that
PB programs have been designed to function. This evidence suggests
that we must be wary of claims that PB is transforming Brazilian politics
because in Blumenau, Rio Claro, and Santo André, the delegates themselves do not believe that they have much of an impact on policy-making
outcomes. In Blumenau and Rio Claro, the government that has adopted

33. Baiocchi 2005.
34. The municipality of São Paulo was automatically excluded from the model by the spss
application because of multicollinearity.
35. Abers 2000; Avritzer 2002; Baiocchi 2003, 2005; Goldfrank 2003.

Table 11. Authority and Negotiation: Municipal-Level Data

	Power to make rules	Power to establish budget priorities	Power to stop government's own projects	Power to monitor government
Belo Horizonte	−.043	−.021	.071	.206
	(148)	(.149)	(.157	(.161)
Blumenau	−.239#	−.393**	−.133	−.360*
	(.147)	(.150)	(.158)	(.162)
Ipatinga	.531***	.423**	.200	.023
	(.151)	(.150)	(.158)	(.162)
Porto Alegre	.383**	.510**	1.10***	.648***
	(.149)	(.152)	(.160)	(.163)
Recife	−.094	−.043	.117	−.243
	(.148)	(.150)	(.158)	(.162)
Rio Claro	−1.09***	−1.577***	−.750***	−.793***
	(.234)	(.204)	(.215)	(.219)
Santo André	−.324*	−.279#	.409**	−.088
	(.142)	(.146)	(.153)	(.156)
Constant	2.76***	2.71***	1.68***	2.83***
(.061)	(.061)	(.065)	(.066)	
F	7.943***	14.283***	10.593***	6.32***
ADJ R2	.068	.118	.088	.051
N	668	695	695	695

≤ .1.
* ≤ .05; ≤.
** .01.
*** ≤ .001.

VIF tests reveal no significant multicollinearity

Note: São Paulo was removed from the model because it was correlated with the other independent variables.

PB is most aptly characterized as a "policy follower."[36] These governments have been inspired by the electoral, mobilization, and policy successes reported in municipalities such as Porto Alegre, Ipatinga, and Belo Horizonte, but they have not produced high-quality programs, and delegates hold very critical and negative attitudes about their PB programs. The

36. Wampler and Avritzer 2005.

potential danger is that poorly run PB programs may increase cynicism among activists rather than contribute to the inculcation of democratic values.

In Recife and Belo Horizonte, there are no clear trends among PB delegates, which is likely caused by the unevenness with which the programs have been administered. This survey data complements additional evidence that makes them both "mixed" cases (see Chapter 7). In Recife and Belo Horizonte, PB delegates both strongly supported and scorned their PB programs, possibly implying that particular types of citizens and CSOs are able to exercise authority (namely, partisan allies or strategically located communities), but other PB delegates feel that they are systematically denied the ability to exercise decision-making authority via PB.

Accountability and citizenship rights are more likely to be established in Porto Alegre and Ipatinga than in Blumenau and Rio Claro, because Porto Alegre's and Ipatinga's respondents believe that PB involves both citizens and government officials in the decision-making process. If the extension of accountability and citizenship rights are conceptualized as processes that require the active participation of two different actors (citizens and government officials), then Porto Alegre's and Ipatinga's PB are laying firm foundations for the extension of accountability and citizenship rights. Accountability is also more likely to be extended in Santo André than in Blumenau and Rio Claro, as is evidenced by the belief on the part of the former's PB delegates that they can monitor the activity of the government. Recife and Belo Horizonte fall in the middle of these cases because there are some delegates who believe that they actively engage in decision-making processes, while there are many others who believe they are shut out of the process.

It is worthwhile to note that this research project was predicated on the assumption that PB programs would produce significantly different outcomes. The results from Table 11 indicate that this comparative research strategy will enhance our knowledge about the effects of participatory institutions on citizens, CSOs, and governments. The survey evidence analyzed in this chapter provides statistical evidence that helps us to describe and explain why PB programs produce such widely different results. Most important, the survey demonstrates that the individuals who are most active in PB programs—PB delegates—hold widely different attitudes regarding their PB programs. In Chapters 4–7 we will explore in greater depth the reasons why PB delegates hold such disparate attitudes.

Conclusions

Participatory institutions, in conjunction with individuals' participation in csos, are helping to alter citizens' attitudes and encourage them to modify the strategies used to pursue public goods. This finding suggests that participatory institutions can play an important role in the process of revitalizing or deepening representative democracy. PB programs are drawing low-income citizens into an institutionalized political environment in which they are rewarded for their ability to form groups and engage in meaningful negotiations with their fellow citizens and government officials. Participatory institutions can therefore help to mitigate the most intense social, political, and economic differences that sharply separate individuals from different classes and groups in much of the developing world. The evidence presented in this chapter demonstrates that PB may provide the means for individuals to promote intra- and inter-group solidarity, thereby facilitating better representation of the interests of low-income citizens in the public sphere.

PB programs that delegate authority directly to citizens can strengthen democracy, which is vital in new democracies where there is often profound cynicism about politics, politicians, elections, and policy outcomes. Accountability and citizenship rights may therefore be extended, allowing citizens to be more actively engaged in selecting public policies that directly affect their communities and lives. Yet this finding cannot be generalized to poorly functioning participatory programs, in which delegates do not believe they exercise much authority. Under these circumstances we would have to argue that participatory institutions will not encourage increases in pluralistic behaviors.

A significant finding in this chapter is that the most active and successful respondents consistently held the attitude that the support of their fellow PB delegates and csos was more important than support from the government during the negotiation and implementation phases of policy making. This tells us that PB alters the traditional method of distributing goods in Brazil; clientelism is less likely to flourish in a context in which delegates are negotiating with one another in public venues. This strengthens the argument that accountability and citizenship rights are being extended. Citizens are learning how to become more actively involved in public affairs, not as clients of a politician, but as rights-bearing members of their polity.

Of course, the survey used in this book captures the attitudes of PB delegates, who are elected representatives within PB and therefore a political elite. The findings are not generalized to the broader set of PB participants or nonparticipants. However, it is possible to conceptualize the extension of accountability and citizenship, beginning with the most active CSO leaders and diffused to other citizens as a result of the efforts of these same CSOs. An arduous task, to be sure, in a country such as Brazil, but one that Brazilian CSOs are trying to accomplish.

On the municipal level, the most surprising finding is that as a city's population increases, there is also an increase in the attitude that citizens can exercise authority and should negotiate with CSOs rather than with government officials. This indicates that modern, institutionally complex forms of participatory democracy are viable in large urban centers. This is welcome news, since the world is increasingly an urban one, with populations congregating more and more in large urban areas.[37] Although PB may not be the institutional structure that is appropriate in all settings, the findings suggest that participatory democracy is a viable option.

This confounds conventional wisdom in the United States that participatory democracy would find more fertile ground in smaller rather than larger cities. There are two explanations. First, PB is a new institutional type. It is well suited for urban settings because it was created by governments and CSOs for use in large metropolitan areas. PB's founders created rules that take into account how class, education, and social status combine to discourage active participation among low-income groups. PB creates specific incentives for low-income residents to mobilize into groups to secure government resources. Policy makers, academics, and activists who seek to revive citizen participation in public life would do well to study how PB's institutional format offers incentives that allow for increased civic engagement among citizens.

The second reason that PB is more successful in larger municipalities is that CSOs are able to engage in cooperation and contentious politics, a combination that is more easily achieved in larger municipalities.[38] Even though civil society activity in Brazil varies greatly, larger municipalities appear better able than midsized municipalities (one hundred thousand to three hundred thousand residents) to produce CSOs that are able and willing to engage in both cooperation and contentious politics. The diversity and density of organizations in Brazil's larger municipalities is allowing

37. Davis 2006.
38. Baiocchi 2005.

low-income individuals to form organizations, through which they can promote their interests. Therefore, it is likely that efforts to extend account-ability and citizenship rights are likely to find broad support in large, com-plex metropolitan areas. A broad range of public and private interest groups, an active body of community-based csos, the presence of univer-sities, and a larger middle class help to set the conditions for the extension of accountability and citizenship. Chapters 4–7 will provide an in-depth description and explanation of why these eight PB programs produced such remarkably different outcomes.

4

Porto Alegre and Ipatinga:
The Successful Delegation of Authority
and the Use of Contentious Politics
(Among Friends)

> I believe that PB in Porto Alegre is an effort to de-
> mocratize the budget, giving citizens a role in the
> selection of projects and control over implementa-
> tion. This represents a great advance because any
> citizens can now defend their projects in PB meet-
> ings. . . . PB is the prerogative of the government,
> but it depends on the capacity of citizens.
> —PB DELEGATE IN PORTO ALEGRE

> We, the leaders of our communities, are pressured
> by the government and by the community. We are
> caught between their demands, which makes it
> more difficult for us to act.
> —PB DELEGATE IN IPATINGA

Deliberation and Direct Decision Making in Porto Alegre

On April 18, 2004, I attended a first-round PB meeting in the southern
Brazilian city of Porto Alegre. The meeting was held in a regional bus
terminal, with more than six hundred people sitting outside in the damp,
chilly air. We were outside because the terminal was the only public facility in the region that could accommodate such a large crowd. I had last
attended a meeting of this size in Porto Alegre in 1999, so I was particularly interested to see if the tenor of the meetings had changed. Several
observations are in order.

First, when government officials explained the rules, they did so efficiently, thus allowing the meeting to quickly proceed to the main policy
issues under discussion. First-time attendees, however, would be hard
pressed to make much sense of the rules because the complex tasks that

would be accomplished that night were not easily understandable from the compressed presentation. However, as the meeting proceeded, it appeared to me that most people understood what their options and responsibilities were, signifying that many individuals were either repeat participants or were being guided by someone who had a firm grasp of the rules.

Second, when participants took the microphone to speak, they did not focus their attention on government officials. Rather, they spoke to their fellow citizens, imploring them to act or vote in a specific way. This engendered a high-quality debate, as delegates introduced new threads to the discussion but also commented on the ideas and arguments of previous speakers.

Third, during the meeting, former mayor Raúl Pont arrived with little fanfare. Pont was again running for mayor (the election was held in October 2004 and Pont eventually lost in the second round). He took a seat in the audience and listened to the ongoing debate. Twenty to thirty minutes after he arrived, his presence was announced. While this was part political theater by Pont and the PT, as they sought to demonstrate that Pont was no different from the average citizen, the lack of response from the audience to Pont's arrival was remarkable. Citizens remained focused on the debate and the PB process rather than attempting to interact with the former mayor. Over the past decade, I have attended well more than one hundred government-sponsored participatory meetings throughout Brazil. Whenever important government officials arrived, participants more often than not stopped what they were doing to interact with them. The posture of Pont and the participants was remarkable for the lack of hoopla created around his arrival.

When it came time to vote, a participant announced that there would be a single slate of candidates, because the community leaders had forged a unity slate. This meant that participants would vote only for their policy preferences. The unity among the community's leadership had elements of solidarity, as various factions put aside their differences. The intraregional cooperation allows their leaders to better defend their projects to the municipal government and legislative chambers. However, the use of a single slate also has the potential to dampen debate and competition within the region. Coalition-building prior to a PB meeting can be used by political leaders to pursue their own interests to the detriment of their followers' needs. PB was set up to overcome the domination by community leaders over the process, yet the use of a single slate of candidates could undermine these democratizing efforts.

A final note: Toward the end of the meeting, six young men arrived. They were in their late teens and were dressed in the appropriate hip-hop style of the day. They received ballots and spent ten to fifteen minutes discussing what they thought their region needed and how they should vote. Although their second- and third-level preferences were different, they all agreed that their first-order preference should be support for local cultural events, which have not traditionally received strong support from PB voters. PB now occupies an institutional space sufficiently large that teenagers are now trying to use it as a means to gain access to resources for their particular set of interests. Porto Alegre's PB is now the primary policy-making institution in which decisions about new capital investment projects are made.

Direct and Contingent Decision Making in Ipatinga

Ipatinga is an industrial town organized around an enormous steel mill, with some 10 percent of the population living in the outlying rural areas. The majority of the rural population is quite poor, but there are an increasing number of family-run hotels situated in the countryside that cater to the state's upper-middle classes. In 1999 Ipatinga added a "rural" region to its PB, thereby dedicating PB funds specifically to these rural areas. In one of the small valleys just outside town, a group of citizens came together in 1999 to try to secure funding for their principal need: building a milk-processing cooperative so they could pasteurize milk before selling it directly to local stores, hospitals, and schools. The milk-processing group calculated that their project would require the equivalent of U.S.$60,000, thereby consuming 100 percent of the PB funds for all rural areas in any given year. The leaders of this group approached other rural groups to strike a bargain. The milk-processing group made the strategic decision to "trade" its resources in 1999, 2000, and 2001 to other groups, if those groups would support the milk-processing plant in 2002.

These negotiations required the development of intergroup cooperation as well as active leadership support within the milk-processing group for its members to convince their followers to forsake short-term, smaller demands for a larger payoff. Solidarity within and among CSOS was crucial, but so too was belief that the government would actually implement a PB project several years later. Poor, rural citizens were being asked to defer short-term needs to eventually receive a project that could have a transformative impact on their lives. In April 2004, when I visited Ipatinga, the milk-cooperative project was nearing completion. The small producers were already lining up contacts to sell their milk to public schools, day care facilities, and hospitals. This example not only illustrates delegates' perceptions of the government's strong support for PB, but also demonstrates how strong mayoral support for PB can alter delegates' calculus for securing benefits. Participants were willing to defer their short-term interests because they believed that their fellow citizens and the government would honor their commitments three years later. The delegates' willingness to forgo short-term advantages in the hopes of a more lucrative benefit down the road signaled a significant change in Brazilian municipal policy making.

In a political environment long known for clientelism, personalism, and low levels of trust, the milk-processing group was counting on maintaining intragroup solidarity for three years while also trying to build intergroup solidarity. Obviously, it was a tough task but one that ultimately proved successful. Ipatinga's government has had a long and successful track record of implementing projects selected by PB delegates, which clearly lowered the political risk for the milk-processing group.

PB in Porto Alegre and Ipatinga: Successful Delegation of Authority

If PB programs are designed to promote social justice, to encourage citizens to be active in making decisions, to enhance governmental reform, and to make better use of public resources, then Porto Alegre and Ipatinga stand apart from the other municipalities included in this book because their PB programs have delivered results in several substantial ways. In Porto Alegre, from 1996 to 2003, nearly U.S.$400 million worth of PB projects were implemented.[1] Tens of thousands of citizens voted

1. To determine this figure, I analyzed the yearly *Balanço Geral* of the municipality's direct and indirect expenditures to determine which projects had actually been spent. The total includes the proposed value of all projects that were implemented, excluding all projects that were not implemented or were still in a planning phase. I used the annual *Plano de Investimentos*, which is published by the municipal government, to show which PB projects are entered into the annual budget as the basis for analysis. *Diario Oficial de Prefeitura Municipal de Porto Alegre* (1994–2004); *Balanço Geral de Prefeitura Municipal de Porto Alegre* (1994–2004).

for public works; elected PB representatives; and participated in workshops, public debates, and field trips over a sixteen-year period. Participation increased to nearly fifty thousand in 2003 and 2004.[2] In Ipatinga, the dollar amounts are lower, but PB has become the center of policy making as citizens make specific policy decisions that their government then implements. In addition to making specific decisions, citizens also have signaled their policy interests to government officials, who have then sought state and federal resources to implement larger and more expensive projects.

The purpose of this chapter is to more fully account for why PB programs in Porto Alegre and Ipatinga have been more successful than in other cases included in this book and to provide evidence that substantiates these claims. Porto Alegre's PB has captured the attention of activists, scholars, students, and international agencies.[3] Although this chapter undercuts some of the claims that have been used to build a metanarrative on Porto Alegre's PB, the evidence collected demonstrates that Porto Alegre's PB has achieved many positive outcomes.

Ipatinga's PB program is not as well known as Porto Alegre's PB. Ipatinga drew upon the set of rules created in Porto Alegre to craft its own PB in 1990. Ipatinga is a modest city, with a population of 220,000 that encircles a gigantic steel mill, the city's principal employer. Ipatinga is a wealthy city, for the state of Minas Gerais, located in the heart of Brazil's steel belt, but it also has high levels of poverty and comprises migrants from the rural areas of the states of Minas Gerais and Bahia. Ipatinga's PB is more limited in scope than that of Porto Alegre, but it too has proved to be quite successful.

In this chapter, I will first briefly describe the most important characteristics of both municipalities, to better situate the reader. I will then explain how a combination of mayoral interest and action, CSOs' capacity to cooperate and contest, PB's rules, the mayoral-legislative context, and the financial situation produced each municipality's results. The second half of the chapter is exclusively dedicated to presenting evidence that demonstrates why and how Porto Alegre and Ipatinga have managed to create successful PB cases when the efforts of most of their counterparts have been far less fruitful.

2. "Número de participantes plenários regionais do Orçamento Participativo," 2004, 3.
3. Abers 1998; 2000; Baiocchi 2003, 2005; Santos, 2005.

Basic Demographic and Political Characteristics

Table 12 contains key political and demographic data on the two municipalities. Two key differences between them are population size and their overall political importance within their respective states. Porto Alegre is the capital of Rio Grande do Sul and the most important city in the state. It is the anchor of a metropolitan region of nearly 3 million residents and is the financial and industrial center of the state. Porto Alegre's importance also stretches beyond the state of Rio Grande do Sul because it is one of Brazil's most important state capitals.

Ipatinga is an important regional hub in the enormous state of Minas Gerais. Ipatinga was created from scratch in the late 1950s and early 1960s by the federal government to support the steel mill that was built there. Ipatinga is still a one-company town, with all activity based around the steel mill. Instead of ending at a central plaza or square, all roads, physically and metaphorically, lead to the mill. Ipatinga is a relatively wealthy municipality, as evidenced by its professional classes and its unionized labor force, although layoffs in the 1990s and the influx of rural migrants have extenuated differences between individuals employed by the mill and those employed elsewhere or not at all.[4]

Survey Evidence

The survey respondents in Porto Alegre and Ipatinga are far more supportive of their PB programs and believe that they exercise authority at much higher rates than do their counterparts in the other six municipalities included in the PB Comparative Study. (See Chapter 3, especially Table 11). Table 13 includes basic demographic information of the survey respondents. The respondents are representative of Brazil's lower classes. Seventy-eight percent of respondents in Porto Alegre and 62 percent in Ipatinga live in households earning U.S.$400 or less per month. The low levels of education also indicate that the survey respondents are representative of the lower classes. Although Ipatinga has a per capita income that is less than half that of Porto Alegre (see Table 12), Ipatinga's PB delegates are not quite as poor. Ipatinga has been able to draw in larger

---

4. Interviews conducted in Ipatinga suggest that the layoffs were the result of the steel company's privatization during the 1990s. However, I was unable to obtain any corroborating evidence.

Table 12. Demographic and Political Profile

	Porto Alegre	Ipatinga
Residents in 2000	1,300,000	212,000
Human Development Index 2000	0.865	0.806
Per capita monthly income in 2000	U.S.$173	U.S.$71
Municipal government's investment spending per capita, average, 2001–2002	U.S.$29	U.S.$58
Political party that implemented PB	PT	PT
% of mayor's vote in 1996 municipal election (first round)	54.5	52
% of mayor's vote in 2000 municipal election (first round)	48.7	45
Average % of leftist seats in city council, 1996–2004	41	34

Sources: www.ibge.gov.br, www.undp.org, www.stn.fazenda.gov.br, www.tse.gov.br.

Table 13. Profile of Survey Respondents (%)

	Porto Alegre	Ipatinga
Household income of U.S.$400 per month or less	78	62
Less than high school diploma	75	60
Women respondents	71	30
Currently active in associational life	80	70
Current leadership position in community association	57	45
Delegates elected 3 or more times	39	35
Delegates received a direct benefit from PB	91	92

Source: PB Comparative Survey.

members of the unionized middle class (20 percent union membership compared with 7 percent in Porto Alegre).

The data in Table 13 also clearly demonstrate that there is active engagement of citizens beyond PB. PB delegates are engaged in CSOS and in leadership positions in CSOS at very high rates. PB has the potential to serve as a multiplier of information and democratic values because increasing numbers of citizens gain information and knowledge about local politics and are able to make decisions regarding the allocation of funds and the general direction of public policies.[5] Interviews with delegates in Porto Alegre and Ipatinga indicate that PB is a central, although not exclusive, subject of their community meetings.[6] PB has therefore become one focus for the activity of the CSOS, although they continue to engage in both types of social and political organizing (cooperative food banks, working with church organizations, working with state police).[7]

We lack data on the level of participation in CSOS from the late 1980s when both PB programs were initiated, but evidence from Porto Alegre indicates that PB has helped to generate new organizations and increase involvement.[8] Evidence also demonstrates that PB is more likely to be implemented in municipalities that have a greater density of CSOS.[9] We do not conclusively know whether PB participants were already active members of civil society at the time they entered PB or whether PB helped to foster the growth of new activists, but the results of this survey demonstrate that there is a strong correlation between PB and CSO activity.[10]

Although it may be impossible to establish a causal link between the development of PB and the current participation rates of PB delegates in CSOS, we can turn to the survey data to gauge whether each municipality's respective PB program is changing the behavior of its participants. Based on the statistical analysis laid out in Chapter 3, the individual-level factors that are most significantly associated with delegates having more authority are number of times that a delegate was elected as a PB delegate, direct benefits from the PB process, and participation in CSOS. The data from Porto Alegre and Ipatinga demonstrate high levels of these attributes, as reported in Table 13.

Authority

Table 14 lists the varying percentages of survey respondents who responded "always" or "almost always" to questions about their different types of authority in PB. Most delegates in Porto Alegre and Ipatinga believe that they have the authority to make decisions on PB's rules, select PB's policy priorities, and monitor the government's activities in PB.

5. Abers 2000; Wampler and Avritzer 2004.
6. Interviews conducted in Porto Alegre, April–June 1999, June 2000, May 2004; interviews conducted in Ipatinga in March 2004.
7. Dagnino, Olvera, and Panfichi 2006b.
8. Abers 2000.
9. Avritzer 2002; Wampler and Avritzer 2005.
10. See Nylen 2002, 2003; Baiocchi 2005; Abers 2000.

Importantly, the delegates in Ipatinga do not believe that they have the authority to stop government projects, while nearly two-thirds of the respondents in Porto Alegre believe that they "always" or "almost always" enjoy this authority. This is supporting evidence that Porto Alegre's government has delegated higher levels of authority to citizens. The perceptions of Porto Alegre's delegates are confirmed by other types of data as well. For example, Porto Alegre's government allows 100 percent of new capital investment projects to be decided by PB delegates, which means that the government must submit its own proposals for new capital investment projects to be debated and then voted on by PB councilors (supra delegates elected to the municipal-wide PB council). PB councilors do have the power to reject, and have, in practice, rejected, government proposals.

Table 14. Delegates' Perceptions of Their Authority to Make Decisions (% Stating Always or Almost Always)

	Porto Alegre	Ipatinga
Authority to make PB rules	63	77
Authority to define PB priorities	75	75
Authority to define projects	80	60
Authority to add resources	50	30
Authority to stop government projects	61	32
Authority to monitor government projects	85	70
Secured projects outside PB	23	57

Source: PB Comparative Survey.

The final row shows that the vast majority of Porto Alegre's PB delegates do not obtain additional public resources outside PB, while in Ipatinga a significant number, 57 percent, are able to secure government resources from other institutional venues. These perceptions illuminate the way in which PB is at the center of policy making in Porto Alegre, but that it was only one venue among many in Ipatinga.

The attitudes of PB delegates are, of course, just one way to demonstrate the PB programs' impacts. In the remainder of this chapter, I will present complementary types of data that demonstrate PB's effects in each respective municipality. More important, I will move beyond the descriptive presentation of data to explain why these programs appear to be much more successful than their counterparts. I will accomplish this by interweaving complementary sets of data with the explanation.

Porto Alegre

Porto Alegre is widely recognized as being the birthplace of the specific set of rules associated with PB, although there were participatory experiences that preceded it in different regions of Brazil.[11] A Workers' Party (Partido de Trabalhadores, or PT) candidate, Olivio Dutra, was elected mayor in 1988. The PT mayoral administration adopted PB in 1989 and placed it at the center of its governing and campaign strategies. PB has gained international fame largely on the basis of the Porto Alegre experience.[12] The evidence presented in this chapter generally supports the prevailing conventional wisdom that PB has helped to transform state-society relations and altered the distribution of public resources in Porto Alegre. However, this positive evaluation of PB is tempered by my argument that PB's success is based on the initial concentration of mayoral authority and the ability of mayors to provide alternative projects and resources that induce municipal legislators to support the government's policies. Ironically, this participatory institution flourished in large part because of the skillful use of the powers concentrated in the mayor's hands. As the data in Table 11 (Chapter 3) make clear, the attitudes of Porto Alegre's PB delegates concerning their PB are substantially more positive than the attitudes of their counterparts in the other municipalities.

The PT administered PB continuously from 1989 through 2004 (sixteen years).[13] It is the interaction of five factors that produce PB's strong results. Porto Alegre's PB is characterized by high mayoral support, a growing civil society base willing to engage in cooperative and contentious behavior and capable of doing so, relatively benign mayoral-legislative relations, rules that explicitly reward direct citizen involvement in decision-making rules that delegate authority directly to citizens, and a strong financial base.

11. Abers 2000; Fedozzi 1998; Wampler and Avritzer 2004; Baiocchi 2005.

12. The United Nations, the World Bank, the PT, and the World Social Forum have all promoted PB as a deliberative policy-making institution that can transform local politics. In addition, there is a large body of scholarly literature on the topic. Chavez and Goldfrank 2004; Santos 2005; Avritzer 2002; Abers 2000; Nylen 2003; Wampler and Avritzer 2004.

13. This report was finished in August 2004, prior to the elections that were to be held in October 2004. The PT, which initiated PB in 1989, pledged to continue PB if they were reelected, but it is not known if another party would maintain PB.

Mayoral Support

In 1988, the PT candidate for mayor, Olivio Dutra, engineered a remarkable come-from-behind victory, winning office with 34 percent of the valid vote.[14] The leaders of the PT administration in Porto Alegre were labor organizers and progressive members of the middle class, many of whom had participated actively in oppositional politics during the military regime. The PT leadership sought to foster a new political and social consciousness that would replace the traditional leftist reliance on nationalism and clientelism.[15] The PT administration sought to govern with and for the excluded sectors of the population by "inverting the priorities" of previous administrations, decentralizing the local state, and creating viable participatory channels.

The government's commitment to creating a new institutional format is exemplified by the writings of former mayor Tarso Genro (1993–96, 2001–2). Genro describes PB as a "non-state public sphere" (*espaço públio não-estatal*), arguing that PB is a new democratic type, allowing citizens to engage in deliberative decision making without state domination. "To construct a non-state public sphere signifies the reversal, the radical reversal, of the process realized under real socialism, in which the state dominated society. It is a civilizing process of the State, a process in which the State becomes a public entity controlled by civil society."[16] PB thus represents a conscious effort to avoid the state domination of civil society, which is what occurred in the Soviet Union and other Communist states. The hope of PT and many of its CSO allies was to build socialism based on the development of new state-society interactions. PB was initially part of a larger process that its supporters hoped would engender a broader transformation of Brazilian political and civil societies.

The conceptualization of the "non-state public sphere" suggests that individual citizens and voluntary associations develop a strong civil society that places a check on the authoritarian tendencies of the state while simultaneously making governments responsive to the demands and interests of the population. However, Tarso Genro's conceptualization, while theoretically and conceptually engaging, reflects a combination of the PT's ideology and "wishful thinking." Instead of viewing it as creating a non-state public sphere, it is more reasonable to assert that PB represents an

14. Abers 2000; Fedozzi 1998.
15. Baierle 1992.
16. Genro 1995b, 27; 1995b; 1997.

effort to create a *public* state in Brazil. It is *not* a "nonstate" space in the strict sense of the term because state officials organize it and the majority of the discussions focus on state policies, resources, and public works. It is *not* a nonstate space because the information and negotiation skills that participants take back to their community organizations are inspired by direct interactions with the state. Rather, the PT government uses the authority of the state to promote new state-society relations. The government is transforming the face and structure of the state by giving substantial levels of decision-making authority to citizens.[17]

During the Genro (1992–96, 2001–2), Pont (1997–2000), and Verle (2003–4) administrations, the government was able to fulfill its pledges and fund a substantial number and percentage of PB projects. Between 1996 and 1998, the government implemented 68 percent of PB projects.[18] From 1999 through 2003, more than 70 percent of the money allocated to PB projects had been spent on these projects.[19] This is strong and compelling evidence that the government privileges the projects selected within PB. PB delegates in Porto Alegre selected policies that resulted in the implementation of projects totaling more than U.S.$400 million by the end of 2003, indicating that the government is actively carrying out the policy preferences of PB delegates.[20] Projects range in size from small drainage systems and street paving to complex housing projects. As another indication of mayoral support, the government induced the Inter-American Development Bank (IDB) in 1999 to allow Porto Alegre to accept a major loan (U.S.$100 million) for infrastructure development near the airport without having to specify how all the resources would be allocated—not how the IDB normally distributes resources. PB councilors had to first approve the loan from the IDB before delegates could decide where to spend a portion of the resources.

How did PB come to occupy the center of policy making? During the PT's first administration (1988–92), the government prioritized the policies selected through PB. Internal administrative mechanisms were initiated to ensure funding for PB projects rather than the pet projects of

17. Abers 2000; Fedozzi 1998, 2000.
18. Wampler 2004b.
19. Determining this figure was done by comparing the government's proposed budget, the PB proposed budget, and the "Year End" accounts. *Diario Oficial de Prefeitura Municipal de Porto Alegre* (1994–2004); *Balanço Geral de Prefeitura Municipal de Porto Alegre* (1994–2004); see also Marquetti 2003.
20. *Diario Oficial de Prefeitura Municipal de Porto Alegre* (1994–2004); *Balanço Geral de Prefeitura Municipal de Porto Alegre* (1994–2004).

political appointees or municipal legislators.[21] Simply put, the government honored the decisions that were made by participants, creating "binding" budgetary lines.[22] By honoring the decisions made within the PB, the government signaled to the population that important public policy decisions would now be made in PB. This first step shifted decision-making processes away from the private spheres of the government and into the public meeting venues.[23]

The PT government took a second step that increased public trust: the submission of the mayor's policy initiatives for approval by PB participants. Without formal approval in the citizens' forum, the government's own policy initiatives that require new capital spending could not be included in the municipal budget and therefore could not be implemented.[24] This step represents a sea change in Brazilian policy making: Porto Alegre's government now must *publicly* defend its specific projects and submit these projects to a public vote of citizens. The government, of course, has the technical knowledge, political skills, and authority to persuade participants to vote for government projects. Government officials often argue that it would make the mayor and incumbent party—and PB—look bad if the delegates did not approve the spending. Even though the power differential between government officials and citizens is present, I was struck by how a large number of government officials, CSO leaders, and PB delegates provided numerous and very specific examples of when and how PB delegates had been able to block the government's initiatives. The government, however, was able to implement social service policies and other programs that did not require the spending of new capital investment, suggesting that the authority of PB delegates is largely limited to new capital investment spending.

21. Fedozzi 1998.
22. It is difficult to narrowly define "binding" decisions in the case of Brazilian budgets. Approved budget items do not necessarily have to be spent; it is left to the discretion of the executive to allocate resources (beyond personnel and debt payments) where he or she sees fit. However, in the case of PB in Porto Alegre, all the PB decisions are entered in the budget. Evidence demonstrates that the executive spent all available discretionary funds on the projects selected by the participants.
23. Luciano Fedozzi, interview, May 25, 1999, Porto Alegre; Genro 1995a; Fedozzi 1998.
24. An example that was cited by PB participants and government bureaucrats was the case of the expansion of highways, roads, and facilities near the airport. Many PB participants argued that the airline companies and passengers should pay for improvements because air travel is restricted to a minority of the population. The government argued that improvements to the airport would stimulate economic activity and thereby help the working classes. In the end, the government prevailed but the municipality's loan from the Inter-American Development Bank included a provision of infrastructure improvements not related to the airport.

Another indication of strong mayoral support has been the effort of the government and PB council to adjust PB's rules to maintain citizen interest and to mobilize new sectors of the population.[25] After PB participants select projects, the process to implement the public works projects is now more administrative than political. The government initiated internal reforms to make it easier for citizens to follow projects that had been selected but not yet implemented.[26] Each specific project selected by the PB participants receives a tracking number that enables municipal bureaucrats to inform any interested party about the current status of the project. The transparency serves as the basis for engagement in informed deliberation and dialogue by the participants.

In 1999, 2000, and 2004, I attended PB meetings in Porto Alegre. One noteworthy characteristic of these meetings, in comparison with those I have attended in other municipalities, is that they are well organized and not dominated by government officials. Government officials play an important role in setting up the meeting and providing information about its purpose. In my experience, the government did not stray too far from this stated purpose. Information about public policies and budgeting are made available to citizens in a coherent manner. Through the auspices of PB, the government holds additional meetings to provide basic information on issues such as tax revenues, budget allocation, and debt servicing. Citizens have access to vital technical and financial information, which helps them during the decision-making process.

The most important indicator of mayoral support across the four different mayoral administrations is the consistent effort to fund PB at robust levels. Government officials reformed the bureaucracy, updated PB rules when and where necessary, and successfully delegated authority to citizens, but perhaps most important, citizens' decisions have resulted in the implementation of specific public works. Thus it is clear that PB participants are able to determine public policy outcomes.

PT mayors in Porto Alegre supported the delegation of decision-making authority for several reasons. First, the PT was initially a minority political party that needed to build a broader base of support. PB gave the PT direct access to existing and new CSOs. Individuals could be mobilized outside PB to work on the campaigns of PT officials. Abers documents how PB fostered the development of new CSOs, arguing that this helped

25. Abers 2000; Baiocchi 2005.
26. Fedozzi 1998.

to create new, dense networks of social capital. It is important to recognize that many new participants may have become strong supporters of the PT government. Recall that 94 percent of Porto Alegre's PB delegates included in the survey shared a partisan political affiliation with the government. PB delegates, regardless of whether they are new or long-term CSO participants, are aligned with the incumbent party.

Second, PB provided the PT with an opportunity to actively experiment with its ideological commitment to deepening democracy. The base of the PT could be engaged in negotiation, deliberation, and decision making. PB serves as a means for non-elite members of the PT to be directly involved in political decision making. This finding also confirms the work of Abers and Baiocchi. As PT activists are empowered to deliberate, exercise voice, and vote, the PT's most active base is able to realize its long-held goal of participating in an active democracy.

Finally, the PT's leadership in Porto Alegre was ideologically committed to the direct participation of citizens in decision-making venues. In Porto Alegre, the PT's leadership came of political age during the transition to democratic rule, and the principal leaders (Mayors Dutra, Genro, and Pont) were ideologically committed to participatory democracy.[27]

Civil Society

Since 1989, there has been intense and close cooperation between CSOs and Porto Alegre's municipal government. Yet it appears that most CSOs have managed to avoid the co-optation that is associated with this type of close cooperation. How have CSOs in Porto Alegre managed to avoid co-optation? CSOs engage in both cooperative and contentious forms of political behavior. This helps PB participants and CSOs gain access to government officials but also allows them to quickly disassociate themselves from government policies with which they disagree. It is the combination of these practices that minimized the role of co-optation in Porto Alegre's PB.

Social movement and community organizations' activities in Porto Alegre reemerged during the late 1970s and grew in strength throughout the 1980s. Land invasions and demands for the provision of basic social services were the two main poles around which these organizations mobilized.[28] Support for these movements came from the progressive wing of

27. Genro 1995b; Pont 2003.
28. Baierle 1998; Larangeira 1996; Genro and Souza 1997.

the Catholic Church and progressive activists opposed to the military dictatorship as well as those from the official party of opposition, the Brazilian Democratic Movement (Movimento Democrático Brasileiro, or MDB).[29]

One of the most important umbrella organizations to emerge during the late 1970s and early 1980s was the Union of Neighborhood Associations of Porto Alegre (União das Associações de Moradores de Porto Alegre, or UAMPA). This association provided infrastructure, technical, and legal support to assist individual community organizations in presenting demands to state officials. Neighborhood associations took on a number of forms, from Gramsci-inspired neighborhood councils, to the more traditional Sociedade de Amigos de Bairro (Friends of the Neighborhood Associations), to the regional and neighborhood councils, as leaders sought different ways to galvanize support and influence state and party officials.[30] Importantly, UAMPA linked social movements to the leaders of the newly created PT. Bairele demonstrates that middle-class activists helped to organize marginalized communities.[31]

UAMPA identified budgets as a contentious issue that deserved the attention of its members and proposed direct citizen participation in the process of budget making as a step toward democratizing the city. UAMPA's 1986 proposal closely resembles what is today called Participatory Budgeting: "The most important aspect that determines the actions of the city government is prioritizing the allocation of public resources. We want to participate in the decision-making process on investment priorities in each neighborhood, in each region, and in the city in general."[32] UAMPA determined that budget issues are central to political life, and they offered specific suggestions for how new social actors could participate in policy-making processes. The PT and UAMPA leadership jointly shared an interest in creating a vibrant new participatory institution. Cooperation flourished between the government leadership and CSO leadership because they had an overlapping set of interests, but these groups were well acquainted with contentious politics, Porto Alegre being the site of large public demonstrations for the return to democracy (early 1980s) and the impeachment of President Coller de Mello (early 1990s).[33]

29. The MDB was a catchall party that included politicians from many different political stripes, from communists to liberals opposed to the military regime. The MDB became the PMDB and remains one of Brazil's largest parties.

30. Bairele 1998; Avritzer 2002; Abers 2000.

31. Bairele 1998.

32. UAMPA 1986.

33. Bairele 1998.

CSO and Citizen Involvement in PB

The emergence of PB in Porto Alegre was founded on the political strategies of activists who turned from neighborhood issues to the broader concerns of how local government institutions could be renovated to accommodate demands for active citizen participation in policy-making venues. Fedozzi notes that the number of associations participating in PB increased from 250 in 1989 to 614 in 1993. Abers's and Baiocchi's research shows that PB increased the number of CSOs in Porto Alegre throughout the 1990s and the first years of the twenty-first century.[34]

The number of participants in PB increased from 780 in 1989 to an average of just more than 35,000 a year from 2000 through 2003.[35] According to a survey conducted by the NGO Cidade, 60 percent of the participants are involved in at least one community or voluntary organization.[36] The survey evidence conducted for this book shows that 80 percent of the elected PB delegates were active in a CSO—a high rate, although not too different from Cidade's findings of a 60 percent participation rate.[37] The growth of CSOs and the strong rates of participation in PB indicate that citizens are willing to cooperate with government officials to secure their policy preferences. PB delegates and other community leaders are in constant interaction with government officials to set the meetings' agendas, calculate the costs of projects, check on the status of ongoing projects, and monitor implementation. A significant factor explaining in part why PB works well in Porto Alegre is that government officials and elected PB delegates and PB councilors work together to encourage citizen decision making as well as to promote the political space that PB occupies as an institution.[38] Cooperation has been emphasized.

Contentious political behavior was also present in Porto Alegre, because of the presence of unions and CSOs that were initiated during the 1980s. Public mobilization and direct confrontations were a key part of civil society activity during the waning years of the military dictatorship and the initial years of the democratic regime.[39] Since 1989, CSOs and the PT government have had a close relationship, and contentious politics has

34. Abers 2000; Baiocchi 2003, 2005; Fedozzi 1998.
35. Fedozzi 1998, 133; Abers 2000; Baiocchi 2003, 2005.
36. *Quem é o Público do Orçamento Participativo*, 1999.
37. PB Comparative Survey. For an extensive analysis of the survey results, see Chapter 3.
38. Abers 1998; Baiocchi 2001.
39. Avritzer 2002; Wampler and Avritzer 2004; Keck 1992.

not been aimed at the PT municipal government but has been largely focused on the legislative branch and local media outlets.[40] Pressure is placed on municipal legislators during formal sessions as well as during election cycles to allow citizens to make binding decisions in PB without the legislators' interference. CSOs use direct-mobilization tactics to pressure municipal legislators. The use of these tactics increased in the late 1990s as opposition legislators increasingly sought to limit the authority and responsibilities of PB.[41]

Even though the majority of contestation by PB delegates has been focused on the municipal legislature, CSOs and citizens do not shy away from open confrontation with government officials. Participants carry themselves as emboldened, rights-bearing citizens rather than as weak, subservient individuals asking for the government's support. CSOs and citizens use the institutional space afforded them under PB's rules to express their frustration and anger at how the government functions and manages PB. Citizens and delegates use their allotted time to explain why they believe that government officials have been negligent or incompetent. An argument I heard multiple times over three field visits was that PT officials did not really understand the poverty faced by the majority of the residents. It was claimed that change was slow because the PT government did not feel a pressing need to dramatically and quickly improve people's basic living conditions. Government officials often responded to these claims with explanations of how government functions and blaming the limited resources available to them.

CSOs and government officials have also sought to use events such as the World Social Forum and Workers' Day (May 1) to pressure the local media to be more supportive of PB. The local media (print, radio, and television) have been fairly dismissive of PB or downright hostile to it.[42] Repeated public demonstrations were held to bypass the media's stranglehold on information concerning PB as a way to assert the legitimacy of PB as a decision-making venue.[43] Government officials and CSOs cooperated to put on contentious public demonstrations that would appeal to their supporters.

CSOs did not engage in massive acts of contentious behavior against the PT government, but their relationship was not entirely peaceful.

40. Baiocchi 2005.
41. Baiocchi 2005.
42. Baiocchi 2005; Baierle 1998.
43. McAdam, Tarrow, and Tilly 2001.

Contestation by csos and participants against government officials appears to have had specific limits, although these limits have never been precisely defined. The most profound differences were resolved within PB and did not spill over into the broader public. csos and participants often complain about different aspects of PB but ultimately appear to believe that the PT government is vital to the continued success of PB. Likewise, government officials expected a certain amount of contestation, but they also assumed that the delegates would not bitterly contest the mayoral administration to the extent that it undermined PB, the mayor's ability to govern, or the PT's reelection efforts.

Mayoral-Legislative Relations

The PT won four successive mayoral elections, helping them dominate political events in Porto Alegre during the 1990s.[44] Although the PT's municipal and state administrations have faced difficulties in building stable legislative majorities across the Brazilian political landscape, PT administrations in Porto Alegre have been able to build a solid majority of support in the legislature. The PT managed to win only ten of thirty-three seats in the city council in 1988, but they were able to cobble together a majority center-left coalition that held twenty-one of the thirty-three seats. Porto Alegre's long political tradition of supporting leftist candidates helped the PT craft a solid voting majority, since legislators from different parties were initially unwilling to risk alienating the mayor or the "people's will" as expressed via PB.[45]

The factor that most clearly distinguishes Porto Alegre from most other municipalities included in this book is the success of left-of-center parties at the polls. Table 15 shows the electoral successes the left-of-center candidates have enjoyed since 1988. One of the remarkable facts is the absence of centrist political parties. Political parties that tend to be centrist in other regions of the state and country are part of the political opposition to the PT in Porto Alegre. The mayor's party and coalition has controlled one-third of the seats and, when combined with parties with a similar ideological makeup, this coalition ballooned to nearly two-thirds. The PT government therefore had willing partners in the municipal legislature.

The PT had to demonstrate during their first administration (1989–92)

44. Araújo and Noll 1996; Horn 1994.
45. Goldfrank, 2007; Wampler 2000b.

Table 15. Composition of Porto Alegre's Municipal Council

	1988	1992	1996	2000
# in mayor's party (PT)	10	10	12	10
# With similar ideology	12	11	6	7
Centrists	0	0	0	4
Opposition	11	12	15	12
Total	33	33	33	33

Note: For an in-depth discussion, see Wampler 2000b.

that they could competently manage local affairs. They also had to demonstrate their ability to implement projects that would alter the balance of power within the municipality to favor the excluded and marginalized.[46] This latter factor was important because their chief political rival, the leftist-nationalist-populist Democratic Labor Party (Partido Democrático Trabalhista, or PDT), had a significant political following but had a different vision of change from the one advocated by the PT.

During the PT's first administration, one of the most important administrative and legislative efforts was aimed at creating social justice through changes in the property tax system. The mayor introduced fourteen pieces of legislation that would alter taxation (generally raising property taxes on higher-valued property and exempting the poor). Eight bills were approved with no changes and another three were approved with minor alterations.[47] The administration seized upon the taxation laws as a means to make more funds available for its political projects while simultaneously instituting a progressive property tax. The progressive nature of the changes in tax policies appealed not just to their constituency base, but also to the largest party in the municipal legislature, the PDT. The PDT supported the legislation, thereby giving the PT a political victory that would later aid the PT in its broader political project. The passage of these eleven bills demonstrated that the PT had willing partners in the legislature.

To compensate for the decline in "pork" resources available for legislators, the PT worked to reward its allies, PDT legislators, with the principal

46. Genro 1995b; Fedozzi 1998.

47. City council member Antonio Carlos Hoflfeldt identified this as one of the key successes of the first PT administration. Hoflfeldt was first elected to the city council in 1982 as a member of the PT. He left the party during Dutra's first administration and became a member of the Brazilian Social Democratic Party (Partido da Social-Democracia Brasileira, or PSDB). Hoflfeldt, interview, May 31, 1999, Porto Alegre; Goldfrank, 2007.

leadership positions within the legislative chambers. The PDT assumed the chief committee assignments and the Speaker of the Assembly, even though their party's representation had fallen to a low of four seats. This allowed PDT officials to control the agenda, provided extra resources and staff support to the legislators, and gave a certain level of prestige to their members. The cost to the mayoral administration was low, although it was forced to endure increasingly hostile attacks over its policies and participatory programs.[48] By giving power to the PDT, the PT encouraged it to rely on constituency service rather than clientelism. The PDT now had the time, resources, and support of the government to attend to the minor claims and demands of its constituents.

Legislators appear to be turning toward constituency service because they do not have goods and resources to distribute to their constituents. Even though constituency service undoubtedly endears legislators to their constituents, it does little to promote anything resembling active and engaged participation in the public sphere. Porto Alegre's PT governments have stymied efforts to strengthen the legislature. The prevailing attitude within the governing coalition is that participatory democracy should be favored over representative democracy. Porto Alegre's PT administration, which likes to boast about its role as one of Brazil's strongest promoters of democracy, is unwilling to include the legislative branch in its efforts to democratize existing institutions. From 1994 to 1999, legislators approved a total of fifty-three budget amendments, which altered just 0.54 percent of the overall budget.[49] Although there was very public posturing among opposition legislators regarding their interest in budgetary matters, this evidence suggests that few legislators made the effort to draft and negotiate for their budgetary amendments. Although they claimed that PB was "usurping" their budgetary powers, the evidence demonstrates that municipal legislators did little to make use of the legal authority given to them.

48. This was most evident in 1999 as a PDT legislator led a campaign to legalize the PB program in a way that would increase its share of allocation responsibility. The proposal was to divide the amount of available resources evenly between the legislature and community forums. This legislation was introduced to highlight issues concerning the role of representative and participatory democracy. Legislators obviously sought to illuminate their role as elected representatives of the municipality. The legislation presented was unconstitutional because it violated federal statutes that give the executive all power over allocation. PDT and other opposition legislators whom I interviewed acknowledged that their legislation was unconstitutional but were not too concerned because their principal aim was to encourage debate on this contentious issue.

49. *Diario Official de Prefeitura Municipal de Porto Alegre* (1994–1998).

During the late 1990s, opposition to the PB program grew in the legislative chambers. Opposition candidates did better at the polls and began to use their positions to openly question PB and the government's policy.[50] The most common criticism is the assertion that PB subverted the democratic process by taking responsibilities away from legislators.[51] In response to legislators' attacks, PB participants and supporters would fill the legislative chambers when they deemed it necessary to pressure legislators not to cut spending associated with PB projects. The PT government supported, directly and indirectly, the use of contentious politics by PB delegates against opposition legislators. The government sought to discredit the legislative branch by using PB participants as the "will of the people." This strategy helped to demonize an already weak legislature while making an appeal to Porto Alegre's lower classes that PB was the appropriate place for policy making.

Rules

PB's rules and the government's creation of new internal decision-making processes to support PB also account for the successful delegation of authority in Porto Alegre. Citizens in Porto Alegre's PB have two important votes: for specific projects in their neighborhood and for PB delegates, who represent them during interregional negotiations and vis-à-vis the PB council. During meetings, citizens debate and then vote for specific projects. Since the government successfully implements most policies, the decisions made are "binding" ones.[52]

The PB council, which comprises two elected councilors from each region, has been infused with a considerable degree of authority. PB councilors meet biweekly throughout the year and at least once a week during peak the budgetary season (September to November). The council works to reconcile the different demands from the sixteen regions. If cost estimates on projects were too high from a region, the council would have to cancel projects to be under the budgetary cap. If the government proposes projects, council members must weigh the cost and value of the plan against other proposed projects. The council has final decisions on rule changes that are internal to PB. PB council members deliberate on issues such as whether district boundaries should be altered, whether the

50. Baiocchi 2001.
51. Nylen 2003. For an extended discussion, see chap. 7 of Nylen's book.
52. O'Donnell 2004.

voting formula needs to be reconfigured, and whether the government is providing sufficient information.

Between 1989 and 2003, the rules were modified at different times. Government officials and PB councilors worked together to craft a rule set that would accommodate their competing and sometime conflicting interests. No rule change could be applied to PB without the approval, by majority vote, of the PB council. The government's local, national, and international prestige was based on the success of PB, so government officials had to engage in arduous negotiations with PB councilors to ensure rule changes that the government wanted. Although it is possible to imagine that the government had backed itself into a corner by making rule changes dependent on majority vote, we must remember that the PB councilors are elected from the pool of PB delegates. More than 90 percent of the survey respondents in Porto Alegre had a partisan political identification, which means that these delegates are likely to be very sympathetic to the demands and interests of the PT government. Although there are a variety of groups within the PT, PB delegates with whom I spoke consistently mentioned the need to promote the interests of citizens via PB and to strengthen the PT as a political party. Intraparty politics were often downplayed as CSO participants sought to expand the authority controlled by PB delegates, but there were constant declarations of support for the PT.

In 1994, government officials and PB delegates expanded the focus of PB by creating "thematic" (issue-oriented) policy arenas to address broader, municipal-wide problems. Instead of a strict focus on neighborhood issues that looks at pertinent and pressing needs of a particular region, the issue-oriented policy arenas (such as health care, education, transportation, and the environment) draw individuals from a broader range of experiences and backgrounds. Whereas neighborhood associations are more likely to be drawn to the regional, territory-based meetings, issue-oriented social movements are more likely to be drawn to the broader policy arenas. We can conceptualize Porto Alegre's PB as having two distinct tracks: (1) a regional focus that allows neighborhood leaders to mobilize their local communities based on appeals of improving the local infrastructure and (2) a municipal-wide, issue-oriented focus that allows social movement leaders to mobilize their followers around a broader set of issues and interests. This combination allows individuals motivated to participate by different concerns to seek out the appropriate venue to seek redress of their problems.

Porto Alegre's PB rules emphasize the direct involvement of citizens and PB delegates in decision making. In all steps of the process, from the initial informational meetings to the final "year-end report" meetings, there are multiple moments for PB participants to be directly involved in policy making. The government adheres to the rules so that citizens understand their rights and responsibilities at each stage of the process. The combination of adherence to the rules and multiple decision-making moments has given Porto Alegre's participants far more authority than that of their colleagues in the other seven municipalities analyzed in this book. The willingness of the government to legally and politically follow PB's rules has led to a significant delegation of authority.

Financial Situation

Porto Alegre is a relativity wealthy municipality, located in one of Brazil's wealthiest states. Annual per capita budget spending from 1996 to 2002 was U.S.$355 and annual per capita capital investment spending was U.S.$26.[53] Although the municipality's financial situation was in good standing by the mid- to late 1990s, this was not the case when the PT took over the mayor's office in 1989. The municipal government was heavily indebted, with few resources available for investments. As Fedozzi makes clear, part of the reason that the PT initially sought to increase budgetary transparency was to publicly demonstrate the difficult conditions the government faced.[54] Increased transparency was initially in the political interest of PT because the party attempted to attribute its financial difficulties to the debts and mismanagement of previous mayoral administrations (who were, of course, its political opponents). Over time, the emphasis on transparency has been maintained, as government officials feel that they have little to hide.[55]

If the level of financial resources available to the municipal government explains part of PB's outcomes, then Porto Alegre's PB program has been placed in an advantageous position. Although the financial situation was not initially conducive to capital investment spending, the PT's success in passing a series of progressive taxes (described above) significantly added

53. See Ministério da Fazenda. Dollar conversions are based on the average yearly exchange rate.
54. Fedozzi 1998.
55. André Passos, PB administrator, interviews, 1998–2004; especially May 24, 1999; March 30, 2000; April 26, 2004, Porto Alegre.

to the municipality's strong financial position. Thus, while the successes of the Porto Alegre PB are in part directly derived from the electoral and legislative success of the PT and the Left in Porto Alegre, the wealth of Porto Alegre, as measured by its high Human Development Index score and strong per capita income, also contributed significantly. The government had the resources to fund projects, and the large middle class did not rely on the municipal state for basic social services. Porto Alegre's wealth meant that middle-class individuals who use private schools, health care, and security guards do not rely on the municipal state for the provision of basic services. This, in turn, opened up greater levels of resources that could be spent on PB projects. In conjunction with a strong property tax base, which was aided by the municipal legislature's approval of eight tax bills in the early 1990s, Porto Alegre had a relatively high level of resources that they could use to spend on public works projects selected by PB delegates.

Synthesizing the Results

How has Porto Alegre's PB affected the extension of accountability? How has the city's PB enhanced citizenship rights? Because citizens are directly involved in shaping and deciding public policies, PB in Porto Alegre acts as an incubator of rights. Importantly, significant levels of resources are negotiated, which gives participants the authority to make meaningful decisions. Survey evidence also indicates that PB delegates believe that delegates exercise authority. Citizens have the opportunity to participate in institutional arenas in which they are able to debate topics ranging from the salaries of municipal employees, to the revenue base of the municipality, to specific public works. Individuals have the opportunity to learn more about the policy-making process and then are given access to government at various entry points.

There are several ways in which we can see that citizenship rights have been established. First, through PB, citizens have the right to make decisions about general policy trends and specific public works. Second, the municipal administration honors decisions made by the PB participants by implementing the public works selected by PB participants in a timely and transparent manner. In Brazil, implementation is at the discretion of the mayor because individual line-items in the budget do not have to be completed. In Porto Alegre, decisions made within PB have become *binding* ones, since the municipal administrations implemented projects selected by PB participants. By honoring the decisions made within PB, the government signals to the population that important public policy decisions are now made in these institutional spheres. These steps shift decision-making processes away from the private spheres of the government and into the PB meetings.[56]

Third, the municipal administration has begun to submit its own policy initiatives for approval by PB participants. Without formal approval in the citizens' forum, the government's specific public works initiatives could not be included in the municipal budget and therefore could not be implemented. This step represents a major shift in Brazilian policy making, since Porto Alegre's government now must *publicly* defend its specific projects and submit these projects for a vote. Porto Alegre's PB is now a new public arena for deliberation and negotiation that has been crafted through the extensive cooperation among government officials and citizens.[57] Debates can be extremely acrimonious, but there is an effort to promote dialogue and public negotiation as a means to settle long-standing disputes. Citizens are mobilized for a series of local, regional, thematic, and municipal-wide meetings that enable them to interact with one another as well as with public officials. This allows interested and engaged citizens to maintain pressure on the mayoral administration.

With regard to accountability, Porto Alegre provides the most paradoxical results of the eight municipalities studied because it has simultaneously strengthened *and* weakened efforts to extend accountability. Citizens have been directly incorporated into decision-making bodies that exercise authority, transparency has increased, participation has steadily increased, and the implementation of public works follows legal means. This has been accomplished under the auspices of a unified government, led by the PT, which increased the authority of the mayor's office while simultaneously marginalizing the municipal council.

However, Porto Alegre's PB took the municipal council out of the decision-making process by having citizens make all budgetary decisions that are considered to be "new capital investment spending." Horizontal accountability has been undermined because one branch of government (municipal legislature) now has a smaller, weaker role in the budgetary process. In addition, PB still has not been legally constituted, which means that it is technically and legally part of the mayor's office. Although

56. Genro 1995b.
57. Avritzer 2002.

successive PT mayors in Porto Alegre have gone to considerable lengths to ensure that citizens within public venues make most budgetary decisions, final legal authority ultimately rests with the mayor's office. From the vantage point of horizontal accountability, we would have to argue that the mayor's office remains firmly in control of the policy-making process. The municipal administration provides information, allocates the political and bureaucratic staff to conduct meetings, and implements projects. The PT lost the 2004 mayoral election, which was won by the PDT. The PDT has maintained the structure of PB that was created by the PT and their allied CSOs, but preliminary evidence suggests that the government is contributing fewer resources and staff members to administer the process.[58] This preliminary evidence supports the argument in this book that strong mayoral support is crucial to producing strong participatory programs.

From the vantage point of vertical accountability, we must note that PB limits mayoral authority because citizens are making real, important decisions. However, PB is intimately associated with the PT's success in winning four consecutive mayoral elections in Porto Alegre. Citizens may have greater authority, via PB, but the PT, which directs PB, also has benefited handsomely from this new institutional type.

From the vantage point of societal accountability, it is important to confirm that citizens are able to engage in meaningful deliberation and negotiation.[59] This allows them to pressure their government to implement changes in public policies. Individuals act as rights-bearing members of their community, evidenced by how they express and carry themselves during meetings. Individuals demand that the government respect their time and effort, which it by and large does. Again, societal pressures may help to strengthen the mayoral administration by creating short-term benefits for the party in power as well as for the party's supporters. There is no evidence, however, that PB creates a permanent set of checks and balances that can be used by citizens or opposition parties to reign in the excesses or wrongdoings of a mayoral administration.[60]

58. I briefly visited Porto Alegre in March 2006 to conduct interviews and attend meetings. Although a short visit (four days) made it impossible to definitively declare that PB is administered differently, my impression, based on interviews, public policy data, and participant observations, is that the PDT government is managing PB in a distinctly different fashion from that of the previous PT governments.

59. Baiocchi 2005; Abers 2000.

60. Navarro 2002.

It remains unclear whether citizens can legally force the hand of the mayor to provide information or implement projects. Thus PB participants are partially dependent on the goodwill and benevolence of the municipal government, an indication that PB has only partially promoted restrictions on mayoral authority in Porto Alegre. The ability of PB delegates to use contentious politics against the legislative branch and local media outlets does help to act as a significant unused check on the mayor's authority because the mayoral administration is aware that if it is unable to fully support PB, then delegates may use contentious politics against the government.

PB in Porto Alegre is noteworthy for how it has modified and expanded decision-making processes, but the outcomes are somewhat limited because PB's positive results depend on considerable levels support from the municipal government. The involvement of citizens may work to decrease the power of the mayor's office over the long haul, but the mayor's office continues to be the most important political actor in Porto Alegre's PB.

PB is a political space that gives citizens the right to participate in a state-sanctioned institution. Accountability and citizenship rights have been extended, but the substantial role the government has played in this process suggests that maintaining some of these new rights depends on the continued support of the government. These are hardly the ideal conditions under which accountability and citizenship rights can be solidified, but they may provide the necessary steps to allow citizens and community activists to find a solid footing from which they can more actively engage with municipal, state, and federal officials.

Ipatinga

The PT won the mayor's office in 1988 and was returned three consecutive times (1992, 1996, 2000) before finally losing the 2004 election. PB was implemented in 1989 and was continuously managed by the PT for sixteen years. "The PT created, organized, and mobilized PB," according to one delegate who had participated in PB from 1989 to 2003.[61] Chico Ferramento, who was elected mayor in 1988, 1996 and 2000, set the tone for PB as he sought to craft a participatory institution that would educate citizens and produce viable public policy. During the 1980s, he was a local

61. Waldemir, PB delegate, interview, April 9, 2004, Ipatinga.

leader of the Unified Center of Workers (Central Única dos Trabalhadores, or CUT), a labor union that led a series of successful strikes against the military government and the state-owned steel mill during the waning days of the military authoritarian regime.[62] Ferramento advocated a political line similar to that of the PT's national leadership: defending state-owned companies against privatization, social justice for Brazil's poor and excluded majority, promotion of an active citizenship, and the direct participation of citizens in policy-making venues.[63] In this section, as in the previous one, I will demonstrate how the combination of five factors—mayoral support, civil society activity, mayoral-legislative relations, PB's rules, and financial capacity—directly affected the outcomes generated by PB.

The PT established PB in 1989, their first year in office. Ferramento's staff drew from a pioneering participatory program that had been implemented by the PT in Diadema, an industrial suburb of São Paulo.[64] During the first few years the program was officially titled Municipal Congress on Budgetary Priorities.[65] The purpose was to bring government officials and interested citizens into a series of meetings to discuss the municipality's financial situation and have different groups identify spending priorities. In 1990, delegates were elected in one of eight regions. In each region, they selected projects that they wanted the government to implement. The process was driven by the presentation of demands. Although the government attempted to implement as many of the demands as possible, there was no attempt to create specific decision-making procedures. Citizens did not have specific decision-making authority.

Between 1990 and 1996, PB was more of a demand-making than a decision-making process. Citizens participated in meetings in which they received information about municipal revenues and policies and were able to select general priorities that should be implemented by the government. In 1997 PB was overhauled, at the start of Mayor Ferramento's second term, to allow citizens to select specific public works that the government would implement. Ferramento sought to jump-start the participatory process, which had not received the full attention of the mayor who served between Ferramento's 1989–92 and 1997–2004 terms. "We

62. *Revista de COMPOR*, 1999, 1–4; Faria and Prado 2002.
63. Villas Boas and Telles 1995; Genro 1995b; Walter Teixeira dos Santos Jr, secretary of planning, Prefeitura Municipal de Ipatinga, interview, April 8, 2004; Faria 2002.
64. Teixeira dos Santos Jr., interview.
65. *Revista de COMPOR*, 1999, 8.

did not want to create false expectations and sell illusions. To the contrary, our purpose is to bring the community together to create a broad debate and to establish the responsibilities of the government and the citizens. From the government's perspective, we are responsible for the provision of public improvement and citizens are responsible for coparticipating in the governmental process."[66] To this end, Ipatinga's PB process is divided into two specific processes, which I label *PB regional* and *PB priorities*.

PB regional occurs within each of Ipatinga's nine districts (expanded to nine from eight in 1999 to add a rural region). Neighborhood associations organize themselves to ask for specific public works. The majority of these projects are small scale, entailing, for example, street paving, small drainage projects, and the installation of streetlights. The government commits between 5 and 10 percent of the total budget for the selection of these projects, which is well more than half of all new capital investment spending.[67] This level of spending does not match the 100 percent of new capital investment spending in Porto Alegre, but it is far better than the 10 percent of such spending dedicated to PB in Recife, São Paulo, or Belo Horizonte (see Chapters 6 and 7).

PB priorities involves discussions and negotiations about larger projects, often public works that would help to restructure neighborhoods. The government includes these larger public works projects in the budget but must then seek external sources of financing for them. Possible sources of financing include the state and federal government, national lending agencies and banks, and international lending agencies. The government commits itself to trying to secure resources to implement the citizens' policy preferences, but government officials clearly explain that public works will not be implemented if the government is not able to secure external sources of funding. The PB priorities process acts more as a signaling device than as a direct decision-making body. Since Ferramento was elected to Brazil's national legislature between his mayoral terms, he knew where and how to secure funding for municipal infrastructure projects. That allowed this signaling mechanism to work well. Therefore, PB evolved into a partnership between CSOs and the government, a "co-administration" process that was more successful than in any other municipality. Shared interests among the participants and government officials explains why the signaling mechanism functioned.

66. *Revista de COMPOR*, 1999, 21.
67. "Ipatinga Hoje," 2003, 1–2. "Programas de obras 2004: Ate 13° COMPOR," 2004.

Mayoral Support

Ipatinga's mayors were willing to *partially* delegate authority—just enough to make PB a viable, strong institution—but the government never placed its political future entirely in the hands of PB delegates. The capacity and willingness of the mayoral administration to implement PB projects are a strong proxy for mayor support. From 1990 through 1996, the government implemented 65 percent of viable PB projects, a very high percentage in comparison with those of other municipalities.[68] From 2000 to 2003, the implementation rate increased to 71 percent of all projects.[69] (There is no data available for the 1997–99 period). Seventy-four percent of the financial capital allocated to PB projects in the 2001, 2002, and 2003 budgets was spent on PB projects by the end of 2003.[70]

Mayoral support can also be evaluated through the willingness of the government to reform PB's basic procedures. Since PB is a dynamic process that depends on the active participation of government officials and citizens, it is logical that both parties would be interested in tweaking the rules and procedures of PB. One of the most significant innovations in all of Brazil's PB programs between 2000 and 2004 was Ipatinga's development of a government-run Web site that allows citizens to enter their demands into an online database.[71] To provide free and easily accessible access to the Internet, the government places computer terminals in public health care clinics, public schools, and the local shopping mall. This allows interested citizens the opportunity to enter their demands into PB and to be able to analyze other projects proposals. The use of an online system streamlines the demand-making process, allowing for better debates, because citizens are informed about the cost of a project and the range of projects that have been proposed by their fellow citizens.

The government has created a database, easily accessible on its Web

68. *Revista de COMPOR*, 1999, 16; Wampler 2004b. "Unviable" projects are those that could not be implemented by the government for reasons of jurisdictional and engineering problems. During the early issues, 1990–96, nearly 25 percent of projects selected by participants were eventually deemed to be unviable. This high rate was largely the result of inexperience by government officials and, to a lesser degree, participants. Over time, levels of information increased, which allowed government officials to better advise PB delegates on which projects should be avoided because they would not likely be implemented due to jurisdictional or engineering problems.

69. "Programas de obras 2004," 2004.

70. "Programas de obras 2004," 2004.

71. See www.ipatinga.mg.gov.br; Martinez, Vaz, and Carty 2004; Tersca 2004, 76–77; Martinez 2003, 75–78; Faria 2002.

site, of all projects approved within PB. Each project selected by the PB delegates receives a tracking number; an individual can input the number in the tracking system to learn the project's current specific stage of development (such as planning, contract bidding, or implementation). This step helps to increase the transparency of the process, since interested citizens know at any time the status of any given project.

The government's backing for the implementation of projects and its efforts to reinvent its programs, in 1997 and again in 2001, suggests a high level of support. Government officials worked closely with PB delegates, but the government can change PB's rules without a majority vote taken by the PB council. This differs from Porto Alegre's PB. The PT government in Ipatinga has been successful in delegating some authority to citizens, but the scope of choice is clearly set by the government because there is only limited pressure exerted on it by CSOs. The government sets the tone for what is feasible, presenting a sharp contrast with the Porto Alegre experience, in which CSO leaders and PB delegates pushed the government to expand the debate and the type of public policies that would be initiated.

Why was Mayor Ferramento only willing to delegate partial authority? First, PB served as an institution that drew in union members, CSO leaders, and citizens. Ipatinga's PB did not encourage the vast expansion of CSOs, as occurred in the case of Porto Alegre, and it also did not necessarily induce CSOs to change their top-down formats. CSO leaders are the principal actors in Ipatinga's PB and serve as intermediaries between the government and the population. Mayor Ferramento was unwilling to delegate greater levels of authority because his party (PT) did not perceive that it could use PB to build a new base of support among citizens. The PB gave the PT increased access to community leaders, but not necessarily to the broader population.

Second, PB serves as an institution that allows PT activists to be directly involved. These activists used PB as a means to exercise voice and vote within municipal politics, but they did not actively and consistently demand that government officials delegate greater levels of authority to them. Finally, Ferramento was willing to delegate authority because of his deep roots in the PT's founding ideology; Ferramento was also personally committed to the creation of new participatory institutions. But he was unwilling to base the PT's local political future on an untested experimental institution in an environment with a limited density of CSOs. The level of authority delegated to citizens increased between 1989 and

2004, but the PT mayoral administration always reserved the right to not fund PB projects and to engage in alternative public policies.

Civil Society

PT leadership in Ipatinga came of political age during the most visible decade of contentious politics in Brazil, from the late 1970s through the presidential election of 1989. CSOs increased in number in Ipatinga during the 1980s as a result of a political opening offered by the transition to democracy and the strong presence of CUT, a leftist, reform-oriented trade union.[72] Union leaders in Ipatinga formed the basis of the PT government and worked with local CSOs. PT officials widely expected that participants would and, in fact, should use PB meetings to directly confront the government over how it managed the municipality.[73]

Participation rates steadily increased in Ipatinga's PB between 1989 and 2004, as listed in Table 16. The early years witnessed low levels of turnout, with the most significant increase in 1998, a result of Mayor Ferramento's renewed emphasis on participatory policy making. The drop-off in 2002 came about in large part following the government's decision not to have participants select specific projects but, rather, focus on establishing "general priorities."

In 2003, 70 percent of the survey respondents said that they were currently active in a CSO, an indication that there are high numbers of delegates who float between formal participatory institutions and their neighborhood associations. Based on interviews with government officials, municipal legislators, and PB delegates, it appears that cooperation behavior is emphasized by all parties, although delegates are willing to directly confront their opponents in the municipal legislature. CSO leaders in Ipatinga are also willing and able to use contentious politics to pressure their allies in the mayor's office, but this occurs primarily in the context of PB meetings. In other words, acrimonious interactions between CSOs leaders and government officials largely took place within the confines of PB, which ultimately aided the government, as it did not have to face intense criticism from the broader public.

Although contentious politics is present in Ipatinga, the PB process continues to be dominated by a small number of well-organized community

---

72. See Martinez, Vaz, and Carty 2004; Martinez 2003.
73. Teixeira dos Santos Jr., interview, 2004; four additional staff members, interviews.

Table 16. Participation Rates in Ipatinga

	Number of Participants
1989	284
1990	630
1991	470
1992	483
1993	563
1994	572
1995	681
1996	604
1997	683
1998	1,533
1999	2,136
2000	2,018
2001	5,015
2002	981
2003	2,374

Source: Ipatinga municipal government.

associations that seek cooperation with the municipal government. Ipatinga's PB program appears to be unable to break the logjam that community association presidents have traditionally created in Brazilian municipalities.[74] According to one delegate, "Within each neighborhood there is generally one group that helps to decide" which projects will be selected.[75] PB represents an opportunity for the most well-organized groups to present their demands in a public format. There continues to be limited competition among CSOs within PB. Ipatinga's PB is a decision-making venue that is dominated and controlled by groups friendly to the municipal government. Therefore, the government's decision to delegate some authority is relatively low risk because the government's allies are largely in control of these bodies.

Drawing from the PB Comparative Survey (see Chapter 3), 77 percent of Ipatinga's delegates have a partisan party affiliation and 92 percent have received a specific good from PB, which means that the PB delegates

74. Avritzer 2002; Wampler and Avritzer 2004.
75. Waldemir, PB delegate, interview, 2004.

are sympathetic to the PT government for political and policy-making reasons. Even though contestation between the government and PB delegates does occur, it is more appropriately characterized as political disagreements among allies rather than the breakdown of communication and acrimonious politics between government officials and delegates. Cooperation is therefore emphasized because delegates and government officials have similar visions of what types of public policy should be implemented and how politics should be transformed.

This relationship is best illustrated by the 1997 "demand making" reforms. This procedure is essentially a signaling device, whereby PB participants vote for general priorities (often large, expensive projects) and the government then attempts to find federal resources to fund them. The most successful effort of this sort, New Center (Centro Novo), involved a major infrastructure project that included building levees for flood control, building a wastewater system, relocating families living in the flood zone, and constructing new houses for the displaced families. A project of this scale did not fit within PB regional—the cost was U.S.$4 million, four times the amount decided by all PB delegates in 1997.[76] However, multiple groups in this region agreed that this was their first priority and thereby combined their votes. Government officials then successfully secured state and federal funding to implement these public works, relying on a combination of loans and grants. According to the secretary of planning, the government's strategy was based on the idea that "if there are many things in the budget, then we will have a very limited chance of actually securing resources. . . . It is better to select a few projects and try to find resources."[77] Government officials did not promise implementation but promised that they would place the project at the top of their agenda. The effort of government officials to seek additional funding for PB-related projects illustrates why contentious politics is an empty threat rather than a viable political strategy. PB delegates rely on the goodwill of the government, which means that embarrassing the government is not a political option. Delegates assert their rights in PB meetings but are careful not to take their criticisms into the streets.

Government officials indicated that the reason they focused on the New Center project was the willingness of multiple community groups to agree among themselves that this was their region's most important

76. "Ipatinga: Aqui Voce vive melhor," 2002, 1–2.
77. Teixeira dos Santos Jr., interview, 2004.

priority. In all published documentation I was able to obtain, government officials directly credit PB delegates for having selected the New Center reforms. This was partially political theater and electoral politics, since government officials were attempting to gain a base of support for up-coming elections; the complexity of the New Center project meant that the broader vision for change emerged from the government, although PB delegates did suggest many of the smaller projects that became part of the larger set of reforms.

Mayoral-Legislative Relations

The PT won four straight mayoral elections (1988, 1992, 1996, and 2000) before losing to a centrist (Brazilian Democratic Movement Party [Partido do Movimento Democrático Brasileiro, or PMDB) candidate in 2004. Although the PT held the mayor's office, it was never able to obtain major-ity control over the municipal legislature. From 1997 to 2000, the Left controlled just 25 percent of the seats, while centrist parties controlled 42 percent. From 2001 to 2004, leftist parties increased their share of munic-ipal legislative seats to 42 percent, while centrist parties held 32 percent of the seats.[78] PT Mayor Chico Ferramento was elected with 52 percent of the vote in 1996 during the first round of voting. In 2000, he received 45 percent of the first-round vote. Mayor Ferramento's popularity, combined with decent results for leftist candidates in the municipal legislative cham-bers, meant that the mayor was able to govern with only minimal restric-tions placed on him.

To achieve majority support, the government had to help legislators with "constituency service," municipal employment opportunities, and the funding of some small infrastructure projects. This helps explain why the mayor was unwilling to commit 100 percent of new capital invest-ment spending to PB programs. Mayor-legislative relations were never excellent, because of divided government, but the legislative branch was never able to build a political climate that would have derailed PB or the mayor's participatory agenda. There was one period of intense conflict, in 2001, when legislators began to offer budget amendments for projects that had already been selected through PB. Legislators were engaging in "credit claiming" to foster uncertainty among the public regarding respon-sibility for the completion of a public works project. In response, CSOS

78. See Tribunal Supremo Eleitoral de São Paulo.

organized demonstrations to pressure the legislature to reject budget amendments that duplicated projects already selected through PB.[79]

Ipatinga's experience stands in sharp contrast to that of São Paulo and, to a lesser extent, Recife, where municipal legislators have sought to limit PB. Ipatinga's small size and its political tradition of deferring to the mayor have worked to the PT's advantage.[80] Because Ipatinga is a regional hub, rather than a capital city, the political stakes for the government's opponents are much lower. Even though the PT in Ipatinga sought to promote PB as means by which to undermine Brazil's traditional political culture (namely, political subordination to the executive), the mayoral-legislative relations are based on the deference of legislators to the mayor. Ironically, contentious politics was used by CSO activists to pressure the legislators to maintain their already low levels of participation in policy making.

Finally, PB has become embedded as a central policy-making institution, an attitude that extends into the political opposition. A conservative mayoral candidate in 2004, who is also a minister and a member of the conservative PFL, argued that PB should be maintained and actually "deepened." Ipatinga's PB, he argued, needed to be diversified to allow different types of groups to have access to the government. The problem was not PB, but rather not enough direct participation among the population. The eventual winner of the 2004 mayoral race, Sebastião Quintão of the catchall PMDB, stated that his administration would continue PB. These public declarations from opposition candidates that they would maintain PB are a strong indication that PB has become a central part of the decision-making process in Ipatinga.[81]

Financial Situation

Ipatinga's financial situation is quite strong in comparison with those of the other seven municipalities. The annual budget spending per capita from 1996 to 2002 was U.S.\$338 and the annual per capita new capital

79. Manualinha, PB delegate, interview, April 8, 2004; Waldemir, PB delegate, interview, 2004.
80. Nunes 1997.
81. It is beyond the context of this book to explain if Mayor Sebastião Quintão followed through on his campaign promises. I suspect that Quintão's level of support for PB will be much lower than former mayor Chico Ferramento's level of support. The point here is a bit different. It suggests that PB has been sufficiently institutionalized that politicians now feel they must make a public commitment to the program.

investment spending was U.S.$61. The most striking feature of these budgetary figures is that the new capital spending was 18 percent of the overall budget, the highest of all municipalities included in this book.[82] This high level of resources is positively correlated with delegates' belief that they have authority because government officials have been able to fulfill their campaign pledges to support the implementation of projects selected by delegates. Ipatinga clearly represents a case in which substantial availability of funds helps the government implement projects favored by PB participants.

When the PT government took office in 1989, the financial situation was fairly bleak, just as it had been in Porto Alegre. High debt was the principal problem. In Ipatinga, the government cleaned up the financial situation through belt-tightening and a greater emphasis on collecting tax revenues that were already on the books. This new financial health of the municipality has increased the government's delegation of authority to delegates. And even though PB does not specifically focus on tax revenues, the emphasis on budgetary issues encourages government officials to identify where and how they can collect additional resources.

Synthesizing the Results

Ipatinga's PB has served as an incubator of rights and has helped to establish the basis for the extension of accountability. However, in comparison with the case of Porto Alegre, the extension of rights and accountability has been more limited. The principal explanation rests not with the PT government's strategies and actions but in the configuration of Ipatinga's civil society. CSOs are limited in number and continue to be dominated by a few individuals, which limits deliberation and negotiations. A single CSO often dominates PB at the regional level. Although the small number of CSOs involved has a constraining effect on the extension of citizenship and accountability, the presence of CUT, a labor union that used contentious politics throughout the 1980s and into the 1990s, has had an unintended and beneficial impact within PB. PB delegates have been able to contest the claims of the mayor and the municipal legislature because there was an expectation that this new public venue was supposed to allow vibrant deliberation and contestation.

Although direct confrontation against the PT government was rarely

---

82. See Ministério da Fazenda.

used outside of PB meetings, PB delegates used contentious politics within PB as a bargaining chip against the government. Yet this political tactic had a limited effect because PB delegates relied on the PB priorities track, which depended on the goodwill of the government to secure state and federal financing. Therefore, the use of contentious politics can be viewed more as posturing between unequal members of the same political coalition. In comparison with Porto Alegre, it is obvious that Ipatinga's PB is much more of a top-down process, explaining why accountability and citizenship rights have been more weakly extended.

In the two weakest cases of PB covered in this book, Rio Claro and Blumenau (see Chapter 5), this "reserve capacity" to engage in contentious behavior is not present, thereby lowering the pressure on the governments to fulfill their PB-related commitments. Even though the use of contentious politics outside PB may be an empty threat in Ipatinga, the combative nature of citizens within PB meetings partially explains why citizens are able to secure resources and their policy preferences.

Ipatinga's PB has partially extended rights, as citizens have the right to make important decisions in public venues. However, this process is driven by the government rather than by CSOs. The government initiated and has molded PB over fifteen years, which has helped foster support in the participatory process and extend the idea that citizens can and should be directly involved in making policy decisions. Within civil society, it also appears that the most active leaders dominated the process, indicating that PB promotes the extension of a new set of political rights to an exceptional body of citizens: the most active CSO leaders, who have been affiliated with the government party, the PT.[83] Ipatinga's PB is now extending a new set of rights to those citizens most able to work with the government and within their communities. As a result, community activists are directly intervening in policy outcomes to the exclusion of the vast majority of their fellow citizens.

The extension of accountability appears to be occurring as a result of the government's commitment to PB. The principal driving factor behind PB, the PT, is also the principal factor that limits the expansion of accountability, because PB delegates and participants seem to rely on the benevolence of a friendly administration, which may also limit the degree to which PB can actually be extended. If we conceptualize accountability as a two-way street, then Ipatinga's PB is restricted because it is mainly community

83. This is similar to Nylen's findings. Nylen 2003.

leaders and not citizens who are working to ensure that government officials fulfill their public commitments. Although community leaders are clearly the first step in the process, their overall impact remains limited because of their small numbers.

Ipatinga has established the basis for the extension of vertical and societal accountability through PB, but horizontal accountability has not been established. The government was reelected to office three times, suggesting that there is broad support in the general electorate for the government's policies and practices. This indicates that vertical accountability is being established between voters and the government. Within PB, the government established dual tracks, PB regional and PB priorities. Vertical accountability was directly established through the former because the government implemented the selected works. The government did what it promised to do. Vertical accountability was also established via the PB priorities route because the government successfully fulfilled PB delegates' demands. The government never promised to implement any of the demands that occurred through PB priorities but merely pledged to try to implement them.

Societal accountability has also been partially established, since CSOs and citizens worked with and against government leaders in public venues. This was more weakly established than in Porto Alegre, but the use of contentious politics was always an option available to CSOs, contributing to the government's responsiveness. Social accountability has also been enhanced, as the public meeting process and the creative use of the Internet via the municipality's Web site have helped strengthen the ability of citizens to monitor the activities of the government.

Since delegates are not sufficiently independent from the government to make full use of PB's oversight mechanism, horizontal accountability has not been established through Ipatinga's PB. The PB priorities process enhances vertical accountability by establishing an interdependence between participants and government officials. But this same interdependence makes it difficult for the PB delegates to pressure the government to ensure that public policies related to PB are being handled legally and efficiently. PB delegates and participants are thus caught in an institutional bind that does not allow them to secure both vertical and horizontal accountability. The survey evidence and interview data both demonstrate that citizens are involved in PB in order to secure policy outcomes for their specific neighborhoods. This suggests that horizontal accountability will not be established in Ipatinga because citizens do not want to risk losing access to funds that may be secured through the PB priorities route.

Conclusions

PB programs in Ipatinga and Porto Alegre have altered their municipalities' decision-making processes, thereby helping to create a new institutional format in which decisions are made. Although many of Brazil's basic institutions are not functioning well, Ipatinga's and Porto Alegre's PB programs established a new set of political rights and have contributed to the extension of accountability. Stalwart mayoral support, active CSOs, and strong financial resources were present in both municipalities. The PT governments' leadership comprised politicians who became politically active during Brazil's transition to democratic rule. For the local PT leadership, the delegation of authority was both a short-term strategy to build a base of political support and a long-term strategy to dramatically overhaul basic state-society relations in Brazil.

In both municipalities, CSOs and government officials cooperated extensively to help the complex PB processes function well. In both municipalities, CSOs and government officials worked together to enable PB delegates to engage in contentious politics against opposition municipal legislators. Public demonstrations in support of PB occurred, especially in Porto Alegre, as government officials and the most strident PB participants sought to show the broader public the value of the new institution.[84] However, the most significant difference between Porto Alegre and Ipatinga rests in the composition of their civil societies. In Ipatinga, there were far fewer CSOs than in Porto Alegre (per capita and absolute), and Ipatinga's CSOs were dominated by a few individuals. The effort to "democratize" or "open up" CSOs in Ipatinga has been stunted by the interests of the CSO leaders, who want to occupy the role of intermediary between their fellow citizens and government officials.

The most notable impact of this difference between Ipatinga and Porto Alegre is that Ipatinga's citizens have access to a small group of new rights while Porto Alegre's citizens are privy to a broader range of rights. Porto Alegre's PB delegates make many meaningful decisions that directly shape how their government acts. The efforts and activities of these PB

84. Abers 2000; Baiocchi 2005; Avritzer 2002.

delegates not only have transformed their communities by bringing in millions of dollars of infrastructure to poor neighborhoods, but also have shifted the balance of power. Municipal legislators are no longer able to negotiate privately with the mayor over the distribution of public works projects. Instead, all new capital investment spending decisions are made by citizens and PB delegates in public meetings. Ipatinga's PB delegates, by contrast, make a more limited number of decisions. Some of their decisions are "binding," thereby formally establishing standardized processes of implementation. Yet many of their decisions require the government to secure outside (state and federal) financing, which means the government can pick and choose among the projects it really wants to support. This decreases the authority of PB delegates and keeps it in the hands of the government. It also decreases the willingness of PB delegates to hold their government accountable, because the delegates need the support of the government to secure these "optional" projects.

Political opposition to PB in both municipal legislatures was a troubling irritant to PB, but there was never sufficient opposition to undermine PB as an institution. The PT governments had enough political support among leftist and centrists parties to allow for the delegation of authority to citizens. In both municipalities, the PT government "deepened" democracy through PB by explicitly bypassing the municipal legislature. This encourages the formation of vertical and societal accountability, but horizontal accountability was not well established in either municipality. Horizontal accountability may be the most difficult form of accountability to establish via PB for two reasons. First, citizens and government officials must engage in extensive cooperation. Extensive cooperation between unequal partners favors the government, thereby weakening the ability of PB delegates to use PB's rule to force compliance. Second, government officials and PB participants sought to bypass the municipal legislature, thereby curtailing the ability of the legislative branch to act as a check on the executive.

PB programs in Porto Alegre and Ipatinga have been able to successfully delegate authority to citizens, as evidenced through the selection of projects to be included in the annual budget, the implementation of these projects, the survey of PB delegates' attitudes, and my observations of participants. Porto Alegre's PB extended greater levels of authority, which is why it has had a greater impact on citizens and public policy outcomes than Ipatinga's PB. This chapter generally confirms the positive analyses of Porto Alegre's PB program. One important caveat is that the concentration of authority directly in the mayor's office played a vital role in producing these positive outcomes. The following chapter, which covers Rio Claro and Blumenau, focuses on two cases in which the concentration of authority in the mayor's office has been associated with unwillingness on the part of the mayors of these municipalities to delegate authority to citizens.

5

Blumenau and Rio Claro:
Weak Mayoral Support and
the Absence of Contentious Politics

> PB rests entirely in the hands of the mayor. He
> decides whether or not to fund projects.
> —VICE MAYOR OF BLUMENAU

> We implemented those projects that were supported
> by the mobilization of the greatest number of peo-
> ple. . . . When resources are low, it is up to each
> department head to decide which projects should
> be done.
> —ANA BEATRIZ DE OLIVERA, SECRETARY OF PLANNING,
> RIO CLARO

Dense Civil Society with Close Cooperation in Blumenau

In 2000 and 2002, nearly 10 percent of Blumenau's adult population attended PB meetings, the highest rate of popular participation among all PB programs analyzed in this book.[1] High levels of participation are often associated with the active engagement of citizens in PB. However, during my field visits to Blumenau, I noticed a peculiar and unique phenomenon: my government and civil society contacts strongly and consistently emphasized that their PB was poorly run and weak and was producing few tangible results. In other municipalities, individuals might emphasize specific weaknesses of their PB, but they would usually place the perceived problems in the context of a "learning experience." In Blumenau, a government official complained, "PB has always been weak here. . . . They [government officials] do it because they are supposed to . . . but the

---

1. "Orçamento Participativo: A vontade do povo via mostrar a sua força," 2002; "Prestação de contas do Orçamento Participativo," 1999; *Diario Oficial de Prefeitura Municipal de Blumenau* (1997–2003); *Balanço Geral de Prefeitura Municipal de Blumenau* (1997–2003).

government doesn't support it."[2] Interviewees quickly and frequently cited PB's failures and sought to explain why the program is so weak. Lack of mayoral interest, political infighting within the PT, and the cozy relationship between CSOs and government leaders were all cited as reasons for PB's breakdown.

The density of CSOs in Blumenau is high, but the absence of contentious politics precluded the development of a robust PB program. High participation rates, in this case, indicate the ability of CSOs to mobilize their fellow citizens. This case demonstrates that if CSOs and citizens are unable to strongly promote and defend their own interests within P B, there is little chance that PB will become a decision-making body independent of the mayor's direct control. The close relationship between CSOs and government officials (PT's mayor) is perhaps best captured by the fact that in 2003 the government allocated more resources to neighborhood associations for their own specific projects (for example, renovating their meetings halls, sports tournaments) than it spent on PB projects.[3]

No Contestation, No Delegation, in Rio Claro

In Rio Claro, low levels of participation in PB and in CSOs led to a weak PB. Low turnout, because civil society is weak, did not encourage the incumbent Green Party government to invest more time or resources in PB. Government officials in Rio Claro do not keep specific figures on the number of attendees at PB meetings, but they do claim that roughly 1 percent of the population participated in PB.[4] This figure is impossible to verify and, quite frankly, is highly unlikely because some of the basic participation data presented to me do not support this figure. The government's support for PB is weak, but government officials continue to insist that the program is working well and that its problems are transitory in nature. This stands in sharp contrast to Blumenau, where government officials and citizens alike acknowledged that their PB is not working.

In Rio Claro, there is a single municipal-wide meeting that all PB administrators and PB delegates attend. This end-of-year event is designed to promote accountability because it gives PB delegates an opportunity to

2. Sadi, former PB delegate and current PB administrator, January 10, 2004. She was a former community leader hired by the government on a part-time basis to help run PB.
3. *Balanço Geral de Prefeitura Municipal de Blumenau* (1997–2003); Andrade 1996, 2000.
4. Ana Beatriz de Oliveira, Rio Claro's secretary of planning, interview, September 12, 2003.

interact directly with PB administrators as well as the mayor himself. Unfortunately, the year-end meeting is dominated by the mayor and his appointed officials. In 2001, 2002, and 2003, the mayor opened the meeting with a forty-five-minute discourse, followed by another forty-five minutes of presentations by his political appointees. PB delegates were given thirty minutes to raise questions and present their concerns, but the government did not respond to their demands or questions. This event encapsulates the problems with Rio Claro's PB: a mayor and his staff appear to be interested in participatory politics but are unwilling to delegate any real authority to citizens. Rio Claro's PB is an empty shell compared with the case that it was modeled after—Porto Alegre.

PB in Blumenau and Rio Claro

The municipalities of Blumenau and Rio Claro appear, at first glance, to have the perfect vortex of conditions that should produce strong, vibrant PB programs. Both municipalities have leftist mayors, both are relatively wealthy municipalities, their PB rules were copied from Porto Alegre's PB model, and their mayors have good interactions with the municipal legislature. Yet neither program was successful. The analytical framework employed in this book aptly demonstrates why both the PB programs are extremely weak, in spite of Blumenau's very strong levels of participation compared with Rio Claro's weak participation rates. The purpose of this chapter is to explain why the experiences of these two municipalities should be categorized as unresponsive, weak, and clientelistic despite political and social conditions that are commonly associated with successful participatory outcomes. The inclusion of these two case studies demonstrates the difficulties faced by government officials and CSO leaders as they attempt to create a new decision-making process.

This chapter follows a format similar to that of the previous chapters. Mayoral support, role of civil society, mayoral-legislative relations, PB's rules, and the financial situation of each municipality are analyzed to explain the results. Before turning to the explanation, some basic demographic and political information on each municipality is in order.

Basic Demographic and Political Characteristics

Blumenau, with a population of 260,000, is an important regional hub in the southern state of Santa Catarina. It is the financial, medical, and educational center for the surrounding agricultural areas. Blumenau and the surrounding areas have a significant German-origin population, which turns this usually sleepy town into a two-week-long party during Octo-berfest each year.

Rio Claro is a midsized city with limited statewide political importance; there are many larger and wealthier cities in the state of São Paulo. Rio Claro is a rather unremarkable small city, located in the heart of São Paulo's agricultural region. A state university sited in Rio Claro has a solid reputation; its presence distinguishes Rio Claro from similar munic-ipalities in this region.

As Table 17 demonstrates, both municipalities are in good financial shape, with fairly high standards of wealth (both are in the top half of 1 percent of all Brazilian municipalities). Investment spending per capita is similar to the resources available in Porto Alegre (see Table 12). Thus, we cannot attribute the weakness of PB in Blumenau and Rio Claro to a resource supply-side argument; these two governments have resources comparable to those of Porto Alegre and Ipatinga.

The political environments in both municipalities show strong sup-port for the leftist mayoral candidates, but weak support for leftists in the legislature. This indicates robust support for the mayor as an individual politician, as well as weak party organization. This weak support means that it is less likely that either mayor would be able to implement far-reaching reforms, such as the delegation of authority directly to citizens,

Table 17. Demographic and Political Profile

	Blumenau	Rio Claro
Residents in 2000	260,000	168,000
Human Development Index, 2000	0.856	0.825
Per capita monthly income 2000	U.S.$124	U.S.$114
Municipal government's investment spending per capita, average, 2001–2002	U.S.$29	U.S.$26
Political party that implemented PB	PT	Green Party
% of mayor's vote in 1996 municipal election (first round)	52.9	46.4
% of mayor's vote in 2000 municipal election (first round)	62	47.5
Average % of leftist seats in city council, 1997–2004	24	21

Sources: www.ibge.gov.br, undp.org, www.stn.fazenda.gov.br, www.tse.gov.br.

because both mayors need to attend to the political demands of municipal legislators in order to build a legislative majority to pass other parts
of their political agenda. Neither mayor enjoyed a broad base of support,
which is necessary to overhaul basic decision-making processes.

Survey Evidence

As demonstrated in Chapter 3, Blumenau and Rio Claro stand apart from
the other municipalities in this book because their survey respondents
consistently held the attitude that PB delegates have little authority and
that their PB programs are not working well. Table 18 contains basic demographic, civil society, and PB-related statistics from Blumenau and Rio
Claro.

Several facets of Table 18 deserve mention. First, the survey respondents in Blumenau clearly represent the lower classes, but the delegates
in Rio Claro are wealthier and are more representative of the lower middle classes. Blumenau's PB has turned into a policy-making venue that
incorporates low-income residents, but Rio Claro's delegates are dominated by middle-class activists. The percentage of women involved is quite
low, suggesting that PB has not disrupted traditional forms of political
incorporation. The percentage of women delegates was far lower in these
two municipalities than in the other six localities surveyed (average of 34
percent in Blumenau and Rio Claro versus 55 percent in the other six
municipalities).

Table 18. Profile of Survey Respondents (%)

	Blumenau	Rio Claro
Household income of U.S.$400 or less per month	58	46
Less than high school diploma	62	40
Women respondents	33	35
Currently active in associational life	61	36
Current leadership position in community association (of those currently active)	28	43
Delegates elected 3 or more times	10	17
Delegates received a direct benefit from PB	68	71

Source: PB Comparative Survey.

Second, Blumenau's percentage of delegates who are active in csos is high, a factor that supports research and anecdotal evidence that Blumenau has a dense civil society.[5] The survey responses in Rio Claro indicate low levels of activity in csos, which also confirms research and anecdotal evidence that Rio Claro has a weak civil society.[6] For pb to flourish there must be csos and individuals active in debates and negotiations. The presence of a dense network of csos in Blumenau indicates that it meets one of the necessary conditions for pb success, and the lack of a similar density indicates that Rio Claro does not meet one of the necessary conditions.

Delegates in both municipalities acknowledge that their communities have received benefits from pb at fairly high rates (68 and 71 percent), but overall these rates are the second and third lowest of the eight municipalities. Few delegates have been elected three or more times, thus creating substantial leadership renewal. Since many delegates have received a direct benefit but have been elected only once or twice, we can infer that the respondents have participated in previous meetings at which benefits had been negotiated. pb had been established for seven years in each municipality at the time the survey was applied, a sufficient period for the government to implement a significant number of projects. Although roughly 70 percent of the survey respondents' community had received a direct benefit, respondents also believe that delegates have little authority, as is demonstrated in Table 19. This suggests that the survey respondents have not reduced their perception of pb to a simple cost benefit analysis (pb benefit in their local community is not equated with their ability to exercise authority). Rather, they are considering how the overall tenor of their pb program is managed and, in particular, the ability of pb delegates to have a role in making significant decisions.

Survey Results

The final table in this section shows the percentage of responses from the delegates in each municipality. The results demonstrate that Rio Claro's delegates believe that they hold little authority. The responses are more mixed in Blumenau, where nearly half the survey respondents believe that delegates do enjoy some authority.

Blumenau and Rio Claro are the only two municipalities where the

5. Andrade 1996, 2000; Rolim 2001.
6. Teixeira and Albuquerque 2005.

figures in the first two rows, "PB rules" and "PB priorities," drop below 50 percent. In Blumenau, less than half the respondents believe that they have power and authority to make decisions "always or almost always," indicating that some delegates believe they have at least some authority. Blumenau's delegates recognize clear limits to their authority, with only 20 percent believing that PB can act as an institutional venue to stop government projects. In other words, Blumenau's respondents perceive that PB is a demand-entry institutional venue whereby they have the right to vote on specific and narrowly tailored projects, but they do not have the authority to affect the government's larger policies and programs.

The results from Rio Claro are much more negative: delegates do not believe they have the authority to make decisions or to intervene in policy making via PB. A strong plurality (43 percent) believe that they can "always or almost always" monitor the government, but only 10 percent believe that they can set public priorities within PB. Therefore, PB is viewed as providing some authority to investigate governmental activity, but not the authority to decide. This is even weaker than in Blumenau; it implies the absence of belief that there is even a "demand-entry system."

The evidence presented above confirms the findings from Chapter 3 (see Table 11). The aggregate responses from Rio Claro and Blumenau are statistically significant and negatively signed on authority questions. The percentages listed in Table 19 demonstrate that Rio Claro's respondents hold negative opinions about their PB programs. The responses in Blumenau are somewhat more positive. A plurality believes that they can make decisions that affect PB and public policies. Importantly, there is a

Table 19. Delegates' Perceptions of Their Authority to Make Decisions (% Stating Always or Almost Always)

	Blumenau	Rio Claro
Authority to make PB rules	46	24
Authority to define PB priorities	42	10
Authority to define projects	47	10
Authority to add resources	22	0
Authority to stop government projects	20	3
Authority to monitor government projects	47	43
Secured projects outside PB	37	71

Source: PB Comparative Study.

significant falloff because only 10 percent believe that Blumenau's delegates have the authority through P B to stop any government projects. P B
is therefore a limited decision-making venue, as the mayoral administration is careful never to delegate substantive decision-making authority to
participants. The reminder of this chapter is dedicated to explaining why
Blumenau and Rio Claro have such weak P B cases.

Blumenau

Blumenau's P B was initiated in 1997 after the PT mayor was elected in
1996. Mayor Decio Lima won an upset victory in the second round of
voting. His electoral victory is attributable to an economic downturn in
the local economy, allegations of corruption against one of his chief rivals,
and the inability of the center and conservative parties to form a stable
electoral coalition.[7] Within the PT, there were two groups that promoted
the implementation of P B. One group comprised community associations that had been aware of the groundbreaking efforts in Lages (Santa
Catarina—same state) and Porto Alegre (Rio Grande do Sul—neighbor-
ing state) to incorporate citizens directly into budgetary decision making.
This group relied on networks of community organizations in Santa Catarina to stay informed about different policy innovations that were occurring throughout the state.[8] The second group that advocated for P B's
adoption comprised university professors and students.[9] This group was
well informed about the successes of Porto Alegre's P B and sought to re-
create it.

Mayor Lima, however, was not as keen a supporter of P B as were the
other members of the coalition. This is similar to the case of São Paulo,
under Mayor Suplicy (2001–4), when Suplicy provided only the most minimal levels of support (for an in-depth analysis, see Chapter 6). Mayor
Lima initiated P B, but the political group closest to him did not support
P B; this is the first indication that mayoral support would be rather
weak. Mayor Lima formally followed the PT's "way of governing," which
emphasized the direct involvement of citizens in decision making and

7. Edinara Andrade, interview, January 10, 2004; Jean Klunderman, interview, January
12, 2004; Walner Costa, interviews, January 3, 2005, and February 26, 2004; Vice Mayor Inácio da Silva Mafra, interview, January 22, 2004.
8. Costa, interviews; Andrade 1996.
9. Andrade, interview; Pedrini, Andrade, Rolim, and Muller 1999.

transparency in governmental practices, but he never demonstrated much enthusiasm for making these ideals the basis for governing.[10]

Mayoral Support

Although Mayor Lima initiated PB in 1997, the program never had his full support, which undermined the initiatives of some CSOs and one faction within the PT.[11] This lack of support can be demonstrated in several different ways. During the first year, delegates were able to negotiate nearly a third of all new capital investment spending, but by 2003, this dropped to just 11.5 percent.[12] The 11.5 percent of new capital investment spending was only 1 to 2 percent of the total budget.[13] The low level of resources is compounded by the fact that the absolute value PB delegates could negotiate each year remained stagnant, while the overall budget increased by 150 percent from 1997 to 2002. The amount of resources, therefore, decreased in relative terms each year as a result of budget increases.

The second sign of Mayor Lima's weak support occurred in 1999 when the government then suspended the yearly selection of PB because the backlog was tremendous after just two years (1997 and 1998). Blumenau adopted a policy of selecting new projects every other year, which were, coincidently, election years (2000, 2002, 2004). Although this eased pressure on the government, it did little to increase the power of PB delegates.

Third, of the 11.5 percent of investment funding negotiated, less than half was actually spent.[14] Not only did the government allocate low levels of resources, they did not follow through on their commitments to implement publics works selected through PB. As the vice mayor remarked, "Power in PB rests with the mayor. He has the power to decide whether or not to spend the money."[15] In a midsized municipality such as Blumenau, the investment section of the municipal budget is sufficiently small that the mayor personally makes decisions on the allocation of new investment spending. The lack of spending on PB projects while government was successfully funding other "new investment" projects suggests

10. Hunter 2004; Guidry 2003.

11. Andrade 1999.

12. "Plano de Investimentos do Orçamento Participativo," 1998; "Orçamento Participativo: A vontade do povo via mostrar a sua força," 2002.

13. "Prestação de contas do Orçamento Participativo," 1999.

14. "Prestação de contas do Orçamento Participativo," 1999. Analysis of the annual budget and final report on spending, 1997–2002.

15. Da Silva Mafra, interview.

that the mayor was personally responsible for deciding *not* to fund PB projects.

Mayor Lima successfully secured large investments from Brazil's National Development Bank (Banco Nacional de Desenvolvimento Econômico, or BNDES). The mayor specifically kept this pool of resources separate from PB. The mayor had a broader vision of restructuring Blumenau and he did not want to open his plan up to comments or feedback from PB participants. Although this political and policy-making strategy helped the mayor to secure financing and advance a major restructuring project, one consequence was that PB was relegated to a decision-making space for the distribution of small projects. This strategy helped the mayor win reelection in 2000, but it did little to initiate a new decision-making venue.

Ironically, PB's focus on small projects had the effect of easing political pressure on the government to engage in constituency service.[16] The government no longer needed to work hard at securing the support of citizens by attending to basic needs in each community. Instead, it became each community's responsibility to work within PB to secure a few benefits. According to one government official, "The head of the Department of Public Works likes PB because he can now tell the public, 'Don't complain to me. Take your demands to PB.'"[17] The vice mayor stated that PB is "a form of removing the government's responsibility. The government can now just say, 'Take your demands to PB.'"[18] Even though the government did little to promote PB, it uses PB as a means to direct the demands of the population to a participatory institution, thereby absolving the government of responsibility. PB became a convenient way for the mayor to sidestep responsibility by using the "new participatory program" as the means to do so. These attitudes reflect the sentiment identified at the beginning of the chapter: mayoral disinterest in supporting PB helped produce a weak PB program.

Why was Mayor Lima's interest in PB so low? First, the PT's political base in Blumenau was weak. The limited number of PT activists were unwilling to use any form of contentious politics or direct pressure politics against the PT government for fear of driving a public wedge between the different factions of the government. Second, PB was partially captured by rival, conservative CSOs (see following section), which meant the PT government did not believe that PB could be used to expand the PT's

16. Andrade 2001.
17. Costa, interviews.
18. Mafra, interview.

weak base of support. In other words, if PB was not a viable strategy to expand the base of the party, then why would an incumbent mayor support it? Mayor Lima was unwilling to delegate authority to an institution that was partially controlled by his political rivals.

The third and final reason relates directly to the obvious question, Why did the mayor implement PB if he was not going to support it? The answer, in short, is the PT. All PT-governed municipalities during the 1997–2000 period in municipalities with a population of at least one hundred thousand residents adopted PB. Although in the PT there are multiple factions divided along ideological, regional, and interest lines, there was sufficient unity and centralization to produce a 100-percent adherence rate to the party's most visible municipal-level success. Mayor Lima adopted PB in 1997 in Blumenau, in part because of the pressures exerted on him to conform to the "PT way of governing."

Civil Society

Blumenau has a dense civil society, but CSOs emphasize cooperation to the exclusion of contentious forms of political behavior. Participation in PB is very high, starting at fifty-four hundred in 1997 and climbing to more than twelve thousand in 2000 and 2002.[19] This second figure represents roughly 10 percent of the adult population.[20] PB's high level of participation results from dense networks of social clubs, neighborhood associations, and self-help groups.[21] Blumenau's ethnic heritage is largely German, and immigrants initially established the types of associations that flourished in Blumenau. The dense network of social clubs is more akin to Robert Putnam's "bird-watching clubs" than to social movements that promote social and political change.[22] The evidence from Blumenau gives weight to Putnam's critics who assert that there is no direct connection between the density of civil society and democratic participation. CSOs can be mobilized for nondemocratic as well as democratic purposes.[23] This is not to suggest that Blumenau's CSOs were undemocratic, but rather to underscore that their behaviors did not support the implementation of a complex participatory process.

19. De Souza 2003, 65.
20. See Instituto Brasileiro de Geografia e Estadística.
21. Pedrini, Andrade, Rolim, and Muller 1999; Andrade 1996.
22. Putnam 1993; Andrade 1996, 2000.
23. Armony 2004.

The municipal government continues to maintain a close relationship with Blumenau's sport and social associations by supporting the clubs' activities. In 2003, for example, the mayor proposed and the municipal council approved legislation that directly funded a number of associations. Funding ranged from financially supporting an intramunicipality youth volleyball tournament to rebuilding an association's meetinghouse.[24] Therefore, csos did not discontinue their practice of seeking out the mayor and his staff; PB did not replace the existing forms of governmental-cso relations. Rather, PB was an institutional space that promoted competition among groups within a government-sponsored venue rather than a challenge to existing political behaviors.

The lack of contentious politics in Blumenau is striking, because the PT's base of support in urban areas is usually situated among labor unions and social movements that are willing to engage in contentious politics. The PT's base of support in Blumenau is weak, with university students and state-unionized professionals making up the main base of support. Neither group was likely to engage in contentious action against the municipal government on PB-related issues, as middle-class professionals tend not to benefit directly from PB.[25] Community organizations, which engaged in contentious activity in Recife, Belo Horizonte, and Porto Alegre, were unwilling to publicly pressure the government for its lack of support for PB. PB was not a forum for criticizing and attacking the government; rather there was an explicit effort made to confine PB to debates and discussions on the distribution of small public works. "Conciliatory" or "cordial" politics dominated Blumenau. The unwillingness of csos and citizens to use any form of contentious politics sharply limited their ability to pressure the mayor. The mayor worked closely with csos, but not necessarily through PB.

Blumenau's dense civil society but weak PB outcomes speak to a broader theoretical debate that was reignited by Putnam in his seminal work on the density of civil society in Italy.[26] The findings from Blumenau suggest that a dense civil society is not a sufficient condition for creating a vibrant participatory democratic institution, because PB relies on debate and competition rather than accommodation. Blumenau has a dense civil society, but its csos lack the means to push their own issues to the front of the political agenda.

24. Kleettenberg 2002.
25. Andrade, interview; Rolim 2001.
26. Putnam 1993.

Mayoral-Legislative Relations

The political Left and the PT are not traditionally strong in Blumenau, a factor that also helps to account for the weak results generated by PB. Centrist and conservative parties dominate the municipal legislative chambers, which means that the PT mayor had to dedicate additional political capital to shore up his base of support in the municipal legislature. The mayor, however, was able to build a base of support by giving legislators the means to engage in basic constituency service and by supporting various community associations. The data presented in Table 17 show that the Left only controlled 24 percent of the seats in the municipal legislature. This small minority made it difficult for the mayor to initiate a broad reform agenda. Centrist legislators occupied 35 percent of the seats, which meant that it was possible for Mayor Lima to secure support for different aspects of his agenda. The low presence of the Left in municipal legislative chambers compounded the difficulties faced by PB, as the mayor had to attend to his legislative bases rather than delegating authority to citizens. Again, successful PB cases depend on a series of factors converging to support the delegation of authority.

However, the political activism of one municipal council member reveals an additional reason that the mayor was not very supportive of PB. In Chapter 1, I described the political activities of a young activist and future municipal legislator, Jean Klunderman. In 1997, fresh out of college, Klunderman devised a political strategy to pack PB meetings with his allies and then distribute their votes to maximize their representation and PB public works projects.[27] Although legislators often lend support during the mobilization phase of PB, what is striking about this case is the conservative political affiliation of Klunderman. He is affiliated with the conservative PFL, a party not commonly associated with support for the direct participation of citizens in policy-making venues. Klunderman's ability to turn out voters and to "capture" four of PB's eight regions in 1997 contributed to the mayor's weak support for PB. The mayor had a clear disincentive to support a program that was partially captured by political rivals.

This case, along with Recife (see Chapter 7), undercuts the claims of PB's strongest proponents that PB is equally open to all citizens and that

---

27. Klunderman, interview. His claims were substantiated by PB Coordinator Costa and Vice Mayor Mafra.

governments will support PB regardless of who participates. As the cases of Blumenau and Recife (again, see Chapter 7) demonstrate, mayors who do not receive full support from PB participants are likely to decrease their support for PB. The "capture" of four of PB's eight regions in Blumenau and the subsequent distancing of the government from PB suggest that governments are acutely aware of who is participating and how this participation likely will affect both parties in the larger political environment. These findings lend credence to the claim that PB operates as a political institution that depends on basic political agreements between the government and CSO activists to ensure that the decisions made within PB are mostly amenable to the political needs of the government. Blumenau is the negative case that demonstrates how the presence of positive political relations in six of the other cases plays an important supporting role.

PB's Rules

PB's rules in Blumenau largely mirrored Porto Alegre's rules. There were two rounds of voting, for specific policies and for PB delegates. The number of delegates was determined by the number of participants, so there was a direct incentive for CSOs to mobilize as many of their fellow citizens as possible. Resources were distributed to each of the municipality's nine regions, the amount based on the same combination of need and population density. Blumenau also adopted a PB council that was charged with making final budgetary decisions regarding which projects should actually be included. This meant that citizens voted on projects, but they had to rely on the political skills and interests of their elected PB councilors to ensure that their project would enter the budget. This is a significant rule change from what occurs in Porto Alegre, where the PB council's authority over specific projects is much more limited. The effect of this rule change in Blumenau is that CSO leadership enjoy increased authority over the policy-making process, since they can disregard or block policies that they do not support.

Blumenau's PB also employed a unique feature regarding implementation: citizens living on a street selected for pavement must contribute 20 percent of the cost. The contribution can be in the form of labor. The government supplies the paving stones and the neighborhood associations' members do the work. Or the neighborhood association can collect money directly from homeowners and pay 20 percent of the cost. Collecting rents is a tricky enterprise in Brazil because of the absence of clear legal title in many low-income neighborhoods. This rule shifts a basic state duty (tax collection) away from the municipal government and onto neighborhood associations, which may be why this rule is only present in Blumenau.

The fact that PB's rules in Blumenau are virtually identical to those in Porto Alegre indicates that how the rules are interpreted and followed is more important than the formal rule structure. Blumenau's government adopted PB's basic rules but did not adhere to the rules. The significance of this finding is more about what it demonstrates in the case of Porto Alegre than in Blumenau. Brazil's political and institutional environments have long been dominated by considerable flexibility in how rules, laws, and legislation are applied. The fact that Blumenau's government ignored the rules that they themselves adopted should be no surprise, but the fact that Porto Alegre's government adhered to the rules is a significant finding.

Financial Situation

Blumenau's financial situation is relatively strong, although it is not stellar. The annual per capita investment spending for 2001 and 2002 was U.S.$29, a figure at the upper end of all eight municipalities. The government secured funding from Brazil's National Development Bank to initiate a major urban revitalization project. Blumenau's per capita monthly income was U.S.$124, which also placed it in the middle of all eight municipalities. A substantial middle class meant that the government could focus its demands on creating public policies that attended to the needs of the poor. The relatively high level of financial resources in Blumenau indicates that a "supply side" argument does not sufficiently explain outcomes. If high levels of resources were sufficient to make PB function well, Blumenau's PB would be one of the stronger cases rather than one of the weakest.

Synthesizing the Results

Blumenau's PB program has not contributed to the inculcation of citizenship rights and has done little to extend accountability. Mayor Lima chose not to delegate much authority to PB, thereby creating a weak and limited participatory process rather than a vibrant and deliberative decision-making venue. The weakness of Blumenau's PB stems from the lack of mayoral support, a mobilized but accommodating base of CSOs, low support for the Left in municipal elections, a conservative party's partial "capture" of PB, and a lack of funds being dedicated to PB. PB did not transform policy-making processes, but it did provide an additional venue in which citizens could press their demands on the state.

The inculcation of citizenship rights via PB depends on citizens being able to engage in policy-making processes in which they make decisions that result in governmental action. In Blumenau, citizens' decision-making authority is limited and the types of projects implemented by the government have been small and limited in scope. PB has not extended political rights. As I mentioned at the outset of this chapter, one of the most surprising aspects of Blumenau is the consistent criticism, from top to bottom, regarding how poorly PB functions. Blumenau's PB has produced cynicism rather than concrete results. The government's failure to invest in PB led to increased cynicism about democracy because the government was unwilling to delegate any meaningful authority to citizens, even though this was a central part of the government's campaign rhetoric. Blumenau's PB mirrors a long history of Brazilian politicians' advocating and campaigning on reform, but then investing little effort to ensure that the reforms will succeed. Similarly, the government did not adhere to the rules that it proposed, and the interested participants appear to have lacked the political will to openly contest these shortcomings.

Blumenau's PB did not contribute positively to the extension of accountability. Societal accountability has not been extended, as a result of the absence of CSOs that were willing to publicly pressure government officials to fulfill their commitments to PB. The high participation rates (10 percent of the adult population) created a political opportunity for CSOs to pressure the government to pay closer attention to their demands, but no groups were willing to risk alienating the government. Political accommodation was favored over contestation, which had the effect of limiting accountability.

Horizontal accountability was not extended through PB. Legislators ignored PB rather than engaging the new institution as part of a new checks-and-balance system. PB became a means for legislators to demonstrate how many citizens they could mobilize to attend meetings, which meant that PB became a barometer for measuring the electoral strength of competing politicians. In early 2003, potential mayoral candidates for the 2004 election were being discussed in terms of how many "PB delegates" different parties and candidates could turn out.

Finally, vertical accountability was only weakly extended. Citizens have not been given decision-making authority that allows them to direct the mayoral administration to act. Delegates are not able to create an environment of "binding decisions" because the mayor personally decides which projects should be funded. Therefore, PB is best characterized as a "demand entry" program through which delegates signal their preferences to the mayor, rather than an institutional body that allows decisions to be made.

The PB program in Blumenau was initiated in seemingly ideal circumstances. A PT mayor, a dense civil society, and a strong financial situation are commonly thought of as key ingredients that would produce a strong program. However, the interactions between the mayor and CSOs did not develop in a fashion that would support the delegation of authority. CSOs affiliated with the PT did not learn how to make effective use of PB. Rather, CSOs affiliated with conservative politicians made the most effective use of PB, but they did so in a method that allowed them to pack the meetings and use strategic voting strategies to dominate outcomes. These groups have not emphasized deliberation and negotiation. Blumenau's mayor has chosen to downplay PB as a decision-making venue that could challenge long-standing traditions and ways of doing business. PB was added to an existing policy-making system, one dominated by the mayor, with no real effort made to use direct participation as a means to transform how policies are made in Blumenau.

Rio Claro

PB was established in Rio Claro in 1997, following the election of Mayor Claudio de Mauro of the Green Party. The Green Party in Rio Claro comprises environmentalists and former PT members who split from the local PT because of ideological differences. Thus, the roots of PB in Rio Claro can be traced back to the PT and the previous PB experiences in Porto Alegre, Belo Horizonte, and Santo André. In Rio Claro, just as in Blumenau, the principal group within the Green Party that advocated the adoption of PB was affiliated with the local university (State University of São Paulo, Rio Claro). The Green Party mayor was a university professor and a longtime environmental activist, two roles that drew his attention away from PB and toward other policy projects. As Teixeira and Albuquerque observed, "The arrival of the mayor to power—and the implementation of PB—had little relationship to the history of CSO mobilization.

The mayor's individual political trajectory is more important—a charismatic leader, a university professor, who inspires confidence from a broad range of social classes."[28] Rio Claro's PB was implemented at the behest of one faction within the Green Party on the basis of the belief that direct participation in decision-making processes was a viable strategy for producing good public works and enhancing the quality of democracy. However, the majority faction within the government did not strongly support PB, leading to the implementation of a weak program that had little impact on policy-making processes. In this section, I will again look at how mayoral support, civil society, mayoral-legislative relations, PB's rules, and the financial situation of Rio Claro affect PB's outcomes.

Mayoral Support

There was generally weak mayoral support for PB. Mayor Mauro introduced a series of policy reform projects; PB was one of many initiatives employed by the government to "remake" Rio Claro.[29] This broad reform package resulted in limited financial and organizational support for PB. PB had two staff members, one full time and one part time. The level of resources was very low. Delegates negotiated just 30 percent of all new capital spending projects, which was 1.3 percent of the overall budget.[30] Furthermore, the government could not provide an accurate accounting of projects that had actually been implemented.[31] There is no way to verify if the 1.3 percent of the budget that was negotiated within PB was actually spent on PB projects.[32] Although it is impossible to definitively assert that the government was not spending resources on PB, there also is no way to conclusively demonstrate that they were spending the resources. In my research in Brazil on participatory institutions, I found that a lack of transparency is an indication that the government is implementing far fewer projects than the delegates are negotiating. When governments are successfully implementing projects, they have a clear set of data that they are able and willing to share with delegates and researchers. The Rio Claro

28. Teixeira and Albuquerque 2005, 20.
29. "Orçamento Participativo: Democratizando o Dinheiro Público," 2002; "Venha Participar do Planejamento de Rio Claro," 2001.
30. De Oliveira, interview; Silviana Pintaude, interview, September 12, 2003; Fabianne Pizzirana, interview, November 2, 2003; "Orçamento Participativo 1997–2000: Rio Claro," 2001.
31. Oliveira, Pizzirana, interviews.
32. "Orçamento Participativo: Democratizando o Dinheiro Público," 2002; "Venha participar do planejamento de Rio Claro," 2001.

government's published pamphlets do little to illuminate budgetary processes related to PB.[33] The fact that there were only two PB administrators also indicates a lack of internal processes that might move projects
from the drawing board to implementation stages.

Another indication of low mayoral support is the limited number of
meetings that the government sponsored each year. Rio Claro was divided
into sixteen regions, each of which had only one meeting per year. This
indicates that Mayor Mauro did not envision PB as a means to jump-start
civil society activity. The mayor was interested in environmental and
health care reforms, both of which are more technically oriented than the
types of projects requested by Rio Claro's PB residents. The kinds of policies and programs initiated by Mayor Mauro were designed to overcome
basic problems faced by Rio Claro, but these programs were not predicated
on citizen involvement. As Teixeira and Albuquerque recount, "The
department heads study and deliberate over the selected projects, analyzing which projects are 'welcome,' or not." Furthermore, "the mayor
left it clear that PB is a moment of consultation with the public about the
public works that would be completed in each neighborhood."[34]

The purpose of this line of analysis is not to criticize the mayor's
choices and strategies. It is reasonable to assume that a university professor from Brazil's Green Party is going to privilege environmental and
health care projects for political, ideological, and personal reasons. However, the emphasis on these projects has a detrimental effect on PB because the mayoral administration did not invest the necessary time and
resources to reform basic decision-making. There was a series of new
policies implemented by new politicians, but these were implemented
within the traditional decision-making process in which the mayor was
at the center of all key decision making.

Why did the mayor delegate so little authority? Or, stated differently,
why would the mayor even implement PB if he did not really support it?
The reason that Mayor Mauro did not delegate authority was that Rio Claro
has a weak civil society (see the following section) that did not strongly
demand the expansion of its role in policy making. Access and accommodation were preferred by Rio Claro's CSOs. Mayor Mauro and the Green
Party did not try to build up Rio Claro's weak civil society because they did
not believe that it could provide the base of support necessary to expand

33. "Orçamento Participativo: Democratizando o Dinheiro Público," 2002; "Venha participar do planejamento de Rio Claro," 2001.
34. Teixeira and Albuquerque 2005, 12, 13.

their political influence in Rio Claro. Second, the Green Party activists, who provided the key mobilization support for Mauro, were more focused on environmental and health care issues than on participatory forms of decision making. Participatory democracy is of interest to the Green Party, but it is tangential, rather than a central, core feature. Finally, and related to the above feature, Mayor Mauro and the Green Party do not have a strong ideological commitment to the deepening of democracy. Their adoption of PB situates the Green Party and Mauro in Brazil's broader political left field, since the vast majority of municipalities that adopted PB during the 1997–2000 period were from the political Left.[35] However, the Green Party and Mauro's adoption of PB appears to be driven by the desire to experiment with policy types that had been successful for the Left in other political settings. Unfortunately for the most ardent supporters of PB in Rio Claro, Mayor Mauro was unwilling to delegate any real authority.

Civil Society

Rio Claro's civil society is limited because there are few organizations or unions that organize citizens. Rio Claro is a large, fairly rural municipality with a strong agricultural base. The state university is one source of CSOs, which are mainly unions made up of state employees. The survey results, presented in Table 18, confirm the low involvement in civil society, with just 36 percent of the respondents reporting current involvement in a CSO (lowest of all eight municipalities included in the study). This low percentage, combined with PB's low participation rates, is indicative of a weak civil society that has few ties to political society.

Rio Claro's political history shows that CSOs formed during the 1930s, 1940s, and 1950s adopted a clientelistic model.[36] Although there was a limited renewal of civil society during the 1980s and 1990s, the principal form of political organizing in Rio Claro continues to be based on the clientelistic form of CSO activity first initiated during the 1930s. Since there are few new groups, it has been very difficult to disseminate new ways of doing politics. Therefore, when PB was initiated, there were few CSOs that were prepared to engage in the complex decision-making processes embedded in PB.

---

35. Wampler and Avritzer 2005.
36. Teixeira and Albuquerque 2005, 13.

This limited number of csos places their leadership and the mayoral administration in a bind. For csos that participated in PB, their principal political ally is the Green Party government. The csos' strategy was to work with the government in the context of PB rather than trying to develop PB as an autonomous decision-making venue. Cooperation is thus favored at the expense of any type of contestation. This may strengthen ties that link the csos to the Green Party, but it does not support the establishment of a participatory institution that contributes to the extension of accountability and citizenship rights. Thus, broader political interests trump PB because of the electoral concerns of government officials and activists. Government officials have an obvious incentive to focus on elections, which occur every two years. For activists, their incentives to cooperate include trying to build a broader political movement, electing officials who will help with constituency service, and investing in the possibility of state jobs based on their involvement in the campaign.

The absence of qualified citizens and csos to adequately manage the complexities of negotiations within PB makes it difficult to see how government officials might have been able to cultivate a base of support through PB. csos and citizens were not prepared to take control of policy making. Teixeira and Albuquerque effectively summarize this: "The debates [in PB] are restricted to small groups, with low levels of information, and with little broader discussions; decisions are made based on the government's technical reports, which are not questioned by the PB delegates."[37] The Green Party was unwilling to delegate authority because of its own electoral interests. Why would the government want to delegate authority when so few people participate? The government claims that "1 percent" of the population participates in PB, which would mean that roughly seventeen hundred individuals participated each year. Unfortunately, not only is the government's claim unverifiable, there is some evidence to suggest that it only gets a fraction of this turnout.

Rio Claro's PB was broken down into sixteen regions, with roughly similar populations in each region. If there was an even distribution of participation, there should be roughly one hundred attendees per regional meeting. Each region has only one meeting a year, so there is no "double counting" of participants. However, the meeting lists that I saw and the interviews I conducted hinted at meetings of twenty to forty people.[38]

37. Teixeira and Albuquerque 2005, 32.
38. Pizzirana, interview.

The low participation means that the government does not really have a significant incentive to hand authority over to such a small minority. If Rio Claro's PB mobilized greater numbers of citizens, the potential for positive demonstration effects would be much greater, which would provide increased incentive for the government to delegate authority. Absent stronger participation rates, there is little incentive for government officials to expand PB.

As a result of the low mobilization, Rio Claro's government did not face pressure from CSOs and citizens to increase the importance of Rio Claro's PB. Contentious politics was not in the repertoire of CSOs. PB was initiated by the government, but there was no faction within either civil society or political society that promoted PB as a new way to establish new policy-making processes.

Mayoral-Legislative Relations

The Green Party's Mayor Mauro won a strong plurality but never gained a majority of the valid vote (46 percent of the vote in 1996 and 47 percent in 2000).[39] His support in the legislative chambers was also fairly limited—just 21 percent of the seats were held by leftists during the 1997–2004 legislative periods (see Table 17). The lack of majority support from the electorate and weak support in the legislature made it difficult for the mayor to delegate authority to citizens. Since PB was not a high priority for him, resistance from the municipal legislative branches contributed to the lack of attention PB received. Although the leftists controlled only 21 percent of the legislature's seats, centrist parties controlled 58 percent, which meant that the mayor could strike deals with the moderate center.[40] It is easier for mayors in smaller municipalities to work with centrist legislators because the municipalities are not at the center of their state's political life.

Mayor Mauro needed to establish a voting majority in the municipal legislature in order to pass other projects, such as the People's Bank (Banco do Povo) and Families of Citizens (Família Cidadã), as well as infrastructure projects that were more environmentally sensitive. The former project

39. There is a second round of voting for mayors only in municipalities with more than two hundred thousand residents or that are state capitals. A simple plurality is all that is necessary to win elections in municipalities that are not state capitals and have fewer than two hundred thousand residents.
40. See Tribunal Supremo Eleitoral de São Paulo.

was a lending program that was funded with municipal resources, and the "families" program was a cash-payment program to the municipality's poorest residents. To fund these projects, the mayor needed majority-vote support. Mayor Mauro engaged in trade-offs of small projects in order to establish a stable voting majority. Since less than a third of new capital investment spending was dedicated to PB negotiations, and since an even lower amount was implemented, the mayor had between two-thirds and three-fourths of new capital investment spending that could potentially be used to secure the support of moderates in the municipal legislature.

Therefore, mayoral-legislative relations neither undercut nor boosted the functioning of PB. The mayor had to attend to the needs of centrist and leftist legislators to ensure legislative approval of his projects, but the relationship was never so contentious that the government's own programs were put at political risk.

PB's Rules

Rio Claro was divided into sixteen regions to facilitate PB's administration and to distribute goods and services. Each region was allowed to pick one project per year that would be included in the budget. According to pamphlets produced by Rio Claro's government, the annual budget "will include suggestions of the community."[41] PB was therefore geared toward bringing people into a "debate and feedback" venue rather than a decision-making venue.

A second type of rule that severely limited PB was the stipulation that there was only one meeting per region per year. Citizens' formal involvement in PB was limited to this one meeting, at which they entered their demand and elected PB delegates. Each district elected one member to a PB council, which meant that sixteen councilors were largely responsible for negotiation and interaction with the government. There were no informational and educational sessions, and as a result the possibility for public learning and deliberation was quite low. Teixeira and Albuquerque assert that "there are no opportunities for participants to speak publicly about their ideas, their arguments, or their criticisms of the government."[42] Based on a single meeting per region per year, Rio Claro's PB is less a

41. "Orçamento Participativo: Democratizando o Dinheiro Público," 2002, 1.
42. Teixeira and Albuquerque 2005, 12.

deliberative, decision-making body and more of an entry point at which citizens submit their demands. PB becomes a channel for demand making, which allows signals to be sent between CSOs and government officials. Citizens make demands, and then the government decides if it is interested in implementing this or that particular public works project.

Thus Rio Claro's PB is not a process through which citizens are actively engaged, but rather one that reinforces the direct relationship between community leader and government officials. The rule structure reflects the limited capacity of Rio Claro's civil society to organize itself and the mayoral administration's pragmatic decision to open up participation to those individuals and groups that were prepared and willing to take advantage of it. Between 1997 and 2004, there were no major rule changes, precluding the opportunity for political renewal. The government has been uninterested in making PB's rules more dynamic, and CSOs have been unable to convince government officials that rule changes would vastly improve the program.

Financial Resources

The new annual capital investment spending available to the municipal government, U.S.$26 (see Table 17), was relatively strong in comparison with that of the other seven municipalities. This, therefore, means that a strict resource supply argument does not account for weakness of PB in Rio Claro. The municipality's Human Development Index (HDI) score and per capita monthly income were lower than in most other municipalities, with the exception of Recife and Ipatinga (see Tables 17, 12, and 24). The lower HDI score and the low household per capita income, however, may partially account for the government's decisions to invest lower resources in PB. The government has had to invest greater resources in providing direct aid and public policies to its residents. This would then give some credence to a supply-side argument, since the government was unable to dedicate the necessary financial resources while they were attending to so many other urgent social and political problems.

Synthesizing the Results

PB's impact in Rio Claro was, at best, negligible and, at worst, corrosive. PB was never a high priority for the government, a circumstance that limited its impact. CSOs are relatively scarce and weak in Rio Claro, a combination that precluded the development of an independent force that could advocate on behalf of PB. Contentious politics was not an option. PB's impact was negligible because so few citizens participated and very limited numbers of projects were implemented over an eight-year span. PB's impact can be viewed as corrosive because the government laid out an ambitious participatory agenda but did not provide adequate support for it. This had a negative effect on the participants. The survey results were unambiguous in Rio Claro: respondents believed that they lacked decision-making authority, which in turn suggests that PB did little to overcome attitudes of alienation and powerlessness, which have long been associated with Brazil's lower classes.

Rio Claro's PB did little to expand a greater sense of active citizenship rights. Most participants attended a single meeting, where they received information about PB and the prior year's spending, voted for a new set of policies, and elected PB delegates. One hundred and twenty PB delegates were elected each year, but most attend only one additional meeting. From the 120 PB delegates, 16 (one from each region) were elected to a municipal-wide council. The very low level of engagement, the low quality of debate at meetings, and the low numbers of participants mean that there was little positive interaction in Rio Claro that might lead us to believe that citizenship rights were being extended.

From the vantage point of accountability, the results do not look much better. Low participation rates and the lack of contestation indicate that societal accountability has not been effectively established through PB. The paucity of meetings did not allow participants to engage in lively debates or to press issues. The government provided little information to the participants; as a result, delegates lacked an informed base from which they could hold the government accountable for its inaction. Beyond the institutional design and low support from the government, perhaps the most important factor that limited the extension of societal accountability was the absence of CSOs willing and able to play this role. If CSOs and their most active leaders do not view contentious politics and direct confrontation as a viable strategy, there is little likelihood that societal accountability can be extended.

Vertical accountability, too, was weakly extended, because citizens did not make binding decisions that might have forced the government to carry out their policy preferences. Instead, PB was a demand-making format. The government took the demands that the citizens voted on and then created its own priority list for the implementation of projects. PB served as a signaling mechanism rather than a decision-making body. Finally, horizontal accountability was not extended. The policy decisions made through PB did not affect basic mayoral-legislative relations. PB was a sideshow rather than a central part of a new decision-making process.

Conclusions

A cursory glance at Blumenau and Rio Claro might lead an observer to believe that the necessary conditions were in place to allow PB to flourish. They share political and economic characteristics of Porto Alegre and Ipatinga: leftist mayors publicly committed to direct participation and a decent financial record. Blumenau looks even better, since its participation rates were robust. These two cases illustrate why researchers and policy makers should be careful regarding claims that decentralized, participatory policy-making institutions will transform basic state-society relations. Blumenau and Rio Claro's PB programs have not transformed the decision-making process, have not promoted social justice, have had limited effects on the inculcation of citizenship rights, and have not contributed to the extension of accountability. The outcomes produced by PB in these two municipalities are weak, despite being "advertised" as successful.

The mayors' weak support for the direct delegation of authority to citizens was the principal factor in both municipalities that accounts for the weak outcomes. Although PB is a participatory institution, it is also a government-sponsored decision-making venue that requires an inordinate amount of time, energy, and resources to function well. Weak government support undermines any capacity of citizens to begin to make meaningful decisions because the citizens lack basic information, are negotiating over small pots of resources, or do not have their policy choices implemented. This evidence suggests that PB programs should not be thought of as an independent institutional sphere of direct democracy or as a "non-state public sphere."[43] Rather, PB should be conceptualized as a government-sponsored policy arena in which citizens are making choices in an environment heavily conditioned by the government's own interests. PB is neither independent nor autonomous vis-à-vis the government, but instead depends on the shared interests of politicians and CSO activists.

The second factor that strongly contributed to the weak PB results was

43. Genro 1995b.

the absence of csos that were willing to engage in contentious forms of politics. If csos are reluctant to confront the policies of the government, there is little pressure on the government to further delegate decision-making authority or to implement the policy choices selected within PB. Rather than contestation, the politics of accommodation and cooperation best characterized the interactions between csos and government officials in these two municipalities. Blumenau and Rio Claro are midsized municipalities, and neither has a history of contentious forms of politicking. Mayoral support, already weak in both municipalities, was not likely to increase without political pressure being applied by csos.

It is the combination of these two factors—low mayoral support and lack of contentious politics—that most significantly affected PB's weak outcomes. This finding helps to refute claims that PB is "direct democracy" or "a government-sponsored sham." If PB was direct democracy, then the involvement of a mayoral administration would not be a strong explanatory factor. In Rio Claro and Blumenau, mayoral support was weak to nonexistent, which greatly contributed to failed programs. It also refutes notions that PB is merely a government-sponsored sham, as csos need to be able to engage in, or at least threaten, the use of contentious politics.[44] In Rio Claro and Blumenau, the absence of contentious politics demonstrates that when csos do not apply public pressure on government officials, there is little that can be done to induce governments to remain committed to PB (or increase their commitment to it). "No contestation, no delegation."

44. This is in accordance with Nylen's findings. Nylen 2003.

6

São Paulo and Santo André:
Co-optation, Limited Delegation, and Signaling

> As the coordinator of PB, I had to find equilibrium between the demands of the population and the government. The demands of the population tend to be immediate issues, while the government is interested in larger projects. . . . If the government and the population shared the same project proposal, we left the project to the citizens to usher through PB.
> —TERESA SANTOS, PB ADMINISTRATOR IN SANTO ANDRÉ

> The bureaucracy knows that PB is not a priority of the government.
> —CARLOS THADEU C. DE OLIVEIRA, PB ADMINISTRATOR
> IN SÃO PAULO

> Our submayor is from the Liberal Party. He doesn't like us and he doesn't even return our phone calls, because he simply doesn't want to. . . . Even though we supported Marta [Mayor Suplicy] and the PT, we are not welcome in our local government offices.
> —PB DELEGATE IN SÃO PAULO

Signaling and Electoral Politics in São Paolo

In 2000, a PT candidate, Marta Suplicy, won the mayoral election in São Paulo, Brazil's largest city, returning the PT to power after an eight-year absence. Following the election, when the political spoils were being distributed, the Socialist Democratic faction of the PT successfully convinced Mayor Suplicy to adopt PB even though PB had not been featured prominently during her mayoral campaign.[1] During Suplicy's four years in office, PB was hamstrung by inadequate funding, poor organization, and

1. Felix Sanchez, coordinator of São Paulo's PB, interview September 17, 2003.

limited decision-making authority for citizens.[2] PB became a marketing tool used by government officials to demonstrate that they were open, transparent, participatory, and democratic. Two vignettes demonstrate the limitations of PB in São Paulo.

In October 2003, I was attempting to trace the Suplicy government's internal decision-making process for the allocation of resources to different policy projects. The government officials administering PB were unclear about how funding decisions were made, but they assured me that PB had a representative in the Department of Finance, which was responsible for green-lighting projects. I scheduled an appointment with the PB administrator in that department. I was surprised to discover, upon my arrival, that the official in charge of PB was a college student, working part time to fulfill a component of an internship program. A few quick questions revealed that he did not really understand how projects were approved for implementation. I then made an appointment with the deputy secretary of finances (second in charge) to examine how PB projects were approved. According to the deputy director, the department had no internal processes for funding PB projects.[3] Decisions regarding the funding of public works projects came directly from Rui Falcão, the mayor's right-hand man. Under Mayor Suplicy, PB was a policy-making process that did not reshape how funding decisions were made. Instead PB-approved projects were part of an intense bargaining process that took place within the government over the distribution of resources. A small faction within the PT that strongly supported PB expended its limited political capital to ensure that PB projects would be implemented. This small faction competed with legislators, party officials, and career bureaucrats for the limited pool of resources. There were no new rules or processes that might have reshaped the distribution of resources and authority to ensure that projects selected through PB would be implemented. Informality and flexibility, both long-standing characteristics of Brazilian politics, were defining characteristics of São Paulo's PB.

A second example of PB's ambiguous role in Suplicy's administration is

2. Mayor Suplicy governed from 2001 to 2004. PB was reinitiated by her government in 2001 after an eight-year hiatus. Mayor Luiza Erundina (PT), who governed from 1989 to 1992, implemented PB in 1990, but the program was abandoned by Mayors Maluf (1993–96) and Pitta (1997–2000). When Suplicy assumed office in 2001, many of the administrators, most notably Felix Sanchez, who had previously worked on PB, returned to run PB, thus allowing for continuity between administrative periods.

3. Jose Police, deputy director of Finances Department of the São Paulo municipal government, interview, November 6, 2003, São Paulo.

related to one of her principal policy initiatives: the creation, in low-income areas, of large schools that each would be equipped with a theater, a swimming pool, and computer facilities (Unified Education Centers [Centros Educativos Unificados, or CEUS]). These schools would provide an infrastructure equivalent to that seen in private schools catering to the middle and upper classes. The CEUS took on an almost mythical status among PB participants. "Best thing that happened in our neighborhood. . . . As nice as a shopping mall." "The only reason that people are opposed to the CEUS is because they don't want poor people to have good schools."[4] This project was initiated by Suplicy in 2002. By 2003, rather than exercising the right to promote their own projects, PB delegates were voting on where they should locate these schools. In other words, PB was being used to legitimize the interests of the Suplicy government rather than serving as a political venue in which citizens could propose, defend, and debate their own policy initiatives. PB evolved into a top-down system, controlled by government officials.

During a focus group held in the low-income neighborhood of Perus, these schools became the subject of a fairly heated exchange among the participants. Some delegates insisted that their region was getting a CEU because of their mobilization efforts and negotiation skills. Others differed; as one PB delegate aptly put it, "I don't understand why we choose the CEU as one of our region's projects when the government has already purchased the land to build the CEU," implying that it was already a "done deal."[5] Under Mayor Suplicy, São Paulo's PB had evolved into a forum that had given the government an opportunity to legitimize its own policy choices by claiming that citizens were choosing public policies.

Co-Administration and Limited Transparency

Celso Daniel, Santo André's popular, charismatic mayor (elected three times) strongly promoted the direct involvement of citizens in policy-making processes. The government sought out allies in civil society during his first term in office (1989–92) and sought to directly incorporate them into government decision making. Empowering citizens, building new state-society relationships, and overcoming traditional barriers that sharply divided the local state and CSOS were ever-present themes in

4. Focus group, November 19, 2003, Perus district, São Paulo.
5. Focus group, November 19, 2003, Perus district, São Paulo.

Daniel's governing strategy. Daniel sought to treat citizens and participants as equal partners in their PB program. There were, unfortunately, two crucial problems that sharply limited this vision for remaking Brazil.

First, government officials and citizens were formally equal partners within Santo André's deliberative body, but they were not equal. Government officials had access to greater levels of information, had broader understandings of the problems faced by the municipality, and were learning how to use the local state to exercise political power. Government officials were powerholders, whereas citizens were trying to make use of the limited authority given to them by the state. The citizens were dependent on the government for information and access, whereas government was not dependent on the citizens. Second, government officials had a more unified set of interests than the heterogeneous group of CSOs involved in PB. There were divergences between the positions of government officials, but they had specific incentives (such as elections, party unity) that would unite them. CSOs had a broad set of interests that made it difficult for them to unite. Therefore, the government was able to steer its proposals through PB, when it deemed it necessary.

Santo André's PT government sought to establish new mechanisms that would allow for the establishment of new state-society relationships. But government officials did not understand how the rule structures they established for their PB program would actually undermine the ability of citizens to make meaningful decisions. By ignoring the basic differences in social and political powers held by citizens and government officials, they actually undercut citizens' power rather than producing the empowerment of citizen leaders.

PB in São Paulo and Santo André

Santo André's PB is remarkable for the government's emphasis on a "co-administration" process, designed to bring government officials and citizens together into a single format to make policy decisions. Although co-administration may have been the intent, in practice the government did not delegate authority to citizens. Santo André's PB has been emasculated as a decision-making process because the "co-administration" process allows the government to dominate the decision-making venue. Santo André's PB lacks basic transparency and openness.

This finding came as a great surprise to me—Santo André's PB program

has been recognized on numerous occasions as groundbreaking and successful.[6] Mayor Celso Daniel represented PB programs when PB was recognized as one of the top-forty policy programs in the world by the United
Nations at the Istanbul Habitat Conference in 1996. What explains the lack
of transparency? What explains why citizen-participants appear to demand
so little of their government? Most of the scholarly analysis on Santo
André's PB has focused on the positive shifts in values that PB has appar-
ently been creating in the delegates (for example, public learning, empowerment).[7] Researchers, with some exceptions, appear to have fallen into
the same trap as PB delegates: an assumption of goodwill on behalf of
the government, rather than an independent verification of the results.

Santo André's PB has a unique rule structure that creates a PB council comprising twenty-six government officials and twenty-six elected citizens. This body was created to encourage deliberation and joint, or "co-,"
decision-making processes. In practice, however, it has allowed government officials to dominate all decision making, thereby emasculating any
political role that citizens may have. "Empowerment" and "public learning" that are unconnected to the actual delegation of authority are rather
hollow concepts.

The purpose of this chapter is to explain why São Paulo and Santo
André's PB programs underperformed and should be considered weak
cases. Both PB programs are better described as "signaling devices" rather
than as decision-making venues. This finding is rather ironic because the
PT have hailed these two programs as examples of how Brazil could be
transformed through participatory processes.[8] These programs are stunted,
but they have had a more significant impact on public policies than that
of either Blumenau or Rio Claro (see Chapter 5). These programs lacked
the delegation of authority and establishment of transparency practices
seen in Recife or Belo Horizonte (see Chapter 7). Although São Paulo's
and Santo André's PB programs have underperformed, the program of
neither locality has been a complete failure. In this chapter, I will also
explore the positive effects generated by PB in each municipality in the
hopes of illuminating how contradictory processes affect the extension of
accountability and citizenship rights.

6. Harvard University 2003; Acioly, Herzog, Sandino, and Andrade 2002; Teixeira and
Albuquerque 2005; Pontual 2000; Ricci 2004.
7. Pontual 2000; Teixeira and Alburquerque 2005.
8. See Fundação Perseu Abramo.

I will follow the same format that I used in the previous case study chapters. Mayoral support, the role of civil society, mayoral-legislative relations, PB's rules, and the financial situations of both São Paulo and Santo André will be analyzed to detail the results. Before turning to the explanation, some basic demographic and political information on each municipality is in order.

Basic Demographic and Political Characteristics

São Paulo is Brazil's largest city and continues to be the economic engine driving the country. São Paulo's economic basis has shifted from heavy industry to finances and services. The sheer enormity of the city (10 million residents, with 20 million in the wider metropolitan area) means that it dwarfs all other municipalities included in this book. This created additional complexities for the government as they sought to implement a participatory decision-making program. The municipality of Santo André borders São Paulo. It was in the heart of São Paulo's industrial expansion from the 1930s through the 1970s, but is now a decaying industrial city.

The Human Development Index (HDI) score is high in both cities, with the presence of a large middle class. Both São Paulo and Santo André have substantial sectors of the population living in poverty, but large majorities of the population also have access to basic schooling and medical care.

Table 20. Demographic and Political Profile

	São Paulo	Santo André
Residents 2000	10,400,000	650,000
Human Development Index, 2000	0.841	0.836
Per capita monthly income, 2000	U.S.$176	U.S.$142
Municipal government's investment spending per capita, average, 2001–2002	U.S.$19	U.S.$19
% of mayor's vote in 1996 municipal election (first round)	n/a[1]	62
% of mayor's vote in 2000 municipal election (first round)	38	70
Average % of leftist seats in city council, 1997–2004	31	45

Sources: www.ibge.gov.br, undp.org, www.stn.fazenda.gov.br, www.tse.gov.br.

1. The election results for 1996 are listed as n/a because the mayor elected in 1996 chose not to implement PB. There were, however, two rounds of voting, indicating that São Paulo is a contested political environment.

Although the H D I score, per capita monthly income, and tax base are strong in comparative perspective, both governments' investment spending per capita is low. Of the eight municipalities covered in this book, Santo André and São Paulo ranked fifth and sixth, respectively, in terms of the level of resources available for new capital investment spending. The budgets in São Paulo and Santo André are eaten up by high debt payments, bloated bureaucracies, and high maintenance costs (street repair, trash collection) because of decaying infrastructures. A supply-side argument partially explains the lack of successful outcomes in both P B programs. However, Belo Horizonte and Recife both had lower investment spending per capita, yet both these municipalities produced more successful P B programs than those of either São Paulo or Santo André, suggesting that a supply-side argument has limited explanatory power.

The political climates of these two municipalities are quite different. Since 1988, São Paulo's political environment has been marked by ideological polarization, with the PT winning mayoral elections in 1988 and 2000, and its conservative rivals, the PPB, winning in 1992 and 1996. Mayor Suplicy won in 2000 with a majority in the second round of voting, but she had only a weak plurality, 38 percent in the first round. The political Left also did moderately well, controlling 31 percent of legislative seats. The election results suggest that São Paulo has not necessary been an ideal place in which to initiate broad reform, as the electorate did not strongly stand behind the leftist mayor.

In Santo André, the PT has been the dominant political party since Brazil's return to democracy. The popular Celso Daniel, a university professor and longtime advocate of government reform, led the PT. Daniel was elected mayor in 1988, 1996, and 2000. As shown in Table 20, he won elections with substantial majorities during the first round of voting. He also enjoyed strong support from leftist legislators in the municipal council. Santo André's government received multiple awards for innovations and policy outcomes during Daniel's tenure in office.[9] The broader political conditions were largely supportive of P B, which should have allowed P B to flourish.

Daniel was murdered in 2001 under what can at best be described as murky circumstances.[10] At the time of his death, he was the campaign manager of the PT's presidential candidate, Luiz Ignácio Lula da Silva. Lula

9. See Gestão Público e Cidadania; see Fundação Perseu Abramo; Carvalho and Felgueiras, 2000.
10. Rother 2004.

was elected president in 2002, following his fourth presidential campaign. The investigation into Daniel's murder brought allegations of corruption upon Santo André's municipal government. It is noteworthy that Santo André's PB focused more on citizen empowerment and education than on the development of new decision-making processes. In particular, there were few efforts made to reform the internal processes that would lead a project from policy proposal to implementation. There was also little emphasis on increasing budgetary transparency.

Survey Evidence

The survey data in Table 21 demonstrate that the majority of the respondents are from low-income households. In São Paulo and Santo André, 63 percent of the respondents live in households that earn less than U.S.$400 per month. Although the HDI score in both municipalities is relatively high, the households from which the majority of participants originate are lower class. In neither municipality, however, do substantial numbers of the poorest segments of the population participate. In both municipalities, delegates participate in CSOs at comparatively high rates, indicating a fairly dense civil society and tight connections betweens the PB programs and organized sectors of civil society. Of those active in CSOs, more than three-quarters of the respondents in Santo André hold a leadership position within a CSO. This indicates that Santo André's PB is dominated by civil society leadership, rather than comprising interested citizens.

Table 21. Profile of Survey Respondents (%)

	São Paulo	Santo André
Monthly household income of U.S.$400 or less	63	63
Less than high school diploma	46	37
Women respondents	61	52
Currently active in associational life	78	72
Current leadership position in community association (of those currently active)	55	77
Delegates elected 3 or more times	18	25
Delegates have received a direct benefit from PB	54	89

Source: PB Comparative Survey.

In Santo André, 89 percent of the respondents indicate that their communities have received a direct benefit from PB. This finding is comparable to those of Porto Alegre and Ipatinga, further complicating the explanation of why survey respondents have such weak evaluations of their PB program. (Statistical evidence presented in Chapter 3 showed that delegates who have received direct benefits from PB have strong and positive evaluations of their PB programs.) In São Paulo, just half of the respondents indicate that they have received a direct benefit from PB. This figure is the lowest of all eight municipalities, a factor that is partially explained by PB's life cycle in São Paulo. São Paulo's PB functioned from 1990 to 1992, was followed by an eight-year hiatus, and then resumed in 2001, which meant that many PB delegates selected projects for the first time in 2001.

Survey Responses on Authority

The delegates' responses on the types of authority they exercise illustrate the difficulties faced by both PB programs.

In São Paulo and Santo André, the PB delegates agree that they have authority over PB's rules. In Santo André, respondents do not believe that they have much power over resources or policies, indicating that horizontal accountability is not being extended. The explanation for this lies in Santo André's unique set of PB rules that established a "PB council" that draws half its membership from citizens and half from government officials. Through this council, government officials can block the agenda and interests of PB delegates by creating a simple majority. PB delegates

Table 22. Delegates' Perceptions of Their Authority to Make Decisions (% Stating Always or Almost Always)

	São Paulo	Santo André
Authority to make PB rules	58	55
Authority to define PB priorities	56	42
Authority to define projects	51	28
Authority to add resources	19	20
Authority to stop government projects	21	34
Authority to monitor government projects	60	55
Secured projects outside PB	37	64

Source: PB Comparative Survey.

can stop government projects as well, since all approved projects need two-thirds support.

In São Paulo, survey respondents believe that they have the power to select projects and define policies, but fewer than a quarter view P B as a political venue in which they can effectively confront the policy directives of the government. The majority of the respondents indicate that they do not believe that they have the authority to stop government projects or to select public works projects whose costs exceed the amount allocated by the municipal government. In other words, respondents do not believe they have the authority to contradict the basic agenda of the municipal government, but they believe they can select policies within limits established by the government. This suggests that São Paulo's P B is a government-driven participatory process in which the participants are able to debate policy programs that the government already supports. The delegates have been induced to propose projects that the government would be interested in implementing.

Sixty percent of respondents in São Paulo claim that they are able to monitor the government's administration of P B-related projects. This robust majority should be approached with a healthy dose of skepticism, because 82 percent of the delegates had been elected for the first time in 2003, the year that the survey was applied (see Table 21). The delegates were elected in June or July, which means that they are claiming to have developed the necessary skills and knowledge to monitor the government in just five months. Without wanting to claim "false consciousness," I suspect that it is entirely likely that the delegates are absorbing one of the oft-repeated claims about P B: citizens and delegates have the right and responsibility to monitor the government through P B. I have attended numerous meetings at which this mantra was repeated, but there was little corroborating data provided in São Paulo to actually allow delegates to actively monitor the government.

Although 60 percent of the delegates claim that they could monitor the government, my own research efforts during this same period encountered significant obstacles. The government did not have any systematic, organized records of the current status of P B projects selected in 2001, 2002, or 2003. For example, in December 2003, government officials were madly trying to pull all of this information together, but the sheer volume of data made it difficult for them to provide easily digestible information to citizens and delegates. Turning to the case of São Paulo, the argument and evidence demonstrate that the government had low levels of interest in the delegation of authority and that csos were induced to limit the intensity of their claims on the government so as not to embarrass the incumbent mayor.

São Paulo

The task of delegating authority directly to citizens is extremely complicated in a mega-city such as São Paulo because of its polarized ideological and political environment, the municipality's importance in national politics, the sheer number of residents, combative and restless csos, and a financial crisis that engulfed the city during the late 1990s. It is made even more complicated when the delegation of authority has, at best, the lukewarm support of the mayor. São Paulo's politics are never just about São Paulo, since the size and wealth of the city place it at the center of Brazil's political life. When Marta Suplicy of the PT won the mayoral election in 2000, the PT needed to build a solid voting majority in the municipal council; implement programs that would strengthen the 2002 presidential bid of the PT's candidate, Luiz Ignácio Lula da Silva, and Marta Suplicy's 2004 reelection efforts; craft programs that would appeal to the base of the PT; and build support beyond its traditional base. The PT implemented PB at the behest of one of its internal factions as well as csos and advocacy nongovernmental agencies.[11]

Significant Rules Updates

When the PT returned to political power in São Paulo in 2001, they were able to draw on successful models of PT that had been implemented in more than one hundred municipalities during the 1990s.[12] Because of São Paulo's size and the existence of successful models of PB, the government opted to slowly phase in PB to increase the likelihood that policies selected by PB participants would be implemented in a timely manner.[13] This strategy is premised on the findings of scholars, policy analysts, and

11. The PT government released a fifty-five-page document titled "90 dias de reconstrução" (90 Days of Reconstruction), which detailed the problems faced by the municipality, what they had accomplished, and what the government was planning to accomplish. It is noteworthy that there were only two brief mentions of PB, thereby suggesting that PB, as of April 2001, was not a high priority of the government. "90 dias de reconstrução," 2001.

12. Ribeiro and de Grazia 2003; Pires 2002.

13. Felix Sanchez, PB administrator, interview, October 22, 2003.

practitioners who have established a strong association between government outputs and citizens' support for the participatory institution.[14] Participation will remain steady or increase if the government is able to follow
through on its commitment to implement public works.

As Table 23 demonstrates, São Paulo's PB program expanded the
breadth of its responsibilities, policy areas, and forms of representation
during each year of its existence. Government officials wanted to slowly
phase in PB so that the delegates would see a direct connection between
their efforts and public policy outcomes.[15] In 2001, delegates could only
select projects in the areas of health care and education.

In 2002, each region voted for a third area in which they would also
be able to select policies. The housing movement was the first organized
group to recognize this political opportunity and turned out in high
numbers.[16] Of the thirty-one regional districts, housing projects were chosen as the additional policy arena in twenty-three regions (74 percent) in
2002. Groups in the housing movement responded more quickly than
other CSOs to this political opportunity. They were also more organized
than other CSOs, allowing them to successfully "capture" most of the available resources. Although this rewarded the most active and astute members of civil society, it also excluded the vast majority of individuals who
are unorganized and have limited access to government officials. A year
and a half after the housing projects were selected, construction had not
begun on any of the twenty-three projects. The government sought to move
forward on some projects, but it simply ignored others that were selected
by PB delegates.[17] The housing movement took advantage of the political
opportunity offered by one section of the municipal government, but the
principal leadership of the government was not prepared to expend the
necessary financial and political capital to implement the works selected
through PB.

In 2003, the government, in conjunction with the delegates, again
redefined the basic rules of how PB would function. The number of policy arenas dramatically increased as "issue-oriented" (*tematicos*) forms of
representation were created. The delegates were able to select new public works or public services in all departmental areas. A second shift in
2003 was the inclusion of new forms of representation. The government

14. Nylen 2002; Wampler 2004b; Wampler and Avritzer 2004.
15. Felix Sanchez, coordinator of São Paulo's PB, interview, October 10, 2003.
16. McAdam, McCarthy, and Zald 1996.
17. "Prestação de Contas," 2003.

Table 23. Policy Areas and Representation

Year	Number of Participants	Policy Areas	Types of Policies	Type of Representation
2001	34,000	Health care and education	New public works	Regional
2002	55,000	Health care, education + a third area defined within each region	New public works + policy services	Regional + issue-based meetings
2003	80,000	All municipal departments	New public works + policy services	Territorial + issue-based meetings + minority representation

Source: www.prefeitura.sp.gov.br.

identified groups that have historically been discriminated against and underrepresented (women; blacks; the elderly; youth, children and ado- lescents; gay, lesbian, bisexual, and transgender [GLBT] people; Indians; the homeless; and people with disabilities). Individuals who self-identify as members of these groups have lower thresholds when it comes to being elected as PB delegates and municipal budget councilors. This "affirma- tive action" policy was an attempt to solve one of the problems that has long plagued PB programs: groups that face the highest obstacles to par- ticipation, such as the poorest of the poor, have very low levels of partic- ipation in PB programs.

However, São Paulo's new form of representation does not link the election of "socially vulnerable" PB delegates to the allocation of resources. During PB sessions, delegates and councilors negotiate and compete with other delegates for the provision of scarce resources. Since the percent- age of affirmative action delegates and councilors is low in relation to the vast majority who were elected through regional or thematic channels and, because of the extreme differences in their interests, individuals who represent these minority groups face tremendous difficulties in having their demands approved. The affirmative action representation has pro- vided individuals from these groups with access to decision-making ven- ues, but it has not provided any additional mechanisms to ensure that they receive resources.

Institutional Location of Decision Making

PB delegates and participating citizens were organized into thirty-one regions that corresponded to the *subprefeituras* (administrative districts, akin to boroughs, previously know as regional administrations).[18] Com- petition among citizens and groups participating in PB is at the sub- prefeitura level. Resources are divided among the different regions based on the logic of an "inversion of priorities." Poorer regions with more pre- carious infrastructure and higher population densities are allocated higher levels of resources than those of wealthier and less dense regions. Indi- viduals and groups compete against individuals and groups within their region, which is designed to dampen the impact that income and edu- cation have on the distribution of resources through PB.

The administrative support provided by each subprefeitura is crucial

18. Couto 1995.

to helping citizens and PB delegates understand the types of decisions they can make.[19] Since PB operates in a decentralized format, one of the principal challenges faced by PB administrators is coordinating policy and actions within each subprefeitura. Each subprefeitura has one PB administrator who manages the local PB projects. However, there are at least seven other political officials in the subprefeitura who are appointed by the mayoral administration. The PB administrator in each subprefeitura must compete with them for the scarce resources. Since the mayor did not strongly back PB, and many of her political appointees share her position, PB administrators were working with a bureaucracy that was largely uninterested in PB.

Since the subprefeituras have been the subject of intense political competition within the PT and among its allies, PB has became embroiled in basic political conflicts over the distribution of jobs, authority, and resources. São Paulo's PB is a participatory decision-making process grafted onto an existing political-spoils system, which limits PB's impact. São Paulo's PB does not represent a turning point in how public policies are debated and distributed, but serves instead to allow PT (in particular, the Socialist Democratic faction) to directly connect with interested citizens and CSOs leaders. The apparent disinterest of the mayoral administration to carve out political and policy-making independence for PB produced a participatory process that does not delegate decision-making authority to citizens and does not create a universal set of rules that guide how policies will be implemented.

Mayoral Support

PT candidate Marta Suplicy won the 2000 election in the second round of voting. She won 38 percent in the first round and then soundly defeated the PT's longtime rival, Paulo Maluf, in the second round, with 59 percent of the vote. Marta Suplicy's victory marked the return of the PT to the mayor's office. In 1988, the PT's Luiza Erundina was elected mayor with just 33 percent of the vote. Suplicy thus increased the PT's first-round vote share (38 percent in 2000 versus 33 percent in 1988), indicating that the PT had a slightly broader base of support in 2000 than it had enjoyed in 1988. However, the PT was still only the first preference for just more than a third of the electorate. In 1988, there was not a second

19. Ricci 2004.

round of voting, so we do not know if the voters' choice in a second round of voting would have been for Luiza Erundina. The PT could not govern just for its base (only 38 percent of the electorate) but would need to reach out to different sectors in order to increase its share of future votes, especially with the all-important presidential election coming in 2002.

Mayor Suplicy's government has been committed to the "reconstruction" of São Paulo, a pledge that did not initially place too much emphasis on participatory programs.[20] Suplicy's political trajectory, and her rise through the ranks of PT, did not occur through union or social movement sectors. And in Suplicy's administration, the core political group that surrounds her does not have deep ties to CSOs that were strongly supportive of participatory politics. Suplicy had few connections to São Paulo's participatory publics, the grouping of CSOs that are committed to using participatory processes within their internal organization as well as to promoting the direct inclusion of citizens in state-sanctioned policy-making venues.

PB delegates formally negotiated projects in 2001 worth U.S.$160 million; in 2002, U.S.$220 million; and in 2003, U.S.$233 million.[21] The absolute level of resources is quite high, indicating that PB has, at least on paper, the potential to be a strong new decision-making venue. However, a careful analysis of the 2003 and 2004 budgets reveals something quite different. For projects selected in 2002 to be implemented in 2003, U.S.$75 million, or 35 percent of the total PB budget, comprised projects that had been initiated by the upper echelons of government.[22] For projects selected in 2003 to be implemented in 2004, this figure increased to nearly 50 percent. The Department of Health was the worst violator, with 69 percent of health projects being programs that were initiated by the mayoral administration.[23]Thus, PB delegates were competing against one another to try to secure government-approved projects for implementation in their neighborhoods rather than selecting and defending their own projects. PB in São Paulo is best conceptualized as an institutionalized competition that allows citizens to vie for government-approved projects.

20. "90 dias de reconstrução," 2001.

21. "Orçamento Participativo," 2003, 169. This document represents the results of six months of negotiations in 2003. It shows that the budget proposal for 2004 was U.S.$233 million. However, in 2004, PB administrators claimed that PB delegates had selected more than U.S.$350 million worth of projects. The sharp increase is additional evidence of a high degree of informality in the PB process, since the new figures cited by the government were a 66 percent increase over what the delegates negotiated.

22. "Plano de Obras e serviços do Orçamento Participativo 2003," 2003.

23. "Plano de Obras e serviços do Orçamento Participativo 2003," 2003.

It did not become a decision-making body that allowed citizens to exercise voice and vote.

São Paulo's PB lacked mayoral support for the delegation of authority to citizens. PB was initiated by a minority faction within the PT, and PB never seriously challenged the basic decision-making processes that concentrate authority in the mayor's office. Mayor Suplicy used the traditional spoils system, which gives local political bosses (at the subprefeitura level) decision-making authority (more on this below), as the basis for her governing and campaign strategy. The expansion of "authority" within PB was part of a deliberate effort to co-opt the most active members of civil society and use their mobilization to legitimize the government's policy preferences. PB was forced into an existing decision- and policy-making process that was geared to the 2002 presidential election and Mayor Suplicy's 2004 reelection bid, rather than being developed as an independent space that could be used for overhauling basic decision-making processes.

Mayor Suplicy and the PT were unwilling to gamble her political future, or, for that matter, the party's political future, on the success of a municipal participatory institution. Suplicy did not use PB as a means to build a base of support among interested citizens. Rather, PB was used as a vehicle to allow interested citizens, many of whom were already sympathetic to the PT government, to direct resources within the government's chosen parameters. PB helped legitimate the government policies rather than serving as a political venue that might alter basic policy-making processes. One faction of the PT supported PB, but it was a minority group, which made it difficult for it to carve out the necessary support within the government.

Civil Society

São Paulo has a long history of cooperation and contentious forms of political organizing by CSOs, which helps to explain why CSOs and the government supported the implementation of PB.[24] During the 1940s and 1950s, Mayor Janio Quadros helped organize "Friends of the Neighborhood" associations, which linked middle- and working-class neighborhoods to his political machines. The relationship between the associations and politicians is best described as being based on accommodation and

24. Jacobi 1989; Dagnino 2002, 1998; Avritzer 2004.

clientelistic exchanges.[25] During the 1964–85 military government, many of these associations acted as intermediaries between their communities and members of the military government's official party, ARENA. Cooperation between the Friends organizations and the military government was quite strong.

Contentious forms of political behavior in São Paulo have their roots in the anarchist and labor movements of the 1910s and 1920s.[26] Italian immigrants employed in the rapidly expanding industrial center employed direct confrontation in their attempt to win wage and working-condition concessions from their employers. Strikes and other forms of collective action were used by labor unions in São Paulo during the New Republic, the 1946–64 democratic interregnum, and the 1964–85 military regime.

Contentious forms of political organizing were also present in neighborhood associations as groups that were marginalized used direct-action techniques to pressure government officials to attend to their demands.[27] However, police brutality and government oppression limited the willingness of CSOs to use direct action as a means to influence public opinion and government officials. During the military regime, São Paulo was the site of intense social movement activity. Starting in the 1970s, neighborhood associations broke free of the accommodation style of political organizing favored by the Friends of the Neighborhood associations and agitated the government for the provision of government services to areas that had an exploding population and limited provision of resources.[28]

São Paulo was a center of political mobilization that demanded direct elections for the office of the president (1984) and for the impeachment of President Fernando Collor de Mello (1991), based on allegations of widespread corruption and misuse of power. Public protests were more prevalent in the 1980s than they were in the 1990s or during Mayor Suplicy's term in office (2001–4). Even though there has been a decrease in the number and intensity of public demonstrations by CSOs in São Paulo since the end of the 1980s, many CSO leaders remain willing to directly confront government officials over broken promises, the lack of basic services, and the continued marginalization of large sectors of the population.

São Paulo has had fairly strong levels of participation in PB. In 2001,

25. Gohn 1995.
26. Wolfe 1993; French 1992.
27. Weffort 1984.
28. Jacobi 1989.

thirty-three thousand people participated. This increased to fifty-five thousand in 2002 and sixty-five thousand in 2003.[29] These figures are the highest of any of the municipalities included in this book, but São Paulo's large population (10 million residents) means that a relatively low percentage of citizens have actually participated—less than 1 percent. The government was able to attract mainly interested allies. Eighty percent of the survey respondents who had an identifiable political identification were on the left. In the meetings I attended, as well as in the focus groups that we conducted, there was a strong PT presence.

One of the PT's early bases of support in São Paulo was CSO activists.[30] Many government officials in charge of PB were drawn from the ranks of social movements, placing many of them in a strange bind. They encouraged cooperation with CSO leadership but also believed that direct confrontation and contentious politics were effective tools for CSOs. As government officials, they discouraged the use of contentious politics, often arguing that it was not appropriate to use these tactics in a polarized political environment. In São Paulo, CSOs and government officials had to strike a careful balance between contestation and cooperation. Contestation was recognized as a potential tool to gain the attention of Mayor Suplicy, but it was considered a risky strategy because too much contestation could embarrass her politically and decrease her already low levels of support for PB. Cooperation was therefore preferred by many PB delegates, as they supported her mayoral candidacy and sought to work with her to "reconstruct" São Paulo. Delegates expressed fear that cooperation could turn into a politics of accommodation, whereby the administration's interests supplanted their own, but there were few concrete steps taken by PB delegates to publicly contradict the government.

This tension is best illustrated by an exchange that occurred in a PB meeting on October 10, 2003. The PB administrator, Felix Sanchez, grew increasingly upset as PB council members leveled a series of complaints and accusations based on the government's weak support of PB. They were contesting his leadership and the PT government's commitment to participatory politics. Sanchez sharply rebuked the PB councilors' criticisms of PB, declaring that "no party has ever done more for São Paulo than the PT." Sanchez yelled and berated the PB councilors who "dared" to criticize the hard work of their team. It was a stunning outburst that indicated that

29. "Orçamento Participativo," 2003, 169.
30. Keck 1992; Jacobi 1989.

contentious politics within PB would not be tolerated. Cooperation was emphasized, which came to mean that the government dominated PB to the exclusion of citizen-participants.

What types of cooperation were emphasized? First, PB delegates have worked with PB administrators to expand the arenas in which PB operates. PB was initially limited to the policy areas of education and health care, but delegates and administrators created political alliances to pressure Mayor Suplicy to dedicate more resources and spending to PB.

Suplicy's government generally set the range of issues that could be debated, although PB delegates have occasionally pushed the government to consider other projects. The area of health care best illustrates how the government has helped to set the agenda. During negotiations in 2001, PB delegates prioritized the construction of new basic-health-care facilities and hospitals. The Family Health Program (Programa de Saúde Familiar, or PSF), a policy program advocated by the then secretary of health care, was included as one of four basic priorities. In 2002, delegates were told that the construction of basic-health-care facilities was no longer available for negotiation, but that the focus would be on the distribution of PSF teams among different regions as well as the reform of existing health care facilities.[31] This meant that the primary policies selected by PB delegates in 2002 were PSF teams. The government set clear boundaries on what project could be selected. During the 2003 negotiations, many delegates came prepared to work on the expansion of the PSF program. They were told by government officials that no new PSF teams could be selected. PB delegates were now instructed to focus on the reform of basic-health-care centers and the construction of emergency centers, ideas that came directly from Mayor Suplicy.[32] There was a strong backlash by the PB delegates. They applied intense political pressure on the secretary of health care to include an additional one hundred PSF teams to be allocated to the different regions (each team cost around U.S.$200,000 per year). This example illustrates that the PB delegates can force the government to make changes in the types of public policies that it wants to implement, but the types of changes are conditioned by the municipal administration. Unfortunately, the lack of transparent information, as produced by the government, made it impossible to know if these additional

31. Focus group, November 19, 2003, Perus district, São Paulo; delegate forum focus group, November 1, 2003, Capella de Soccorro, São Paulo; Eleine Cordeiro, municipal employee in health care and in charge of PB projects in health care, interview, October 13, 2003, São Paulo.

32. Gonzalo Vecina Neto, secretary of health, interview, December 14, 2003.

one hundred teams were actually funded. It is quite possible that they were included in the budget, but never funded. São Paulo's PB maintained an informal or nonstandardized form of moving projects from the drawing board to implementation. This made transparency virtually impossible, creating a weakened PB system. Citizens have to work throughout the year to ensure that the projects selected through PB are actually implemented.

The preceding example demonstrates that PB delegates have exerted some influence over the shape of public policies in São Paulo. Yet the space of decision-making authority has generally been restricted to policy arenas where the government wanted delegates to be engaged. Decision-making authority has been partially extended, as PB delegates helped decide when and where resources would be spent, but the process has been tightly controlled by government officials. The majority of PB projects from 2003 and 2004 were more closely identified with the government's initial reconstruction package than with the policy preferences expressed by PB delegates in 2001.

Mayoral-Legislative Relations

Mayor Luiza Erundina's (PT) administration (1989–92) sought to implement participatory decision-making bodies, but the government got bogged down in an internal dispute between issue- and territory-based participatory programs.[33] Even as the internal disputes within the PT government limited the impact of Erundina's participatory institutions, the acrimonious relationship between Mayor Erundina and the municipal council further undercut reform efforts.[34] Erundina's weak support—more than half of the legislative chambers were strongly opposed to her—contrasts with the 2001–4 legislative period under Mayor Suplicy. During Erundina's term, the PT controlled sixteen of fifty-five seats (29 percent), affiliated leftist parties held seven seats (13 percent), and centrist parties (PMDB, PL, and PDT) controlled an additional eleven (20 percent).[35]

Mayor Suplicy had a far more favorable political environment than did Mayor Erundina, with just more than 60 percent of the municipal council

33. Paulo Singer, professor at University of São Paolo and secretary of administration under Mayor Luiza Erundina, interview, May 30, 1997, São Paulo; Jacobi and Teixeira 1996; Wampler 2004c.

34. Couto 1995; Erundina 1990, 1991; Singer 1996; Kowarick and Singer 1993.

35. Tribunal Regional Eleitoral de São Paulo.

members being potential allies. Crafting a stable governing majority has never been easy in São Paulo because of the ideological divisions, the diversity of special interest groups, and the municipality's political importance on the national scene. To guarantee the support of a solid majority in the municipal legislature, Suplicy made use of the traditional spoils system, which former Mayor Erundina had rejected. The spoils system used in São Paulo is based on the unofficial annexing of regional administrations to politicians.[36] This system began in the 1950s when Mayor Janio Quadros responded to high population growth at the time by decentralizing the functions of the government. The intent was to allow decisions to be made locally. Of course, politicians affiliated with the government were in charge of local decisions, thereby undermining the rational administrative reasons for decentralizing service delivery and decision-making responsibility.

To maintain support in the municipal council, Suplicy allowed allied council members, state representatives, and even some federal deputies from São Paulo to name upward of seven political appointees in each of the thirty-one subprefeituras. This political strategy helped to ensure that the mayor would be able to pass her preferred legislation and her budgets while also avoiding the legislative investigations that had crippled the administration of her immediate predecessor, Mayor Celso Pitta.

A detailed analysis of the spoils system is not under review here, but the use of the system is important to understand because the PB program is administered within each subprefeitura.[37] Thus, the politician or political group that "controls" the subprefeitura has a tremendous influence on how the PB operates. If a PB-friendly politician controls the subprefeitura, there will be organizational and operational support to arrange the complex process, as well as a focus on the implementation of public works projects and services that have been selected through the PB process. If the politician does not support PB, there will be limited support (if not outright hostility), making it difficult for PB delegates to influence policy outcomes.

In a focus group in the Perus region, delegates complained bitterly that they were longtime supporters of the PT, but were treated shabbily by their local submayor, who was from the conservative Liberal Party (PL). As one delegate declared, "Our submayor is from the PL. He doesn't like

36. Couto 1995.
37. Couto 1995; Couto and Abrucio 1995.

us and he doesn't even return our phone calls because he simply doesn't want to. . . . Even though we supported Marta [Mayor Suplicy] and the PT, we are not welcome in our local government offices."[38] In the southern region of Capella de Socorro, PB delegates refused to work with the PT-appointed officials in reaction to allegations of corruption and misuse of power. The PB delegates were PT militants, but they were unwilling to allow PT government officials to attend any of the PB meetings. This shows a remarkable degree of independence asserted by these PB delegates, but it also made it unlikely that their projects would be implemented, because the PT-appointed officials did not appreciate having their authority challenged.

The use of the traditional spoils system promotes informality within PB and the bureaucracy. Reliance on the spoils system allows for short-term alliances, helping the mayor to secure a solid majority in the municipal council. This weakens the standardization of policy-making and administrative purposes, which are central components of successful PB programs. The standardization of policy processes refers to the negotiation process that leads up to the selection of a public works project *and* to the implementation of the public good. These processes are not standardized in São Paulo because there has been a wide variation in local politicians' interests related to how "their subprefeitura" should manage PB. One PB administrator claimed that it was necessary to maintain "flexibility" and "informality" in PB, as Brazilian politics has long been based on informal-exchange relationships.[39] This administrator's analysis of local politics suggests that the government was more interested in political expediency than in attempting to transform the local decision-making process. PB was initiated in 1989 as an attempt to end the informality that had long plagued Brazilian governments.

Since control of the subprefeituras represents an important political resource, many politicians are unwilling to delegate authority to citizens through PB. The lack of consistency has meant that groups more closely aligned with the government have had a distinct advantage over less organized or more politically distant groups. CSOs face clear dilemmas: they need to develop closer alliances with the government to increase the likelihood that their projects will be implemented, but this "cozying up" to the government limits their ability to use PB to hold the government

38. Focus group, November 19, 2003, Perus district, São Paulo.
39. Carlos Thadeu C. de Oliveira, PB administrator in São Paulo, November 27, 2003.

accountable. The desire to investigate (*fiscalizar*) governmental action in a rigorous way has been weakened as a result of the csos' need to work closely with the government to secure their preferred policy outcomes.

Financial Situation

São Paulo's financial situation was not very positive, another factor that weakened the overall impact of PB. Mayor Paulo Maluf, during his 1993–96 administration, incurred massive debts that severely limited his successor's administration (Celso Pitta, 1997–2000) as well as the administration of Marta Suplicy (2001–4). Suplicy attempted to address the issue of municipal solvency by raising taxes and limiting spending. She was able to pass several tax increases, but these steps undermined her popularity, and her political opponents found a label for her that stuck: Marta-taxa. The English equivalent would be Marta-tax, hardly a nickname that a candidate wants to take into a campaign.

The other route pursued by Mayor Suplicy was to decrease spending. This proved quite difficult for the government to tackle because one of its main bases of support was from municipal unions. The unions not only resisted trimming positions; they placed intense pressure on Suplicy to increase wages, which had eroded significantly during the previous two administrations. An additional pressure on Suplicy, limiting her ability to control spending, was the 2002 presidential election. Her administration was on display during the campaign, since the PT sought to use São Paulo to demonstrate that they could effectively administer a complex municipality.

The limited financial resources available in São Paulo were directed to programs other than PB. Suplicy's administration was not interested in investing scarce resources to help create a new decision-making venue that might or might not provide political dividends. Suplicy focused on the 2002 and 2004 elections, which ultimately meant that PB was drastically reduced in scope and importance.

Synthesizing the Results

São Paulo's PB was implemented by the PT in a polarized political environment during a tense political moment in which the PT needed to simultaneously "reconstruct" São Paulo and show that it could govern a complex city in an efficient manner. When the PT came to power in 2001, they not only needed to appeal to their traditional base (unions, social movements, progressive middle class), but also show that their governing strategies were viable. The PT and Mayor Marta Suplicy sought to strike a balance between the need to develop policies that would demonstrate their efficiency and the demands of their organized bases to "deliberate" over policies.

During the initial phase of PB, the policy-making arenas were narrow in focus because the government wanted to act quickly (something that complex policy-decision-making arenas do not allow for) and have PB delegates select projects that could be implemented in the short term in order to draw repeat participants. This latter concern is consistent with most research on PB and participatory programs: individuals will continue to participate and encourage their neighbors, friends, and family to participate if there is a specific benefit that will be achieved through participation.

Yet the types of policies debated each year shifted depending on the government's political and policy considerations rather than on the delegates' interests. Delegates needed to be able to correctly surmise the government's policy interests and then change their positions in order to more closely match the interests of the government. This suggests that Suplicy's administration sent signals to PB participants regarding what was feasible and politically desirable. The more astute leaders followed these signals and requested projects that corresponded with the government's interests. This, of course, suggests that São Paulo's PB was becoming a vehicle for co-optation: the government set the agenda and CSO leaders modified their own policy preferences to more closely match those of the government.

Yet it is important to bear in mind that PB occupied a much larger role in São Paulo's policy making in 2004 than in 2001. PB participants successfully pressured the government's *núcleo duro* (inner circle) to expand the influence that PB delegates would have on public policy outcomes. However, the government's use of the traditional spoils system demonstrates that PB participants had to compete against politicians and citizens who were using extrainstitutional means to secure resources, greatly restricting PB's broader impact on the decision-making process. PB did not transform São Paulo's decision-making process, but it provided an additional public space for contestation.

The initial foundations for the extension of citizenship rights were limited. PB administrators sought to empower participants by holding a series of workshops that would help to educate individuals about their rights and how the government works. For example, individuals identifying themselves as a member of a disadvantaged group had access to PB forums and workshops. The focus of these workshops was on the financial issues, the rights and responsibilities of citizens, and the PB process. Although these workshops were an important first step, the results were limited because there was a weak connection between participants' work within PB and the public policy outcomes. The process allowed individuals to learn about their rights and responsibilities as citizens but did not allow them to actually exercise these rights.

For individuals and groups actively engaged in politics, São Paulo's PB has been an ill-defined institutional venue. It has produced a form of "conceded citizenship" because the government set the conditions under which PB operated.[40] PB participants were able to use the decision-making process as a means to signal their policy preferences to the government. But this is a very stunted form of citizenship rights, since citizens do not actually exercise much decision-making authority.

Turning to vertical, horizontal, and societal accountability, we also see mixed results. When considering vertical accountability, citizens have been able to use PB's formal institutional structure to successfully change some government policies. PB has worked as a signaling device. However, vertical accountability has been ultimately quite restricted, as the signals being sent were confined to very specific policy-making areas. The government's upper echelon made broad policy decisions that established the general direction of policy; PB participants had the authority to decide where public works could be located, but they were unable to select policies beyond the mayor's preferences.

With regard to horizontal accountability, PB was inserted into an already existing decision-making process. PB did not develop into an independent and autonomous decision-making venue, but instead was forced to compete with existing methods of distributing resources. Perhaps more than anything else, it is this "add-on" approach rather than the creation of new programs and institutions that most sharply limited PB. PB is housed in São Paulo's subprefeitura system. Each subprefeitura has at least seven political appointees. By 2003, PB had one administrator (also a political appointee) in each subprefeitura, which often meant that the PB administrators and delegates were in direct competition with other political appointees for control of scarce resources.

40. Sales 1994.

Finally, was societal accountability established through PB? PB delegates used threats of contentious politics against Mayor Suplicy outside
PB and used direct contestation within PB meetings against the government to try to hold government officials accountable for their practices
and politics. The threat of their going public with their demands helped
hold government officials accountable, given the officials' worries about
the possible negative repercussions. However, this was largely an empty
threat; PB delegates were acutely aware of the larger political issues and
were unable to use their political positions to embarrass the incumbent
government. The 2002 and 2004 elections came up repeatedly during
focus groups and informal conversations, and many delegates expressed
the belief that they should not take actions that might be detrimental to
Mayor Suplicy. As one delegate stated, "Look, we think that PB is the best
thing that has happened to us. We can participate. We are learning how
to do this. But we must reelect Marta [Mayor Suplicy]. There are many
other programs that we would lose if she loses."[41] Delegates were unwilling to publicly pressure Mayor Suplicy in light of the potential negative
consequences, a situation that may have helped the mayor politically, but
also had the effect of weakening PB.

Societal accountability has also been limited because CSOs have been in
constant and direct competition for resources in an ever-changing policy-
making process. Intergroup alliances, vital to creating enough support to
publicly pressure a government, have been difficult to construct because
groups have been uncertain about how to pursue their interests. Political
uncertainties, combined with informality in the decision-making process,
made it very difficult for CSOs to develop a coherent strategy to pressure
the municipal government. It has been my experience, verified through
observation of participants rather than through survey research, that most
disgruntled activists simply left PB in order to work on other political and
policy projects rather than trying to devise political strategies that would
force Mayor Suplicy to fulfill the commitments made thrOugh PB.

Santo André

Santo André's PB program is often cited in the academic and policy literature as one of the most successful PB cases because of its commitment

---

41. PB delegate Fatima, from Capella de Soccoro, interview, November 11, 2003.

to public learning, empowerment, and the "co-administration" process.[42] Mayor Celso Daniel was instrumental in promoting PB nationally and internationally; his leadership and three terms as mayor helped draw researchers to Santo André. Santo André's PB has a municipal-wide PB council that divides representation between the government and citizens. Government officials hold half the seats and the other half are held by elected PB councilors. Its unique set of rules has encouraged intense debates and negotiations among government officials and delegates, but an unintended consequence was the emasculation of decision-making authority exercised by citizen-delegates. According to Teresa Santos, administrator of PB from 1989 to 1992, "The problem with the council was and still is the degree of preparation of citizens. Citizens don't have the skills to argue against the government."[43] This case demonstrates unequivocally that PB's rules do matter. In Santo André, the effort to create a "co-administration" process, based on shared power, had the unintended consequence of undermining citizens' capacity to carve out their own base of power from which they can direct and monitor governmental action. This section begins with the rules because they are sufficiently different from those of the other seven municipalities.

PB's Rules

Santo André's PB is divided into thirteen regions. In each, participants vote for policies that they would want to have implemented, but final decision making rests with the PB council. There has been no attempt to create a binding decision-making process that would give citizens authority at the local level. Each region elects two members to the council, which means that there is fierce competition among CSOs to secure these highly coveted spots. All elected delegates bring several priorities from their region to the PB council, where they negotiate with their fellow delegates and government officials over which projects will be included in the annual budget.

   The PB council includes fifty-two voting members—twenty-six citizen-delegates and twenty-six government officials. Although the goal of the PB council has been to help empower citizens, the rule structure has had a perverse effect. Why? First, only twenty-six citizens, out of more than

---

42. Pontual 2000; Teixeira and Albuquerque 2006.
43. Teresa Santos, interview, October 14, 2003.

ten thousand who participate annually, have any decision-making authority that directly translates into public policy outcomes. PB participants,
during regional meetings, do not decide which policies would actually be
implemented but rely on their elected PB councilors to negotiate deals
with government officials. Second, to approve a project, a two-thirds vote
of support in the PB council is necessary, meaning that delegates have to
convince at least half the government officials and all citizen-delegates
(or vice versa) to support their project. This sharply undercuts the independence that PB delegates enjoy elsewhere (especially Porto Alegre) and
increases the likelihood that the government can co-opt PB delegates.

Delegates and government officials are clearly aware of these problems.
In 2003, PB delegates were elected for the first time in an attempt to create a layer of local representatives who would be able to act as intermediaries between the PB council and local communities. These PB delegates
have been granted increased decision-making authority and monitoring
responsibilities, although they continue to be hamstrung by the PB council's active role in deciding which projects should be implemented.

Mayoral Support

Mayor Celso Daniel, elected in 1988, 1996, and 2000, was an early and
strong advocate of the direct participation of citizens in governmental
decision-making venues.[44] Under Daniel's leadership, the government
initiated participatory programs in 1989. The emphasis in Santo André
was on the creation of a public forum whereby community leaders and
government officials could discuss, deliberate, and negotiate public policies.[45] Empowering citizens and building democracy after twenty-one years
of military rule were two of Daniel's main goals.

Santo André's PB has had two distinct phases, marked by Mayor
Daniel's shifting emphasis on what PB could and should be. The first
phase existed from 1989 to 1992, when the process was explicitly "consultative," and the second was from 1997 to 2003, when the government
made a more conscious effort to delegate authority. Pedro Pontual, who
directed Santo André's PB from 1997 to 2001 and worked in the original
PB experience from 1989 to 1992, argued that the attempt to create a "consultative" PB (1989–92) was not very successful for several reasons. First,

44. Daniel 1994.
45. Daniel 1994.

because the process was specifically designed to be consultative, the mayoral administration was unwilling to hand decision-making authority over to citizens.[46] This again contrasts sharply with the Porto Alegre experience, in which the government decided that the key to its PB program was to hand authority over to its citizens.

Second, the government did not develop any internal mechanisms to respond to the large number of demands placed on them by participants. There was a high volume of demands, in part because participants had limited access to government officials during the military government.[47] As a consequence, according to Teresa Santos, who directed PB from 1989 to 1992, "Some of the department heads emphasized their own projects and did not implement the projects supported by the government."[48] There were no internal mechanisms that took PB projects from the selection stage to implementation.

Third, the government was unable to gain control over a recalcitrant bureaucracy because bureaucrats resisted efforts by the government to implement participatory processes.[49] "The bureaucracy resisted the program," according to former PB director Santos, which meant that the implementation of projects was an intense struggle between the elected government and the bureaucracy.[50] The bureaucracy resisted the new types of public works and the new procedures associated with PB. This was also a major problem in Belo Horizonte, Recife, and São Paulo. Only in Porto Alegre and Ipatinga were governments able to gain control over the bureaucracy, thereby suggesting the importance of internal reforms as a mechanisms to enhance the quality of the state.[51] It appears that PB's successful outcomes are strongly associated with internal government reforms initiated by interested governments.

Finally, the government lacked sufficient resources to dedicate to PB projects. The government had high debt payments and could not manage to pass any tax increases through the municipal legislature to generate additional revenues.[52] This limited the resources available to PB, which again sharply contrasts with the experiences of Porto Alegre and Ipatinga.

The PT's mayoral candidate lost in 1992, and PB did not function

46. Pontual 2000, 141.
47. Pontual 2000, 141.
48. Santos, interview, October 14, 2003.
49. Pontual 2000, 142.
50. Santos, interview.
51. Fedozzi 1998.
52. Pontual 2000, 143.

between 1993 and 1996. (Daniel could not run in 1992 because, before 2000, mayors were not permitted to run for reelection.) When Celso Daniel was again elected mayor in 1996, he reinitiated PB. There was an explicit effort to change PB from a consultative process to a process "that would guarantee the implementation of public projects selected during budgetary deliberation," as Pontual points out.[53] The government drew from Porto Alegre's experience to create a PB process that would enable the government to more systematically implement the policies selected by participants. To this end, the government created a distinct administrative unit that would manage PB; this unit was in charge of organizing participation and ensuring that projects selected by each region were brought to the PB council. The government also created thematic forums to complement the regional districts.

However, the government also established a parallel participatory process, Future City (Cidade Futura), designed as a deliberative forum that would bring a wide range of interest groups together to develop a long-term plan for Santo André's future. The government created Future City as a mechanism to induce business leaders into a deliberative forum. PB was therefore pigeonholed to focus on smaller projects that were of immediate concern to community activists. Decisions in PB were on a "second order" scale, which emasculated the delegates' authority. Decisions about major investment projects were made in Future City or by the mayor, leaving PB participants to negotiate over only small-scale projects.

The government dedicated low levels of resources to PB. According to official publications and government officials, roughly 50 percent of investment spending was open for debate by PB delegates; the government argued that it needed to have control over the other 50 percent to implement larger-scale projects.[54] However, the absolute level of resources that delegates negotiated over was static while investment spending increased each year.[55] In other words, the amount of resources available to PB was constant, while the overall budget increased, thereby incrementally decreasing the relative and absolute impact of PB on public policies from 1997 to 2003.

The government continued to have extreme difficulties implementing projects that were selected, largely as a result of the government's inability

53. Pontual 2000, 160.
54. Pedro Pontual, interview, September 3, 2003.
55. "Retratos da cidade," 2000; "Você Participa, A Cidade Melhora," 2003; *Balanço Geral de Prefeitura Municipal de Santo André* (1994–2004).

to create internal mechanisms and the bureaucracy's continued intransigence. Pedro Pontual, who directed PB from 1997 to 2002, conceded that "after a project was approved by the PB council and entered the budget, we didn't really follow it anymore. We didn't really understand how a public policy was developed and implemented."[56] In the evaluation of one delegate, "The government did not produce relevant information to make decisions, which undermined confidence in the government. . . . PB was used as a space where the government could have more power, and to create a well-known leadership that had direct access to the government."[57]

A study published in 2000 found that few projects had been implemented in Santo André. The study found that only 10 percent of the projects selected in 1997 had been completed by August 1999 and only 5 percent of the projects selected in 1998 had been implemented at all.[58] A survey conducted by Venturi among PB participants found that their most significant complaint concerned the government's inability to fulfill its promises to implement projects selected through PB.[59] It is notable that our research team was unable to verify the number of projects that the government had actually implemented. It is our experience that the lack of transparent information is a strong indication that little was actually being accomplished.

Mayoral support for PB in Santo André was contradictory. The government invested heavily in mobilizing citizens and engaging in public learning. Pontual argued that there was a "maturing of the government's team and the community leaders with respect to the process."[60] In the most positive evaluations of PB, the focus of the analysis is on the positive steps taken by the government to promote public learning, empowerment, and citizenship. The downside in Santo André is that the government was never able to systematically translate the selected projects into actual public works. Santo André's PB is much better characterized as a "public learning" process rather than as an institutional space that has transformed decision-making processes.

Why was Mayor Daniel unable or unwilling to delegate authority? First, the rules structure produced an unintended consequence, which had the effect of sharply limiting authority. CSOs and government were brought

56. Pontual, interview.
57. Pontual 2000, 175–76.
58. Felgueiras and Carvalho 2000, 60–61.
59. Venturi 1999.
60. Pontual 2000, 236.

together to "co-administer" PB, but this had the effect of allowing PB to be a vehicle for the co-optation of CSO activists. Second, the government enjoyed a strong base of support among a dense network of CSOs, which meant that the PT did not need to use PB as a means to expand the party's support by incorporating previously marginalized groups. Finally, although Mayor Daniel was an early advocate for participatory democracy, the demands of the PT in 1997 were different from those of 1989. By 1997, Mayor Daniel was the most important PT mayor in the state of São Paulo, so the PT needed to use Santo André as a base of support for the 1998 and 2000 elections. Even though Daniel may have been ideologically committed to PB, there were election issues that he and the PT had to confront if they were ever to expand the PT's influence over Brazil.

Civil Society

Santo André has a long history of union activity and civil society contestation, both of which aided in the election of the PT and the establishment of PB. Santo André was "the birthplace of heavy industrialization in the 1950s and the independent union movements during the 1970s and 1980s."[61] During the 1930s and 1940s, Santo André's growth as an industrial center allowed for a wide expansion of union activity. In a 1947 election, the mayor and 40 percent of the city council members came from the Communist Party, although none were allowed to take office.[62] During the 1964–85 military regime, Santo André emerged as one of the centers of strike activity, and the PT was founded in the industrial belt that included Santo André.

Complementing union activity, CSOs developed as legitimate and forceful political actors. According to Mayor Daniel, "Politically and socially, the region has a tradition of contestation by collective organizations such as social movements, religious groups, civil society organizations, etc., which seek to improve the quality of life for the population. Local governments always have to confront these organizations during the daily tasks of managing the municipality."[63] On Santo André's border is São Paulo's famed eastern region, which had a strong expansion of civil society mobilization during the 1970s and 1980s.[64] The PT's base of support

61. Daniel 2003.
62. Pontual 2000, 127.
63. Daniel 2003, 157.
64. Jacobi 1989.

was initially founded on unions and social movements, both of which were strong in Santo André.

The PT had an alliance with CSOS and unions; thus Mayor Celso Daniel could count on these groups' cooperation with his administration. CSO activists were fundamental to the building of the PT, a process that required seemingly endless meetings and mobilizations to refine party positions and attract potential supporters. The social movements and unions associated with the PT in Santo André engaged in contentious forms of political organizing during the 1970s and 1980s, throughout the struggle to end the military regime and establish democratic rule. Leaders and their followers were therefore able to draw on contentious forms of politics when it was deemed necessary to directly confront employers and governments.

Although these preconditions boded well for Santo André's PB, because participants were likely to work with government officials when necessary and also directly confront them when required, there was an even more important force present: building the PT in the hopes of expanding the electoral chances of the party in municipal, state, and federal elections. According to one PB councilor, "The situation was very favorable for the government because the PB participants were organized by PT legislators or because they were progressive and had a specific project to promote."[65] Cooperation was emphasized by CSOS and government officials in the hopes of building a larger political movement that would allow them to fulfill the PT's basic goals of social justice and an inversion of priorities.

Citizen participation in PB has been fairly strong in Santo André. From 1997 through 1999, an average of eight thousand citizens participated in PB's second round.[66] From 2000 to 2002, mobilization levels averaged more than ten thousand a year.[67] Santo André had the highest level of partisan political identification, 92 percent, suggesting that participants had a strong affinity for the government and the PT.[68] Santo André's citizens continued to participate in a context of limited authority, as they were politically and ideologically predisposed to support the government's political initiatives. Citizens had direct access to government officials through

65. Pontual 2000, 172.
66. Pontual 2000, 181; Felgueiras and Carvalho 2000, 26; "As prioridades para 1999," 1999.
67. "A população como parceira," 2003.
68. PB Comparative Survey.

participation in PB, which constituted an important access point, since the process of implementing public works continues to be a nonstandardized process that suffers from opacity.

In Santo André, PB has operated as a political incorporation process through which the PT has been able to build and solidify its base of support. CSOs have rarely engaged in contentious behavior against the government; disagreements were worked out within the PB council and have not spilled out into the larger political environment. This is not to assert that major disagreements are unknown. PB delegates and participants have intensely deliberated over how to best manage PB, but their time and efforts have not resulted in the delegation of specific authority.

Mayoral-Legislative Relations

Of all the municipalities included in this study, the PT has had the strongest electoral support in Santo André, which, ironically, has both hindered and aided the development and functioning of PB. Mayor Celso Daniel, first elected in 1988, was again elected in 1996 and 2000 in the first round of voting, with 62 percent and 70 percent of the vote, respectively.[69] The political Left, Daniel's allies, controlled 45 percent of the seats in the city council. The strong electoral support enabled Daniel and the PT to use Santo André as an example of how the PT could manage change and promote economic redevelopment. The broad support for the PT and Mayor Daniel provided the mayor with a considerable degree of flexibility because he did not have to engage in extensive horse-trading to pass his legislative projects in the municipal legislature. The mayor had strong support in his efforts to establish innovative policies, which could have strengthened PB, but the mayor chose to implement a wide range of policies instead of deepening this particular participatory experience. PB was one of myriad social policy initiatives that the government implemented, rather than being the primary policy and political objective of the government.[70] This contrasts sharply with Porto Alegre, where PB became the primary policy and political innovation of the PT government. This is not to make the argument that Mayor Daniel should have invested his political resources in solely PB, but the point is that a multifaceted reform project takes away energy, time, and resources that might otherwise have

69. See Tribunal Supremo Eleitoral de São Paulo.
70. Daniel 2003, 171–76.

been invested in PB. In contrast, the government in Porto Alegre invested heavily in PB, to the near exclusion of other policy and social reform projects. Thus Santo André offers a clear juxtaposition to Porto Alegre, where the government has supported PB to the detriment of other participatory institutions.

The broad electoral support for the PT in Santo André, however, also partially accounts for why so little authority has actually been delegated. In 1997 Daniel did not have to start from scratch to build a loyal following among organized and active sectors of civil society because these groups were already active members of the PT coalition. Santo André's CSOs were more strongly controlled by the government than CSOs in Porto Alegre, Recife, and Belo Horizonte. PB delegates in Porto Alegre were organized at the neighborhood level, had specific sets of demands that could be directly entered in PB debates, and were willing to use contentious politics against the government. In Santo André, citizens were organized in unions, there was a strong ideological and partisan component to this organization process, and the PT strongly discouraged the use of contentious politics. Mayor Daniel emphasized the "co-administration" process, which gave the most active CSO participants access to government-sponsored decision-making venues. Comparative research demonstrates that the institutional design selected for Santo André's PB had the unintended consequence of never forcing the mayor to actually delegate any authority.

Financial Situation

Santo André's financial situation is similar to São Paulo's. The government in Santo André has access to low levels of resources. There were strong demands on the budget from unions, and the percentage of resources dedicated to general maintenance and upkeep was high. Again, this does give some support to a supply-side argument. Santo André had to confront a decaying infrastructure, while also needing to provide upkeep to keep businesses in the community. Raising additional revenue through property tax increases was unlikely because many private companies had already threatened to exit Santo André unless a more attractive business climate was established.

Synthesizing the Results

Santo André's PB enjoyed only limited success during its eleven years, which is somewhat surprising given the strong emphasis on public learning, direct participation, and co-administration. The PT, which implemented PB in Santo André, has had the highest levels of electoral support of any government among the eight municipalities included in this study, which should have given the government the opportunity to delegate higher levels of authority to citizens. What, then, explains its shortcomings? The answer is weak mayoral support for the delegation of decision-making authority, a rules structure that has not favored direct delegation, the political necessity of using the government of Santo André to help build the PT and, finally, the limited success of the government to dedicate the necessary funds and administrative efforts to implement PB projects.

In terms of extending citizenship, the emphasis on public learning and empowerment have been the strongest points of the program. When PB was administered by Pedro Pontual (1997–2001) the emphasis was on public learning, citizenship empowerment, and co-administration. The government provided information to participants, thus creating more knowledgeable citizens who could engage in public policy debates. From the vantage point of citizenship rights, Santo André's PB appears to have initiated a key first step: providing citizens with the tools to actively engage in policy-making debates. Workshop sessions focused extensively on the rights provided to individuals under the 1988 Constitution.[71] Yet the unwillingness of the Daniel administration to delegate authority limited the types of decisions that the citizens could make. In other words, citizens have been instructed about how to make decisions, but the government does not actually allow them to make many meaningful decisions, resulting in an empty form of empowerment.

Turning to the axes of vertical, horizontal, and societal accountability, Santo André presents mixed results. Small groups of elected citizens can place issues on the public agenda and can stymie governmental projects. Thus, PB has contributed, somewhat, to the extension of vertical accountability. Thirty-four percent of the survey respondents believe that they "always" or "almost always" are able to stop government-sponsored projects. The strength and weakness of Santo André's PB is, in many ways, best illustrated in this finding. Thirty-four percent is low compared with Porto Alegre (64 percent), but it is high in comparison with low-performing PB programs in Blumenau and Rio Claro (20 percent and 3 percent, respectively). The survey respondents indicate that citizens can occasionally promote their own issues and block the prerogatives of the government.

71. Pontual 2000.

Horizontal accountability, the capacity of one institutional body to place checks on another branch of government, has been weakly extended in Santo André through PB. Of all the cases, this is where it could have been highest because of Santo André's PB council. There is a simple reason: insufficient authority has been delegated to PB to alter the political calculations of the mayoral administration or the municipal legislature. Since there has been only limited delegation of authority, municipal legislators are not threatened, as the traditional practices have not been replaced. Furthermore, the PT and the political Left control a near majority of seats in the municipal legislature, which means that leftist legislators use constituency service and direct access to the mayoral administration to build their careers, manage their campaigns, and mobilize voters.

It is in the area of societal accountability that Santo André's PB demonstrates the strongest advances. Through PB, participants have been able to gather information, debate public policies, and initiate a process of gaining access to rights guaranteed to them under the 1988 Constitution. Societal accountability is based on the idea that citizens should act in a collective manner to bring attention to their problems and concerns. PB's meetings and workshops have provided numerous opportunities for citizens to draw attention to their community's most pressing needs as well as to the government's unresponsiveness to basic problems. Contentious debates within PB were common, indicating that PB reflected the ongoing political tradition of Santo André. Rather than "reinventing" the decision-making process, PB served as a means with which to draw interested citizens (often government partisans) into a formal, government-sponsored project.[72] PB extended the number of citizens and the locations where citizens could attempt to hold their government accountable.

Even though Santo André's PB is often lauded, especially in the context of single-case-study analysis, comparative analysis demonstrates the program's fundamental weaknesses. The government has been unwilling to delegate decision-making authority to citizens, which led to a series of cascading negative effects. Despite the tremendous efforts of the personnel associated with Santo André's PB, the program never gained traction because the government's emphasis on a co-administration process allowed the government to dominate citizens rather than permitting citizens to exercise decision-making authority that would lead the government to implement project outcomes.

---

72. Daniel 2003; Pontual 2000.

Conclusions

São Paulo and Santo André's PB programs have underperformed because citizens have been unable to make decisions that translate into specific policy outcomes. PB has, instead, developed as a public space for cooperation and deliberation, thereby allowing government officials to interact with CSO activists and politically engaged citizens. Citizens and government officials work together, but largely on the terms set by government officials. In neither municipality has PB developed into a new decision-making venue that challenges existing forms of distributing resources and power. In short, PB has been incorporated into the municipal government's governing and electoral strategies rather than being a direct challenge to the personalism, clientelism, and informality that condition so much of Brazilian public life. Mayor Suplicy in São Paulo and Mayor Daniel in Santo André did not delegate authority to PB participants, choosing instead to centralize authority to implement different projects.

If little decision-making authority has been devolved, are there any positive aspects? In both cases, the PB administrators have gone to great lengths to hold informational and public learning sessions that have contributed to the knowledge of the participants. The emphasis on public learning can potentially deepen the capacity of citizens to understand how to obtain rights and contribute to policy-making processes. Although this could help "empower" citizens, this empowerment is ultimately enfeebled by the inability of the government to fulfill its publicly stated commitment to implementing the public works projects selected through PB.

The PB programs in São Paulo and Santo André illustrate the central role that the mayoral administration must play in PB programs. In both programs, PB developed into a signaling mechanism through which CSO activists and government officials communicate their political and policy preferences. In both PB programs, the CSO activists had a strong leftist identification, which meant that PB allowed government leaders direct access for individuals who would serve as their base of support during election campaigns. Of course, if the PB programs failed miserably, there is always the possibility that these CSO activists will exit the PT and align themselves with other political parties. To date, this has not happened. The most plausible explanation is that CSO activists do not have another party to which they can migrate. This suggests that the PT leadership is aware that they can be slow to respond to the demands of PB participants because most of the PB participants would not throw their support behind rival parties.

For São Paulo and Santo André, we can assert that formal citizenship rights and accountability were weakly extended as a result of the governments' refusal to give citizens a more active role. The formal trappings of strong participatory institutions are present but the government leaders have been unwilling to gamble their political futures on the decisions made by citizens in PB.

7

Belo Horizonte and Recife:
Contentious Politics and Mayoral Shifts

> We are going to fight against the mayor, but not to
> the point that the government doesn't implement
> our public works project. . . . Today, the PT govern-
> ment believes that it can create the best PB pro-
> gram. We are not going to ask that they do so. We
> are going to demand our rights.
> —PB DELEGATE IN BELO HORIZONTE

> When we were elected, we wanted to break the
> associative tradition that induced CSO leaders to be
> the political operatives of [former mayor] Jarbas.
> —JOÃO COSTA, PB ADMINISTRATOR AND PT
>   OFFICIAL IN RECIFE

> PB is a good program. It is not a bad program,
> although it is being poorly administered. If it were
> well administered, we would have all our approved
> projects already completed. I feel that the key strat-
> egy for us is to unify different community to approve
> our projects.
> —PB DELEGATE IN BELO HORIZONTE

Contestation and Cooperation in Recife

On January 21, 1999, a group of CSO activists and local citizens converged
on Entra Pulsa, a small favela bordering Recife's largest shopping mall,
to hold a public demonstration that would eventually block lunchtime
traffic around the mall. The activists were trying to draw attention to the
municipal government's inability to implement PB projects that would
substantially upgrade the community's infrastructure. Entra Pulsa had
only several thousand residents, so the ability of the demonstrators to
turn out several hundred residents on a weekday morning indicated
strong organization (and high unemployment) within and outside the

community. The residents were located in a geographically strategic position, the southern edge of their neighborhood butting up against one of three feeder roads that led to the shopping mall and their western edge bordering a main avenue that ran parallel to the famous Boa Viagem beach avenue. To draw attention to their plight, the activists sought to shut down the shopping mall road, with this to be followed by an incursion into the principal avenue. The demonstration began just before noon and the hope was that it would block the main avenue for the better part of the lunch rush.

The activists successfully blocked the feeder road initially by force of numbers and then through setting up burning tires that prevented cars from passing. The demonstrators were then able to close off the main avenue, snarling traffic. The protestors were met by a police task force that sought to remove them from the street. The police did not act hastily, which gave the protesters time to enter into contact with the mayor's office to set up a meeting. The protestors held the road and the avenue for nearly an hour before an agreement was reached to hold a meeting between the protest organizers and the mayor. Recife's activists used contentious, extrainstitutional means to try to force the government to adhere to PB's basic rules. This event encapsulates both the strength and the weakness of Recife's PB: Activists were able and willing to engage in direct action, which embarrassed the government because the CSOs publicly demonstrated that the government was unable to honor its political and legal commitments. In response to these embarrassing allegations, the government agreed to fast-track the activists' public works projects, thereby undermining the standardization of practices that PB administrators were trying to implement.

Captured Audience in Belo Horizonte

On Saturday, March 21, 2004, Belo Horizonte held its annual opening rally to mark the beginning of that year's PB. The rally was held in a public theater downtown and was packed with hundreds of delegates, participants, and interested citizens. The event opened with a rousing speech from a woman who had been elected as a PB delegate several times. She extolled the virtues of the PB, claiming that there was not a better program in Brazil. She also presented testimony on the virtues of the government officials, who, she claimed, shepherded the process so well each year.

The woman identified herself as one of Belo Horizonte's poor, asserting that PB had given her the power to help transform her community and city. It was a captivating and stirring speech.

The PT mayor followed. Mayor Fernando Pimental began by recognizing all the elected officials in attendance, primarily municipal legislators but also several state legislators. The mayor then quickly mentioned the white elephant in the room: his reelection campaign. It was surprising that he addressed this issue at the beginning of his talk because most governments that administer PB make an effort to argue that PB's successes are based on the strength of the participants and not related to the electoral interests of the incumbent party. Pimental spent much of his thirty-minute speech arguing that the PT was the only political party capable of administering PB "the way that it deserves to be administered." This was a clear reference to the claims of the mayor's opponents (Brazilian Social Democracy Party [Partido da Social-Democracia Brasileira, or PSDB], Brazilian Democratic Movement Party [Partido do Movimento Democrático Brasileiro, or PMDB]) that they would continue to administer PB the same way that the PT/Socialist Party of Brazil (Partido Socialista Brasileiro, or PSB) coalition had done for eleven years. PB had become a standard part of the policy-making process in Belo Horizonte, so electoral dispute was over who best could manage it.

As Mayor Pimental closed his remarks, he began to talk of PB as a *festa* (party), as a *festa de alegria* (joyful party) and as a *festa de participação* (participation party). The mayor was attempting to create an imagined public sphere where people enjoyed themselves, where they were happy to spend their free time. His comment stood out because the previous day I had been interviewing PB delegates who referred to PB as a *luta* (struggle, fight), as a luta to organize themselves, as a luta to compete against other groups, as a luta to try to get basic infrastructure (such as sewage). It struck me that although government officials and some delegates would talk about PB as a festa in public formats, I never heard PB participants describe PB this way during formal or informal interviews or conversations. The government officials sought to use PB as a springboard from which they would run their reelection campaign, which they won, while CSOs sought to use PB as a means to transform their community. Many PB delegates were frustrated by the overtly political tone of the meeting, but they had limited venues in which they could vent their frustrations.

PB in Recife and Belo Horizonte

Recife and Belo Horizonte's PB programs partially delegate decision-making authority to citizens while also enabling citizens to partially hold government officials accountable for their actions. These programs are more successful than those of São Paulo and Santo André, but fall far short of the results produced in Porto Alegre and Ipatinga. Different political parties have administered Recife's and Belo Horizonte's PB programs, which demonstrates the impact of mayoral administrations on PB programs. Recife's mayors have had the greatest range of political and ideological variation. The mayor who implemented PB was a charismatic leader from the catchall PMDB, who was succeeded by a dry, reserved technocrat from the conservative PFL, who was succeed by a charismatic leader from the leftist PT. In Belo Horizonte, there has been a narrower range of differences between mayors: PB was implemented by a PT mayor and later administered by the PSB and a second PT mayor. The PSB and the PT, while affiliated parties, have different bases of leadership and membership that influenced how PB was administered in Belo Horizonte.

Political strategies of contestation and cooperation were both present in Recife and Belo Horizonte. Cooperation was present because each mayor's office worked closely with CSOs to establish these new institutions. The mayoral administrations that have governed PB in Recife (with one exception) and Belo Horizonte sought to forge close alliances with CSO activists and PB participants, which helps explain their interests in delegating some authority directly to citizens.

Contentious politics never replaced cooperation, but it was used by activists, participants, and CSOs as a political strategy with which to pressure government officials. Contentious politics played a stronger role in PB in Recife and Belo Horizonte than in either São Paulo or Santo André, helping to explain why stronger results were produced in Recife and Belo Horizonte. Contentious politics was also stronger in Recife and Belo Horizonte than in Porto Alegre and Ipatinga because CSO activists had to devise strategies to pressure government officials as a result of the unwillingness of the Recife and Belo Horizonte governments to delegate authority directly to citizens. Contentious politics has been an effective strategy for CSO activists in Recife and Belo Horizonte, helping them to achieve some of their goals, as government officials were partially committed to making PB a viable decision-making venue. Yet the use of contentious politics also had a perverse effect in Recife and Belo Horizonte, since it undermined efforts to create standardized, internal processes through which PB projects could be implemented. In short, contentious politics helped to make PB programs relevant, but it also undercut key aspects of this new participatory type.

Basic Demographic and Political Characteristics

Belo Horizonte and Recife are, respectively, the third- and fourth-largest metropolitan areas in Brazil. Belo Horizonte is substantially wealthier than Recife; the former has a long-standing role as a center of agricultural, industrial, and commercial activity. Recife is an important regional hub in the northeast, but poverty is widespread and economic activity is limited.

Despite Belo Horizonte being a relatively wealthy city, there are few resources available for spending on new capital projects. A key reason for this is that successive mayoral administrations have invested heavily in social programs (such as Bolsa Escola and Programa da Saúde da Família) that have taken a significant share of available resources. This limits the decision-making authority of PB delegates, forced to negotiate over an ever-shrinking piece of the budget. Recife's low levels of spending on new capital investment projects reflect low revenues and high poverty in the municipality; the government must spend a considerable share of its resources on social programs to address the dire poverty faced by a significant portion of the population.

Table 24. Demographic and Political Profile

	Belo Horizonte	Recife
Residents in 2000	2,200,000	1,400,000
Human Development Index, 2000	0.839	0.797
Per capita monthly income, 2000	U.S.$135	U.S.$100
Municipal government's investment spending per capita, average, 2001–2002	U.S.$14	U.S.$12
% of mayor's vote in 1996 municipal election (first round)	41	51
% of mayor's vote in 2000 municipal election (first round)	43.5	36
Average % of leftist seats in city council, 1997–2004	34	18

Sources: www.ibge.gov.br, www.undp.org, www.stn.fazenda.gov.br. www.tse.gov.br.

Politically, the PT and the political Left in Belo Horizonte enjoy broad, though not majority, levels of electoral support. This strong plurality gives the PT and its ally, the PSB, some flexibility to experiment with different types of social and political programs. Electoral support for the Left is not quite as strong as in Santo André, Porto Alegre, and Ipatinga, so that Belo Horizonte's mayors must spend additional time and resources on creating coalitions with centrists and catchall parties. The coalition between the PT and the PSB has become the principal political force in Belo Horizonte, although it has never achieved any sort of hegemonic status. The PMDB and the PSDB, which are the PT's main political rivals, are competitive parties in Belo Horizonte, placing pressure on PT and PSB mayors to negotiate with these parties' legislators and to reach out to their bases of support. In 2002, when the PSB supported Rio de Janeiro's former governor Antonio Garotinho as a presidential candidate, Celio Castro left the PSB and affiliated with the PT. Therefore, although Castro was not a member of the PT, he was closer to them ideologically and politically than he was to the populist-nationalist Garotinho.

Recife's electoral and political life revolved, during the 1980s and 1990s, around Jarbas Vasconcelos, a charismatic politician who began his political career in the MDB, briefly migrated to the PSB, and then became the leader of Recife's PMDB. Vasconcelos's political positions shifted; once a radical democrat, he became a centrist politician who was willing to enter into political alliances with conservative groups. He forged a political alliance in 1996 with the conservative PFL, helping the PFL's Roberto Magalhães to be elected mayor in 1996. In return, the party helped elect Vasconcelos as governor in 1998 and 2002. The PT won the mayor's office in 2000, but it has always been a minority party. Political life in Recife has been dominated largely by centrist and catchall political parties, although the PT's capture of the mayor's office temporarily shifted the balance of municipal power.

Survey Evidence

The survey respondents in Recife and Belo Horizonte are representative of each municipality's lower classes. In Recife, 90 percent of the respondents live in households that earn less than U.S.$400 per month, and more than half the respondents in both municipalities have less than a high school education. The level of civil society participation of the delegates, however, is quite high. In this way they are not representative of the population, being engaged in CSOs at such a high rate.

In both municipalities, a large majority of respondents reported that their neighborhood had received a direct benefit from PB. This is lower than in Porto Alegre or Ipatinga, but higher than in the other four municipalities. The per capita spending is low in Recife and Belo Horizonte, but the PB programs had been in place ten and eleven years, respectively, at the time of the survey, giving the government sufficient time to implement a large number of PB-selected works throughout each municipality.

The respondents in both municipalities believe that they have the authority to be involved in decision making. This perception starts to drop dramatically when the type of authority begins to place delegates in direct competition with government officials. Less than a quarter believe that PB can be used to block governmental initiatives, suggesting that delegates

Table 25. Profile of Survey Respondents (%)

	Belo Horizonte	Recife
Household income of U.S.$400 or less per month	61	90
Less than high school diploma	51	53
Women respondents	48	55
Currently active in associational life	89	72
Current leadership position in community association (of those currently active)	63	55
Delegates elected 3 or more times	47	13
Delegates received a direct benefit from PB	79	79

Source: PB Comparative Study.

Table 26. Delegates' Perceptions of Their Authority to Make Decisions (% Stating Always or Almost Always)

	Belo Horizonte	Recife
Authority to make PB rules	51	54
Authority to define PB priorities	54	53
Authority to define projects	55	47
Authority to add resources	21	28
Authority to stop government projects	23	25
Authority to monitor government projects	71	52
Secured projects outside PB	43	38

Source: PB Comparative Study.

perceive that although they have been given specific types of authority, their votes are limited to what government officials want them to decide.

When assessing their authority to monitor government projects, the delegates' responses show wide differences in attitude. More than half of Recife's delegates believe they have the ability to monitor governmental actions, which places Recife squarely in the middle of the responses for the eight municipalities. In Belo Horizonte, nearly three-quarters of the delegates declare that they have the power to monitor governmental action through PB, the second-highest percentage of all eight municipalities (trailing only Porto Alegre). Belo Horizonte's institutional design best explains this high percentage. In Belo Horizonte, each region is subdivided into districts, all of which have a Monitoring and Oversight Committee. After a project enters into the budget, the municipal bureaucrats, private contractors, or both draw up plans for the proposed project. The district committee must then approve the plan. During the implementation phase, PB delegates monitor the construction. This can be an unwieldy process, especially if a cranky delegate tries to become too involved in project administration. However, interviews with administrators and delegates, combined with participant observation, indicate that committees introduce additional "sets of eyes" into the process, thereby reducing the likelihood of corruption. When projects are completed, the committee meets again to vote on whether the specifications of the projects have been met satisfactorily.

The percentage of PB delegates who responded that they have successfully secured public works outside PB is among the lowest of the eight municipalities. Although there is still a strong plurality, 43 percent for Belo Horizonte and 38 percent for Recife, most PB delegates are working through PB as their preferred institutional channel. This perception falls in line with other types of evidence (implementation records, budgets), suggesting that PB has become a fairly important place for making decisions.

In this chapter, I explain why Recife's and Belo Horizonte's PB programs have been only moderately successful. Their respective PB programs demonstrate better results than those of São Paulo, Santo André, Blumenau, and Rio Claro, but they do not quite measure up to Porto Alegre or Ipatinga. Through an examination of mayoral support, civil society activity, mayoral-legislative relations, PB's rules, and each municipality's financial situation, this analysis will shed light on these mixed success cases. Variation in mayoral support, from one administration to the next, provides additional support for the argument that mayors and government officials' strategies and interests are at the heart of understanding PB's successes and failures. This, in turn, suggests that PB is not an independent "direct democracy" institution, but one that involves a heightened level of interaction between government officials and participants.

Recife

The outcomes produced by Recife's PB are strongly conditioned by the city's history of CSOs' use of contentious politics, intense cooperation between CSOs and government officials, and strong party competition. Recife's PB is distinct from the other seven cases analyzed because three mayoral administrations, each with widely different political bases and policy-making agendas, have administered PB. The first two mayors who governed Recife's PB, Jarbas Vasconcelos (1993–96) and Roberto Magalhães (1997–2000), used a model that limited direct participation to elected representatives, which numbered between three hundred and five hundred delegates. This sharply limited deliberation and demand-making because it largely restricted participation to CSO leaders and discouraged ordinary citizens from participating. As one PB delegate stated in 2003, "During this period, you were elected with only one vote. The *donos* of the associations were elected with only one vote. I thought that it was absurd. Although I was the president of our local association at the time, I refused to be elected to PB under those conditions."[1] In 2001, Mayor João Paulo changed the basic set of rules to make PB a "mass-oriented" process, thereby allowing the election of upward of six thousand delegates a year. This exponential increase in delegates greatly expanded access opportunities, but PB suffered from the lack of clear organization when the surge of demands overwhelmed the administrative capacities of the municipal government.

The shift in strategy from one mayoral administration to the next helps demonstrate the ways that mayoral support affects PB outcomes. In particular, this case demonstrates how the connections between mayoral administrations and CSOs affect how participants are brought into contact with government officials.

---

1. Buzinha, PB delegate and community leader, focus group interview, December 10, 2003.

PB History

Recife's PB program was initiated in 1995 but had its roots in a program developed by Vasconcelos during his first term as mayor (1985–88). Vasconcelos initiated the Mayor's Neighborhood Program (Programa de Prefeitura nos Barrios, or PPB), a policy program that served as a direct link between the mayor's office and community leaders. This program increased the participation of community leaders in the selection of priorities for implementing small infrastructure public works projects.[2] Vasconcelos attracted a loyal following of community leaders and activists after he established direct lines of communication between his administration and these community leaders.[3]

The two principal characteristics of PPB that directly relate to the founding of PB are the direct contact between the administration and community leaders and the organization of the program around specific demands. First, under PPB, Mayor Vasconcelos attended hundreds of meetings in which community leaders presented their demands. He also opened the mayor's office every Friday afternoon to community leaders and the general public, thus earning the reputation of being an open and democratic mayor. PPB was a ground-breaking participatory program in the mid- to late 1980s because of the intense commitment of the Vasconcelos administration to work with the poorer sectors of the population in addressing their needs.

Second, the PPB established a system in which leaders were encouraged to present, and ultimately were rewarded for presenting, specific and immediate demands, such as the need for paving a specific street, cleaning a particular canal, or installing lighting in underserviced areas. The structure of the PPB thus encouraged community leaders to present concrete demands to resolve immediate and specific problems. Simultaneously, it directed these leaders away from a broader discussion of the administration's overall budget priorities; community leaders were encouraged to act principally on behalf of their local environment. In sum,

2. Soares 1998, 1996.
3. During his first administration, Jarbas secured the approval of legislation that legalized the Special Planning Zones of Recife (Plano de Regularização de Zonas Especiais de Interesse Social, or PREZEIS), a participatory program that established specific rights and responsibilities for elected representatives of low-income areas. It is beyond the scope of this chapter to analyze PREZEIS, but it is crucial to point out that PREZEIS is a formal, legalized institution that is beyond the direct control of the mayor's office. See Marinho and Botler 1998; Soler 1991; Fontes 1997; Wampler 1999.

PPB was an institution that captured the demands of community leaders without transferring any authority to them. PPB did not transform decision-making processes in Recife, but it gave the government direct access to the most active CSO leaders.

In 1994 several of Recife's government officials traveled to Porto Alegre to learn from their innovative PB program.[4] Recife's PB was formally initiated in 1995 by Mayor Vasconcelos. The Vasconcelos administration sought to move beyond PPB's "demand presentation" system and implement a PB model that enabled community leaders to present and vote on specific demands as well as discuss the overarching budget priorities of the administration. The goals of the program were clearly stated in the administration's initial publications: "Participatory planning should not be limited just to the formulation and implementation of public policies but, above all, should seek to advance broad and global priorities in order to escape clientelistic ties that mark the participation of community organizations."[5] PB delegates were included in multiple decision-making venues and had authority to influence the general priorities of the administration. Yet the number of PB delegates was limited. Just 320 delegates were allowed to exercise vote during decision-making meetings, an indication that this is a limited political institution. Half these delegates were appointed by CSOs that registered with the government, and the other half were elected in open meetings.[6] Ordinary citizen-participants did not have a direct vote for policies because the vote was restricted to PB delegates. PB delegates were an intermediary between government officials and their communities. This had the effect of granting legitimacy to the community leaders while simultaneously limiting the number of citizens who could have access to the mayoral administration. The administration was thus able to screen out the demands of nonelected CSO leaders.

The amount of resources available for negotiation within Recife's PB was decided in a somewhat haphazard fashion. The amount available for negotiation within PB was established by the secretary of social policy with no input from PB delegates.[7] Department heads who participated in the Mayor's Neighborhood Program (PPB) were asked to estimate the amount

4. Chico de Assis, secretary of social policy for Recife (1997–99), interview, September 8, 1998; Salvador Soler, secretary of social policy for Recife (1993–96), interview, October 6, 1998.
5. "Orçamento Participativo: Metodologia," 1995, 5.
6. "Orçamento Participativo," 1996, 18.
7. Soler, interview.

of resources they had dedicated to the PPB.[8] The averaged response was 10 percent of the administration's new capital spending. The administration thus decided to allow the PB delegates to negotiate projects equal to 10 percent of the funding available for new capital spending projects for the 1996 fiscal year. In 1996, the total proposed budget for Recife was U.S.$558 million and the proposed spending on new capital investments was U.S.$144.45 million (25 percent of the total). The amount of resources thus available for negotiation for the PB delegates was U.S.$14.4 million, or 2.5 percent of the total proposed budget.[9] Under this scheme, PB was only given a small slice of the municipality's budget, suggesting that the mayoral administration was not particularly interested in delegating authority or creating participatory processes.

Under Mayor Magalhães (1997–2000), PB's rules changed. Most important, the electoral system was modified to expand representation and directly include the population in the electoral process. The number of elected delegates increased to 470 from 320. The number of those directly elected by the general public increased to 273 (58 percent of total elected), and the number of delegates elected by registered community organizations decreased to 197 (42 percent of total elected). The first election under these new rules was held in 1998, drawing nearly thirty thousand voters to the polls.[10] The relatively high turnout enabled the administration to publicize its projects and aided in the establishment of legitimacy for CSO leaders within and outside PB. The direct elections had the effect of allowing the new mayoral administration to identify new CSOs and to confirm the strength of existing ones. The ballot box system of electing members placed an emphasis on competition.

The second important modification was the introduction of meetings organized under the rubric of Year-End Report of Activities (Prestação de Contas) in 1997. During November and December 1997 in each region this series of meetings took place in which all participating agencies reported their PB-related activities. The introduction of these meetings was intended to facilitate the ability of the delegates to exercise their right of social control and fiscalization of the program. The meetings were marked by contentious demands from the delegates regarding what was not done

8. The agencies participating in the program include the Departments of Culture, Education, Health Care, Tourism and Development and the city-owned companies responsible for maintenance and infrastructure.
9. "Orçamento Participativo: Plano de investimento regionalizado 1996," 1996, 4.
10. "Fique de Olho," 1998.

and explanations from the participating department heads. These meetings were, by no means, easy for the administration. Delegates were extremely critical of the two administrations' lack of support and failure to implement projects that had been negotiated by the delegates.

Mayoral Support

Mayors Jarbas Vasconcelos, Roberto Magalhães, and João Paulo Lima established a distinct relationship to PB and its delegates. Vasconcelos initiated PB in 1995, impelled by his deep political, moral, and ideological commitment to incorporating Recife's CSO community into government. During the late 1970s, under the military dictatorship, the local Catholic Church sponsored the Commission for Peace and Justice, which worked with the opposition party MDB and local CSOs to craft a moral and legal argument for the legalization of properties in favelas and for the direct participation of citizens in public policy-making venues. Vasconcelos was the local leader of the opposition party, the MDB, at this time.

When Vasconcelos was elected mayor for a second time in 1993, he reinitiated PPB and went on to found PB in 1995. PB was designed to overcome PPB's obvious weaknesses (no elections, no votes on projects, piecemeal approach to policy making). Vasconcelos specifically sought to increase the direct involvement of PB delegates in decision making. He placed great importance on participatory processes, putting them at the center of his administration. However, through his agreeing to limit PB funding to 10 percent of new capital investments (or 1.0 to 1.5 percent of the entire budget), Vasconcelos's strategic choices undermined PB. By allowing citizens to make budgetary decisions but then denying adequate levels of funding, Vasconcelos's policies ensured that PB would have a minimal impact. Although Vasconcelos was formally committed to PB, the rules structure sharply curtailed direct citizen involvement in decision making, and the allocation of low levels of resources did not allow PB to flourish.

The close relationship between Vasconcelos and CSOs remained strong throughout the 1990s and the first five years of the twenty-first century, while Vasconcelos was in his second term as governor of the state of Pernambuco. Vasconcelos, first as mayor and later as governor, was commonly perceived by many CSO activists with whom I spoke as "having done more for Recife than anyone else."[11] Vasconcelos's willingness to

---

11. Tres Carnerios, focus group, December 10, 2003, Recife.

debate and work with csos was a strong part of his draw. csos were able to cooperate with him, but they were still willing to engage in acts of contentious politics against him. Rather than isolating groups that engaged in contentious politics, Vasconcelos chose to negotiate with dissident groups.

Roberto Magalhães was elected mayor of Recife in 1996 with the support of a broad-based center-right coalition and the outgoing Mayor Vasconcelos. Magalhães had been Pernambuco's governor under the military dictatorship and was part of the "modern" wing of the PFL, a conservative political party.[12] His mayoral campaign stressed the modernization of Recife and, importantly, the continuation of projects initiated under Vasconcelos. Magalhães's campaign promises were important for cso leaders, since the previous PFL administration of Joaquim Francisco (1989–91) had deactivated all participatory channels.

Magalhães assumed control of PB, which his political alliance with Vasconcelos obligated him to maintain. Although Magalhães maintained PB, it gradually lost the power and influence that had been established under Vasconcelos. Magalhães maintained the formal structure of PB but limited the resources negotiated and had a poor track record of implementation. In 1996, Vasconcelos's last year in office, 84 percent of PB projects were funded. From 1997 through 1999, only 18.3 percent of PB projects were implemented.[13] This dramatic drop indicates that Mayor Magalhães did not support the delegation of authority. This also meant that the Year-End meetings focused more on the failures of the government than on what had been achieved. Even though PB was extremely limited under Magalhães, perhaps the most positive aspect was the forced interaction between two political groups that traditionally had very little contact with each other. cso activists debated with political appointees from a conservative party (PFL), thereby helping to open up political and policy dialogue between disparate groups.

In 2000, Magalhães ran for reelection. In the first round of the election, he won 48 percent of the vote, far ahead of the second-place finisher, João Paulo Lima of the PT (36 percent) but just short of the 50 percent plus one vote required for victory during the first round of voting. In the second round of voting, Lima came from behind and won unexpectedly.

---

12. For an excellent discussion of the modernization of the PFL's leaders during the 1970s and 1980s, see Araújo 1996. The majority of the important political leaders in the PFL were also members of ARENA, the military's political party during the 1970s.

13. "Quardo da Relação entre o previsto e o executado pela URB/PCR no Orçamento Participativo," 2000, 1.

Although there is no available poll data on how and why people voted, anecdotal evidence gathered in 2003 indicated that many CSO activists loyal to Vasconcelos (elected governor in 1998) abandoned Magalhães and worked on behalf of João Paulo. They refused to support Magalhães because of his lack of support for participatory programs.

Once in office, Mayor João Paulo Lima (2001–4) sought to shake up access to PB decision-making venues by changing the electoral process. The most important rule change concerned the election of PB delegates. The number of delegates elected would be based on the number of citizens mobilized, which is the case in Porto Alegre, but with one key difference. In Porto Alegre, as the number of participants in a regional meeting increased, from one hundred to one thousand, there are higher thresholds for electing the number of delegates (see Chapter 2). In Recife, for every ten citizens attending a particular meeting, there would be one delegate elected. In 2002, for example, more than sixty thousand citizens participated, which meant that more than six thousand delegates were selected. Therefore, Recife's PB went from a cso-leader-dominated process to a mass-based process because of this key rule change. The immediate effect was a sharp decline in the quality of deliberations because many people included in the process had low levels of knowledge about complicated policy-making processes.

Second, the process of introducing projects by PB delegates was modified. The demand-making process would now allow citizens to present a specific project during the first meeting of the yearlong cycle. The purpose was to break the stranglehold that Recife's civil society leaders had on the PB process. This rule change would allow ordinary citizens (that is, nonleaders) to engage in an unprecedented activity: discussing and promoting their preferred policy in a formal, public arena. This potentially would have had a major effect on empowerment-related issues, since citizens would no longer be dependent on their local community leaders for representation. But there were two drawbacks to this new system. citizens did not have sufficient information about the costs of their proposed projects or the likelihood that projects would be implemented if selected; and the government was unable to clearly explain which projects would be entered into the budget, which meant that citizens were under the mistaken impression that their projects, once selected, would be implemented, when this was not necessarily the case.

The third important change under Mayor Lima was a rapid and substantial increase in the number of meetings. The government made an effort to meet with each community or neighborhood association that registered at one of the meetings. More than five hundred meetings were organized by government officials in 2003 with individual community and neighborhood associations so officials could clarify and explain the purpose of PB, as well as listen to the demands of these associations.[14] This was part of the broader attempt to break the hold of traditional CSOs, but it was also a method of deepening the new participants' information on, and knowledge about, municipal policy making. This time-consuming effort was part of a broader education campaign in which the government sought to educate citizens on the government's responsibilities and limitations. It was an effort to enable new groups to signal their preferences, allowing them to bypass traditional leaders.

What explains the variation in mayoral support? The clearest answer to this question lies in the realm of party politics and the personal relationship that each mayor had with Recife's "participatory" CSOs. Mayor Vasconcelos was from the catchall P.MDB, and he had strong, close ties to CSOs that demanded direct access. Members of the PMDB did not necessarily promote direct decision-making, but they did not oppose it, because of the strong interest of Vasconcelos. PB was designed in Recife to reward CSO leaders affiliated with Vasconcelos; PB provided Vasconcelos with an opportunity to expand his base of political support among CSOs.

Magalhães is a member of the conservative PFL, which is not a strong advocate of direct citizen participation in decision-making venues. Magalhães committed his administration to continuing PB because of the PMDB-PFL political alliance that was established to help elect Magalhães as mayor and Vasconcelos as governor of Pernambuco. Little in Magalhães's political trajectory suggests that he would be a supporter of PB. Therefore, PB continued during Magalhães's four years in office, but with lackluster support, which meant that little real authority was given to PB delegates. PB was maintained to keep an electoral agreement in place, rather than because it was an institution that could actually challenge long-standing political practices.

Finally, Mayor João Paulo (PT) placed his political future in PB by seeking to make it a vibrant space for policy making. This interest stems from his desire to replicate what other PT governments had accomplished with PB, but it was also part of a specific effort to build a new base of support

14. There were an additional 150 official PB meetings. "Número de reuniões da Secretaria do Orçamento Participativo e Gestão Cidadã," 2003.

for the PT among Recife's CSOs. PB became the means through which Mayor João Paulo sought to break the close relationship between CSOs and Vasconcelos. PB is now a site of significant political contestation because Recife's leading political parties and CSOs now believe that PB is a legitimate venue for giving citizens and CSOs voice and vote in policy making.

Civil Society

Contestation, mobilization, and electoral successes by leftist political parties and affiliated CSOs mark the post–World War II political history of Recife. The Frente de Recife (Front for Recife) united the Communist and Socialist Parties and dominated the political scene during the late 1950s and the 1960s.[15] The Frente de Recife won three consecutive elections for the mayor of Recife: 1955, 1959, and 1963. The Frente de Recife also won the governor's office in 1958 and 1962 as a result of their electoral strength in Recife. Governor Miguel Arraes of the Frente de Recife was one of only two governors to actively resist the military coup in 1964. Arraes was forced into exile by the military government, where he remained until 1979 when political amnesty allowed him to return to Brazil. Recife can be characterized as having a strong leftist political tradition, based on the electoral successes of leftist parties over a fifty-year period.

During the 1970s, when Communist and Socialist parties were banned and their members actively persecuted, support for political organizing was provided by the Archdiocese of Recife and Olinda. A progressive archbishop provided the moral and logistical support to found the Commission for Justice and Peace (Comissão de Justiça e Paz, or CJP). The CJP played a crucial role in organizing the demands of Recife's poor and disenfranchised by helping to select the appropriate form of legal or political action. The CJP represented many of the basic ideals of liberation theology and thus aided communities in their search for moral justifications for their demands.[16]

The peak mobilization period for CSOs in Recife took place during the late 1970s and early 1980s. Nearly 80 percent of the neighborhood associations that formally registered did so between 1978 and 1982.[17] Although individual neighborhood associations took on different institutional shapes,

15. Soares 1982, 1998, 1996.
16. Soler 1991.
17. Silva, Amorim, and Montenegro 1988.

there can be little doubt that marginalized populations crafted creative institutional designs to overcome problems of representation and participation. One of the most frequent institutional types created was the Council of Neighbors (Conselho de Moradores), which was often considered to be the "representative body of the community."[18] These councils and similar associational types worked on behalf of the interests of the community. Council members were elected by community members, decreasing the likelihood of corruption and backroom political deals. Transparency, openness, and internal democracy were central tenets of the councils as a means to prevent clientelism.

The leaders of the community organizations received the support of the CJP to develop political, legal, and moral claims to their land. One of the most important outcomes of the exchange between community leaders and the progressive clergy was the rearticulation of rights as a result of arguing that housing and land titles fall under the rubric of "the right to have rights." Recife's shortage of decent housing and infrastructure was the material basis for this reconceptualization. The rise and dissemination of new political and social rights appears to have been an outgrowth of progressive liberation theology and the abysmal living conditions faced by the majority of the population.

Contentious politics, competition between political parties and politicians for the support of CSOs, and low levels of citizen "preparation" defined how PB affected and was affected by civil society. Recife's CSOs have long used contentious politics, largely as a means to break the stranglehold that small groups of elite politicians (coroneis) have enjoyed over the political process. Although contentious politics has been a hallmark, so, too, has been the use of cordiality, which emphasizes private political agreements to avoid direct confrontation.[19] Even though cooperation has been stressed, there have been sufficiently high levels of competition between political parties so that no single faction has been able to dominate the political system.

CSOs, especially those willing to engage in contentious politics, did not easily give their support to Magalhães when he campaigned for the mayor's office in 1996.[20] This support had to be negotiated by then-mayor Vasconcelos. During the 1996 mayoral campaign, CSO activists worked on the campaign of Magalhães, which was rather ironic, considering that

18. Moura 1990, 40.
19. Buarque de Holanda 1936.
20. Barbosa 2003.

Magalhães had been appointed governor by the military regime and many of the csos had been formed explicitly to oppose the military's policies. Vasconcelos helped to create this political coalition because Magalhães's party, the PFL, would in turn support Vasconcelos's gubernatorial run in 1998.

Magalhães's relationship with Vasconcelos's base of support was tense because Magalhães was a technocrat unskilled at working with Recife's popular classes. Movement leaders with whom I spoke did not necessarily have high expectations for Magalhães's government. His performance, however, disappointed even the least hopeful. Magalhães systematically underfunded participatory programs and gave csos very little of his political attention.

Upon entering office in 2001, Mayor João Paulo sought to break the stranglehold he believed had been placed on PB through the restrictive participation rules (see previous subsection for a description of the rule changes). João Costa, PB's head administrator, argued that the majority of elected PB delegates were allied with Jarbas Vasconcelos when the PT took over in 2001. Costa stated, "When we were elected, we wanted to break the associative tradition that induced cso leaders to be the political operatives of Jarbas [Vasconcelos]."[21] The government therefore sought to create a rapid expansion of participation in order to create a new base of support.

The expansion of participation under Mayor Lima gave new csos, citizen-participants in existing csos, and ordinary citizens the right to deliberate over public policies. As one delegate stated, "I did not participate in the previous PB programs because it always seemed too difficult and too far away from me. . . . But in João Paulo's [Lima's] administration, PB came to us and I dove in to try something new."[22] The rapid expansion of participation created opportunities for new types of demands to be presented, debated, and eventually voted on, but it also created tremendous problems for the administration of PB. The new system allowed all participants to enter their specific demands in the first round of meeting. The proposed projects were initially ranked, but these decisions were not binding because there would be two additional votes (one regional and one municipal-wide) before final budgetary decisions were made.

The benefit of this approach was to allow citizens to directly affect the

21. João Costa, interview, December 9, 2003; "Orçamento Participativo: 3 anos invertendo prioridades," 2003.

22. Tres Carnerios, focus group, December 10, 2003, Recife.

decision-making process by forcing all participants to consider the proposals of their fellow citizens. João Costa, the PB administrator, argued
that this process would "allow participants to break the tradition of intermediaries, who had become the 'owners' of PB."[23] The creation of a new
deliberative space was seconded by one delegate, who argued that PB "is
a space where we can compete as equals; before only the educated, the
politically connected had a say. . . . With PB, it is people from the hum-
ble class that have the same opportunity to bring a public work to their
community."[24] However, the new process generated considerable problems because it was not clear to the delegates how projects would actually be included in the budget. Another PB delegate, Monica, stated, "I
have gone to many, many meetings that were confusing, never arriving
anywhere. The level [quality] of participation was low. . . . I think that people are still learning how to participate."[25] Elizabeth noted, "If someone
selected a public work and it is not done, then the people stop going,
which is very dangerous. It is for this reason that we work hard trying to
force the mayor to do more, because if they open a space and then don't
deliver, people will be disillusioned."[26]

A prevailing attitude among the participants was that PB was a space
in which they could fight for their political rights and interests, reflecting
Mayor Lima's and other PT officials' language regarding how political
change would occur. Costa, the PB administrator, argues that "political
contestation" must occur within PB because marginalized groups need
to directly confront others. Behind this argument rests the government's
interest in having its disputes with CSOs worked out within the confines
of PB rather than spilling over into public demonstrations. The government actually encouraged heightened contestation, but this support only
extended to confrontation within PB's institutional spaces.

"While we work hard to ensure that we can debate and discuss the
issues," PB delegate Neta argues, "we also work with the government, because we want to see improvements in our community. Because of this,
I spend all of my time working on behalf of my community. Every day I
go to the municipal administration, to workshops, to wherever is needed
in order to get some improvements for my community."[27] Monica asserts,

---

23. Costa, interview.
24. Elizabeth, focus group, December 4, 2003, Recife.
25. Monica, focus group, December 4, 2004, Recife.
26. Elizabeth, focus group.
27. Neta, focus group, December 4, 2003, Recife.

"In order to improve our community, we can't depend on a politician or a party. No, we have to depend on ourselves and constantly fight for some way to improve our community."[28] Although Monica and her colleagues seek to improve their communities, they are working with political leaders who are interested in governing and running for reelection. PB is part of Recife's political and decision-making processes, because each successive mayor has sought to alter the rules and access points to best help his governing and election strategies. Although CSO leaders may choose to be independent from politicians and political parties, PB is inserted directly between government officials and CSO activists, which then induces CSO leaders to act as intermediaries between government officials and citizens.

Mayoral-Legislative Relations

During the 1990s, two parties dominated political life in Recife, the centrist, catchall PMDB and the conservative PFL. For most of the 1990s, the PT was weak; however, it would win the mayor's office in 2000. Although initially there was conflict between the PMDB and the PFL, the rivalry dissipated and the parties' leaders converged during the 1994–96 period to form a stable electoral coalition. Vasconcelos's initial political base lay in the opposition civil society that formed during the 1980s, but his base of support shifted toward the middle and business classes during the 1990s, which drew him more strongly toward PFL voters.

The coalition led by the PFL campaigned and governed through traditional politics. The PFL won mayoral elections in 1988 and 1996. The PFL and the PMDB executives did not face great opposition in the legislature. It should be noted that Recife's legislature is noteworthy for the high number of centrists, mainly nonideological politicians who occupy a middle ground in hopes of receiving targeted goods.

Table 27 shows the distribution of seats in Recife during the four legislative periods (1989–92, 1993–96, 1997–2000, and 2001–4).[29] What stands out is the number of legislators elected from centrists and parties with ideological backgrounds similar to that of the executive's party for the first three periods. This suggests that most legislators would be likely

28. Monica, focus group.
29. The number of seats was calculated at the time of the election and does not take into consideration legislators' exit from city council or their replacements. It also does not consider the movement from one political party to another.

236 Participatory Budgeting in Brazil

to support the various executives' governing projects, to align themselves within the executive administration, and to not make use of their monitoring powers.

Table 27 demonstrates that the first three legislatures were predominately aligned with the mayor. Mayor João Paulo (2001–4) had a much smaller base of support. During Mayor Magalhães's last month in office, December 2000, his political supporters were sufficiently worried about the potential of PB's occupying an expanded role under incoming Mayor João Paulo that they passed legislation to limit PB's possible impact. Specifically, Recife's municipal legislature passed legislation that would give legislators the right to decide where 10 percent of the new capital investment resources would be spent. This would prevent Mayor João Paulo from following Porto Alegre's PB program, where 100 percent of new capital investment spending goes to PB. This municipal law was clearly in violation of Federal Law 4.320 (1964), which regulates how municipalities can legislate budgetary issues. Since the law was clearly unconstitutional, we can interpret this legislation as part of an effort to send a warning to the incoming mayor: make sure that municipal legislators have access to small projects or we will undermine your government. PB has not been codified in law, but Recife's principal political actors now recognize that it is an integral part of policy making.

Mayoral-legislative relations were more difficult under Mayor João Paulo for several basic reasons. First, Mayor João Paulo had weak support in the legislature. Second, centrist legislators could turn to Governor Vasconcelos for resources and campaign support rather than having to rely on Mayor Paulo. Centrist and opposition legislators could block the mayor's

Table 27. Composition of Recife's City Council

	1989	1993	1997	2001
Number in mayor's party	9	9	6	5
Number with similar ideology	8	7	17	3
Centrists	11	18	8	18
Opposition	5	7	10	15
Total	33	41	41	41

Source: www.tse.gov.br.

Note: For a description of the party coalitions, see Wampler 2000b.

initiatives because their political careers were not dependent on him. Third, Mayor João Paulo sought to fortify the participatory structures that could conceivably undermine the clientelistic and pork-barrel strategies used by many legislators. Finally, Mayor João Paulo was a political outsider, representing a wing of the PT that was dedicated to dramatically overhauling how government works at the municipal level. Mayor João Paulo's administration antagonized the legislative branch in 2001 by supporting a march by PB delegates to the municipal legislative chambers, where the protestors actively denounced the municipal legislators. "The PB administrators, together with popular movements, decided to directly confront the legislators. There was a march to the municipal legislature, where there was the symbolic burying of legislators and direct conflict with the municipal police."[30] This public demonstration antagonized centrist legislators and did not result in the ending of legislators' interference in PB.

Mayors Vasconcelos and Magalhães had generally positive relations with the municipal legislature, which did not detract from the mayors' ability to delegate authority to PB, if they had so chosen. Their refusal to delegate meaningful levels of authority is therefore not based on the intransigence of municipal legislators, but on their own political and policy preferences. Mayor João Paulo's experience is substantially different. He had few natural allies in the municipal legislative chambers, and he was forced to distribute pork barrel projects to obtain majority support for his budget. Mayor João Paulo initially used direct confrontation, antagonizing legislators and increased his governing difficulties. However, unlike São Paulo's legislators under Mayor Luiza Erundina (1989–92), Recife's legislators did not undermine Mayor João Paulo. Rather, they were willing to accept partial side payments, which allowed PB to continue to function while also helping them during their election campaigns.[31]

Financial Situation

Recife's financial and administrative situation, in comparison with those of Belo Horizonte, São Paulo, and Santo André, is moderately weak and is much weaker than Porto Alegre's or Ipatinga's. Recife's budget allows for only U.S.$12 of investment spending per capita. The lack of resources

---

30. Silva 2003, 31.
31. Chico de Assis, secretary of social policy for Recife (1997–99), interview, September 8, 1998; João Costa, interview, December 9, 2003; Liberato Costa (PMDB), January 20, 1999.

in Recife is compounded by high levels of need. Recife has a decrepit infrastructure, widespread poverty, and little economic production. In Belo Horizonte, São Paulo, and Santo André, there are large sections of the middle class that do not rely on the municipal government for services, using instead private education; private health care; and, often, private security. Recife's middle class is smaller and relies on the municipal government to provide some of these services, which increases the burden on the government.

Recife's bureaucracy can be described as inefficient and rather uninterested in working with the new participatory institutions. Since Mayors Vasconcelos and Magalhães dedicated just 10 percent of the budgeted investment spending to PB, there were no clear incentives for bureaucrats to alter their internal procedures. Under Mayor João Paulo, the increase in resources that could be negotiated by PB delegates and the mayor's decisions to focus, first and foremost, on implementing projects selected through PB will likely change the bureaucracy's focus. However, at the time of this writing, two years into João Paulo's first term, there have been few discernible changes in how the bureaucracy addresses PB projects.[32]

The weakness of Recife's financial situation is a significant factor in why its PB program is weak. Recife's PB illustrates that even when mayoral administrations and CSOs are interested in deepening democracy through PB, a lack of funds makes this particularly difficult. Although participation has increased under Mayor João Paulo, it is not likely to be sustainable if the government is unable to secure additional resources to implement PB projects. As demonstrated in Chapter 3, PB delegates are more likely to hold positive relationship with PB if they are able to secure basic public works projects for their communities. If Recife's track record of implementation does not improve, it is quite probable that people will be embittered by the process and simply exit PB.

Synthesizing the Results

Recife's PB program has produced mediocre results with regard to the delegation of authority because the successive governments have been unable or unwilling to implement the projects selected by PB delegates.[33] In 1998/1999, I spent six months in Recife, during which time I carefully

32. João Costa, interview, December 9, 2003.
33. Wampler 2004b.

documented what the government had actually implemented since PB began in 1994. I returned to Recife again in 2000 and 2003 to collect additional data. Mayor Vasconcelos implemented a series of PB projects, but Magalhães implemented relatively few projects. When João Paulo was elected in 2000, his administration began by implementing PB projects left by Magalhães. Although there were considerable efforts made to put these projects in place, they were hampered by the lack of resources. The inability to implement projects means that citizens have very little decision-making authority. In the best-case scenario, PB continues to be a demand entry system whereby delegates express their preferences to the government. At worst, it suggests that citizens are dedicating considerable time and energy to a policy-making process that does not affect how the policy outcomes are produced by the government.

The government's inability to make PB an important decision-making venue has undermined efforts to extend citizenship rights. Citizens have had limited decision-making authority, and as a result there have been few new political or social rights established through PB. From 1995 through 2000 PB allowed already active CSOs to formally act as intermediaries between members of the CSOs and the government. PB helped to create a new venue for deliberation, but only among a select few. Recife's PB has not promoted "the right to have rights," but rather has promoted the ability of the most active CSO leaders to become the official representatives of their communities in a government-sponsored venue as well as the official representatives of the government in their respective communities. A controlled, top-down process has done little to promote citizenship among ordinary citizens. The explosion in participation, with more than sixty thousand participants in 2001 and 2003, indicates that there is a vast pool of citizens interested in participating, but at the time this research project was completed, it was still too early to know whether the new PB format would expand rights.

Recife's PB has helped to foster electoral accountability, although not necessarily in a fashion that has always benefited the incumbent party. Vasconcelos was able to help elect his successor, Magalhães. When Magalhães ran for reelection, even though he was the heavy favorite, he lost to João Paulo partly because CSOs did not rally behind Magalhães. There was a widespread perception that Magalhães had invested very little time, energy, or resources into Recife's participatory programs, thereby allowing João Paulo to campaign as the champion of participatory programs. The 2000 election did not hinge on PB, but it was a contributing factor.

Vertical accountability, the ability of citizens to make decisions, has been weakly extended. Citizens, to date, have been unable to make many decisions that direct the government to act. PB delegates select policies but government officials then use an unclear system to decide which policies will be implemented. The lack of clarity in the implementation process, combined with low numbers of projects being implemented, now means that citizens' voice and vote in PB has rather feeble foundations.

PB now occupies an institutional space that mayors and legislators must include in their general policy-making process, which suggests that the foundations for horizontal accountability are being established. However, horizontal accountability has not been extended to the sphere of implementation, since governments have been unable to follow through on their promises. PB continues to suffer from the lack of government support in the crucial area of implementation. PB delegates engage in little "oversight" work because there are actually few projects to closely monitor.

The most important type of accountability that has been fostered is societal accountability.[34] Citizens use the public forums to discuss their problems, denounce government inaction, and build social networks. The material results of Recife's PB have been limited, but there has been a flourishing of societal accountability as citizens have learned to effectively use the new public venues as the first step toward holding the government accountable for its (in)actions. Even under Magalhães, a mayor not necessarily hospitable to PB's format, citizens were able to use the public format to initiate accountability demands on public officials.[35]

Recife's PB is carried by an active group of CSOs that seek desperately needed resources for their communities and by interested politicians who seek to provide citizens and potential supporters (voters) with access to participatory decision-making venues. When their interests overlap, such as under Mayors Vasconcelos and João Paulo, PB projects will be implemented, which helps PB to function well. When the interests of participants and government officials diverge, PB projects are not implemented, thereby weakening PB. Recife's PB has not delegated independent decision-making authority to citizens, but it has allowed citizens to decide where some resources will be spent. The government's uneven role in PB has sharply weakened PB's impact on Recife's decision-making processes.

34. Smulovitz and Peruzzotti 2000.
35. Wampler 2004b.

Belo Horizonte

PB in Belo Horizonte was initiated in 1993 by a political coalition that united the PT and the Brazilian Socialist Party (PSB). Mayor Patrus, of the PT, initiated PB in order to transform basic state-society relationships. The government "sought to stimulate, create, and invigorate diverse participatory channels. . . . The challenge was to democratize the municipal administration through popular participation and create a new relationship between the mayoral administration and society."[36] The mayor was from a reformist camp within the PT, interested in drawing from the purported successes of PB in Porto Alegre to overhaul Belo Horizonte's basic governing and decision-making processes. Although the mayor's office brought the basic rules configuration of PB to Belo Horizonte, CSOS were active participants in the PT, which means that PB is not merely a government-driven program.[37] As Avritzer demonstrates, CSOS in Belo Horizonte used contentious politics throughout the 1980s and early 1990s to draw attention to their demands.[38] Contentious politics were part of the CSOS' "toolbox," but many CSOS are now closely aligned with the PT, thus making cooperation between PT governments and CSOS an integral part of the reason that PB was initiated.

Why did I earlier characterize Belo Horizonte's PB delegates as a "captured audience"? To explain why Belo Horizonte never reached the successes of Porto Alegre and Ipatinga, yet still fared better than Santo André or São Paulo, in this section I pay particular attention to the shifting interests of three different mayors and the way CSOS were incorporated into PB.

PB's Rules

Belo Horizonte's PB program is distinguishable from others in the government's continual effort to improve PB by modifying the rules that govern it. The willingness to alter the rules demonstrates an intense government commitment to identifying a new rule set that will best achieve its goals. In the most optimistic scenario, the constant tinkering with PB's rules means that CSOS and government officials are working together to

36. Azevado 2003; see 23, 61.
37. Avritzer 2002.
38. Avritzer 2002.

strengthen participatory processes. However, the constant shifting of the rules undermines attempts to build a stable institution because participants must change their strategies each year. From 1993 to 2003, eleven years of PB, there was a significant rule change each year that affected how authority and resources would be allocated, thus sending conflicting signals to participants.

In 1993, the government initiated PB and drew over fifteen thousand participants. During the first year, there were three rounds of negotiation and deliberation, the substantial number of meetings leading to government and participant fatigue. During the first year, the greatest difficulty PB faced was the incongruity between the demands made by the participants and what the government could provide. According to a government evaluation of PB's first year, the most basic problems were (a) the selection of short-term projects with little consideration of urban planning, (b) the government's lack of administrative support to implement projects, (c) the weak involvement of bureaucrats during the planning phases, and (d) the lack of a global vision for developing the city.[39] In sum, the basic criticism of the coordinating committee was the lack of administrative and bureaucratic support from the mayoral administration.

In 1994 and 1995, the government sought to overcome the problems encountered in 1993 by dedicating more time to technical issues and by creating district-based oversight committees. Although the government sought to influence the type of projects that would be selected, the level of resources dedicated to PB remained low, just over U.S.$7 per capita. Overall, the level of new capital investment spending was at the rate of U.S.$15 million per year, hardly a figure that would allow the government to initiate a political project that transformed decision-making processes.[40] The resources were sufficient, however, to draw interested community leaders and citizens into the process because the proposed projects could improve their neighborhoods. The emphasis on streamlining projects appears to have been successful because the government increased its ability to implement the projects selected by delegates. Participation increased, rising to a high of 35,194 in 1995.[41]

In 1997, the program was again revamped. A new mayor, Celio Castro of the PSB, was elected to office. Castro had been the vice mayor under

39. Azevado, 2003, 71.
40. "Acompanhamento financeiro Orçamento Partcipativo Regional," 2003.
41. "Plano regional de empreendimentos Orçamento Participativo 2003/2004," 2003; "Belo Horizonte comemora 10 años de Orçamento Participativo," 2003.

Mayor Patrus, as a result of the electoral coalition between the PT and the PSB. The number of PB "rounds" was reduced to two from three. The PB coordinating committee decided to have PB participants select projects only in alternate years in order to address the backlog of projects. Of course, the alternative would have been to increase spending on PB projects, but the government did not choose to do this. Instead, delegates selected projects in 1998, 2000, 2002, and 2004 (coincidently, all were election years). During the "off years," when no projects were selected, PB became an institutional space in which to monitor government (in)actions and to prepare projects for the following year.

Although the government initiated a series of reforms in PB, there was never the development of a PB council that would oversee the PB and make final decisions on behalf of the program. The absence of a PB council was intended to prevent the emergence of new intermediaries who would represent the interests of delegates during negotiations with government officials. Decisions internal to regional districts were made by delegates at the regional level, thereby giving direct control and authority to local citizens. However, the lack of a centralized forum for delegates has had the effect of fragmenting participation. There was no institutional venue in which participants could gather to compare notes and devise strategies to counter the government's claims. Delegates are often of low income, with limited resources, which meant that it is not possible for them to easily meet in the city center. Decentralization of all decision making to the district level precluded the development of a consistent block of delegates and activists who might choose to contest the policies of the government. Ethnographic research from 2000 and 2004 illustrates this point. In 2000, delegates in different meetings with whom I spoke complained about the government's inability to implement the selected projects. In 2004, during the first meeting I attended, a government official provided data that the government had spent the equivalent of U.S.$250 million dollars on projects over a ten-year period. These results were impressive. However, as I conducted interviews and focus groups, it became clear that the delegates continued to believe that the government was substantially underfunding PB.

I then secured data from the PB administration on what had been allocated from 1994 to 2003. The actual capital outlays were less than half of the government official's claims, equivalent to U.S.$125 million during the same period. Government administrators were "informing" PB participants of the figure for what had been budgeted rather than what had actually been spent. One official publication provided a figure similar to the U.S.\$125 million, which meant that there was an astonishing disjuncture between what the majority of participants were hearing in public meetings (which is how most people receive their information) and an official government publication.[42] In Belo Horizonte, the delegates have traditionally relied on the government to provide accurate information. The lack of a unified, centralized institutional venue (for example, PB council) for PB delegates limits the delegates' ability to form a collective, unified response to the government. Instead the delegates were a "captured audience," with each group or region believing that their struggles and difficulties with PB and the government were unique to their district rather than understanding that their problems were likely representative of a larger municipal-wide trend. Let us now turn to the five factors (mayoral support, civil society, mayoral-legislative relations, PB's rules, and financial/administrative costs) that best explain the outcomes.

Mayoral Support

Belo Horizonte's PB has been governed by three mayors who are from different parties (PT and PSB), have different bases of support, and have different levels of commitment to PB. Mayor Patrus, who initiated PB in 1993, came from a wing of the PT that sought to use its ascension into political office as a means for transforming basic state-society relationships. Patrus and his allies drew from the experiences of PB in Porto Alegre, São Paulo, and Santo André to initiate Belo Horizonte's participatory program. Formal support for the PB program was high, but Patrus's team experienced great difficulties in convincing the bureaucracy to work with the new program. Part of the problem stems from a decision made early on: PB would only have access to a minority share of the new capital investment resources. During the last two years of Patrus's administration (1995 and 1996), PB delegates were able to negotiate just one-third of all new capital spending.[43] Patrus, therefore, was unwilling to delegate authority, because he sought to prioritize types of projects that might not be selected in PB. The bureaucracy, therefore, received conflicting signals from the Patrus administration: rhetoric that PB was a centerpiece of the administration, subsequently followed by low levels of negotiated spending.

---

42. "Plano regional de empreendimentos Orçamento Participativo 2003/2004," 2003.
43. "Acompanhamento financeiro Orçamento Participativo Regional," 2003.

Compounding the low levels of negotiated spending was the Patrus administration's difficulties in implementing projects.

If Patrus did not appear to strongly support PB, why was it initiated? PB, by 1993, had emerged as one of the PT's successful projects. It became known as good government that encouraged direct citizen participation, an appealing political, electoral, and governance value that PT and Patrus wanted to be associated with. In addition, the PT's base of support in Belo Horizonte was squarely situated in CSOs. CSOs' leaders demanded inclusion in decision-making venues.[44] Although Patrus's support was grounded in a combination of instrumental and ideological values, his and the PT's formal political rhetoric far outpaced the commitment they were willing to make in actual expenditures.

Mayor Castro, elected in 1996 and reelected in 2000, was vice mayor under Patrus and a member of the PSB. Mayor Castro was a medical doctor and focused many of his reform initiatives on improving Belo Horizonte's public health care system. Castro's vice mayor was from the PT, and members of the that party were the administrators of PB. Castro formally endorsed and supported PB, encouraging the reforms outlined above. Yet, although Mayor Castro formally supported PB, his six years in office (he did not complete his second term in office because of severe health problems) were marked by a continual decrease in the percentage of resources available to PB. In 1997, during Castro's first year in office, the level of new capital investment spending resources available for negotiation dropped to 19 percent of all new capital investment spending.[45] By the time Castro left office, the level of available funding for PB dropped to just 12 percent of all new capital investment spending.

After Castro resigned from office, Fernando Pimental became mayor. Pimental, who had been elected vice mayor in 2000, was a member of the PT. Since the PT was the principal agent behind PB in Belo Horizonte, it was logical to assume that there would be an increase in resources available to PB. In 2003, Mayor Pimental wrote, "It has been ten years since the municipal government has been working with the population to consolidate popular participation through Participatory Budgeting. This is one of the principal instruments that the community can rely on to guarantee its effective involvement in the decision regarding how to utilize a part of the annual municipal budget."[46] Although there have been

44. Avritzer 2002.
45. "Acompanhamento financeiro Orçamento Participativo Regional," 2003.
46. "Plano regional de empreendimentos Orçamento Participativo 2003/2004," 2003.

small increases in the amount of resources that delegates could negotiate, relative to the growth of the budget caused by inflation and the municipality's ability to "capture" new capital investment resources, there was
an actual drop in the percentage of resources dedicated to PB under Pimental. By 2003, only 9 percent of budgeted new capital resources were dedicated to PB.[47] Although Mayor Pimental's government continued to assert
that PB was a centerpiece of its governing strategy, the budgetary data
suggest that this was not the case.

Thus, over a ten-year period, the PT and PSB mayoral administrations
gradually restricted, rather than deepened, the authority exercised by
citizens. Citizens continued to participate in the process—more than forty-
three thousand individuals attended meetings in 2002—but the government sharply limited the influence of PB participants over the decision
making. Understanding this seeming disconnect—decreasing authority
and increasing participation—is best explained by analyzing the relationship between CSOs and the PT.

Civil Society

"Participatory Budgeting is the best thing that has happened to the poor
of Belo Horizonte because we can transform our neighborhood from favela
into city. We can become part of the city."[48] This delegate's sentiment captures a basic incentive that brings many to participate: decisions made
in PB can help to transform neighborhoods, bringing infrastructure and
urbanization improvements that are desperately needed. This delegate
expressed a widely held sentiment: PB allows interested individuals to take
control of their lives.

However, another delegate was much less sanguine about the status
of Belo Horizonte's PB. "PB represents the exclusion of the favela from
the city. We fight among other *favelados* [shantytown dwellers] over the
crumbs. . . . The PT is now the wolf in sheep's clothing. The party [PT]
convinced us that it would invert priorities, but PB doesn't allow that to
happen. Since we helped to build the PT, we now don't have any other
political options. . . . And the PT knows that."[49]

These two positions reflect a broader body of sentiments expressed by

47. "Acompanhamento financeiro Orçamento Participativo Regional," 2003.
48. Focus group, April 7, 2004, Santa Lucia, Belo Horizonte.
49. Mauro, PB delegate, interview, March 25, 2004.

delegates in interviews, focus groups, and meetings, and they have their roots in the way that cooperation and contentious politics developed in Belo Horizonte. Among the municipalities included in this book, the growth of Belo Horizonte's civil society is most similar to that of Santo André and São Paulo.

During the 1940s and 1950s, there was a proliferation of unions associated with Brazil's industrialization and expansion of bureaucracies. There was also the rise of neighborhood associations, although many fell under the sway of ward-style bosses.[50] Unlike in Recife, the political Left in Belo Horizonte never dominated electoral politics. The use of contentious politics by opposition groups during the last decade of the military regime was also widespread. Contentious politics were focused against the military government (such as the *direitas já* campaign in 1984), but were also focused more narrowly on expanding the role that citizens and activists could play in policy making. During the 1980s, there was a rapid increase in CSOs that advocated their own direct involvement in public affairs.[51] This new base of CSOs became one of the pillars of the PT's and the PSB's political organizations during the 1990s.

By the 1990s, CSOs active in PB were closely associated with PT. In the survey carried out for this book (see Chapter 3), 89 percent of the delegates belong to CSOs. Nylen's findings in Belo Horizonte are similar.[52] Seventy-nine percent of those with a stated party identification have a leftist political affiliation. This close alliance means that cooperation is a key component of CSO-government interactions. The PT in Belo Horizonte was built through the significant support of social movements, community organizations, and other CSOs. The PT's style of politics in Belo Horizonte has been similar to that in other major urban areas: an emphasis on internal democracy, extensive meetings with wide-ranging debates, and a willingness to use public displays of contentious politics (marches, demonstrations). These basic features of the PT helped prepare CSOs for the style of politicking that would be part and parcel of PB.

Mayors Patrus, Castro, and Pimental, thus, were able to incorporate groups of citizens and activists into PB, which became a "captured audience." In his 2003 remarks during PB's annual kickoff, Mayor Pimental warned the audience that PB would be poorly served if his main rival

50. Gomes 2004; Schettini 2004.
51. Avritzer 2002; Wampler and Avritzer 2004.
52. Nylen 2002, 2003.

from the centrist PSDB were to be elected (see story at the beginning of this chapter). PB works well, Pimental asserted, because the PT puts so much time and effort into the process. Although Pimental stressed unity and cooperation, delegates were seeking ways to increase their authority. The example in this book's first chapter (a mock funeral to bury PB) is one way that delegates sought to pressure and embarrass the municipal administration in order to secure additional resources. This particular threat was successful, since the government agreed to spend additional resources in the neighborhood.

The initial effort to create a decision-making process that would be free from political manipulation after a policy is selected has slowly eroded in Belo Horizonte since PB's inception. PB delegates used political tactics long employed by the CSOs to shame and frighten governments into act- ing. Although this shows the results that can be produced by PB activists when they engage in contentious behavior, it highlights the informality that remains embedded in the process. The low levels of resources pit poor neighborhood against poor neighborhood, thereby driving wedges between the groups rather than bringing them together. Even though it is true that groups from competing neighborhoods will negotiate with one another (logrolling and solidarity), these neighborhoods are also in competition with one another over the distribution of scarce resources. The example from Belo Horizonte, as told in Chapter I, illustrates that citizens and CSOs will engage in acts of solidarity with CSOs, but they will also work to secure their own particular set of interests.

The unity and solidarity called for by the government appears more focused on extending cooperation between different groups and the PT than it does on the establishment of unity within groups of participants. The rules (no centralized PB structure), low levels of resources (9 percent of new capital resources), and the PT's political interests (elections every two years) have diminished PB as a political decision-making venue. The political question, of course, is why have the PB delegates not exited the PT? Why have they not withdrawn their support? Recall that 79 percent of the survey respondents shared a partisan political affiliation with the PT or the PSB.

The quotation at the beginning of this section best explains why CSOs have not left the PT. There is no other political home for the CSO activists and PB participants who spent two decades building the PT. The centrist PSDB does not have a political tradition in Belo Horizonte that empha- sizes direct participation. Other leftist parties such as the Communist Party of Brazil have pretensions of inverting spending priorities and investing more heavily in PB, but their small size and low likelihood of electoral victory have precluded them from gathering the support of a broader number of PB delegates. CSOS continue to participate in PB and to support the PT because they judge that these are the best political and policy-making options available to transform their communities.

Mayoral-Legislative Relations

Mayors Patrus, Castro, and Pimental never enjoyed majority support from leftist parties in the municipal legislature, which partially helps to explain why these mayors were unwilling to dedicate more resources to PB. The percentage of leftist legislators elected in 1996 and 2000 was 34 percent.[53] The percentage of centrist legislators elected in 1996 and 2000 was 51 percent. The combination of centrists and leftists gave the mayors comfortable majorities with which they could negotiate. Although the relationship between these mayors and the different legislatures was far from harmonious, the relationship did not cripple any of the administrations, unlike in the case of São Paulo, where intense conflict in a multiparty system limited the effectiveness of Mayors Erundina and Suplicy.

There are several reasons why Belo Horizonte's mayoral-legislative relationships were never as acrimonious as those in São Paulo. First, PB has never allocated more than one-third of budgeted new capital investment spending, which meant the municipal legislators were never in direct competition with PB delegates over the distribution of scarce resources.[54] Second, Belo Horizonte is Brazil's third-largest metropolitan region, but its politics are not "national" in the same way that São Paulo's politics are. This meant that other political parties were not as willing to attempt to derail the PT/PSB governments as had been the case in São Paulo. Belo Horizonte's PT had additional breathing room that allowed them to introduce innovative policies. Third, the PT's rise in Belo Horizonte was based on its ability to build a strong electoral and governing coalition with the PSB. The PT leadership, therefore, was accustomed to negotiating with other political parties. The PT did not seek to govern alone.

PB did not directly contest or challenge the traditional processes of distributing resources, which therefore shielded legislators from losing their

53. Tribunal Supremo Eleitoral de São Paulo.
54. "Acompanhamento Financeiro Orçamento Partcipativo Regional," 2003.

access to pork barrel projects. PB slowly evolved into a participatory process that allowed interested citizens to debate over an increasingly smaller share of the budget. Legislators could try to influence new capital investment allocation in two ways: work directly with the mayor regarding how 91 percent of spending would occur or work with citizens and PB delegates to influence how nine percent of the spending would be allocated. At all PB meetings I attended in Belo Horizonte, in 1999, 2000, 2001, and 2004, there were always municipal legislators present. At times, they had helped to organize a bus to bring participants to the meetings, or their *cabo eleitorais* (election ward bosses) organized individuals to support a particular project. Legislators, mainly leftists associated with the government, attend PB meetings because they can identify the most active leaders and the most pressing problems, as well as engage in "credit claiming" for "strengthening" the PB process. Legislators did not try to overturn PB in large part because PB was not a political threat. Mayors Patrus, Castro, and Pimental were therefore able to use constituency service as a means to develop majority support.

Financial Situation

The municipality of Belo Horizonte's financial and administrative situation, in comparison with those of Recife, São Paulo, and Santo André, is moderately strong, although it is in a weaker position than Porto Alegre or Ipatinga. The level of new capital investment spending is relatively high, and the government has exercised fairly strong control over its bureaucracy.[55] Belo Horizonte has the necessary conditions that would allow for PB to flourish. But PB has not flourished, because the government chooses to further restrict it every year. The fact that the government has spent U.S.$125 million on projects selected in PB is impressive and helps account for why the program has been partially successful. More than seven hundred projects were completed over a ten-year span.[56] This wide distribution of projects across Belo Horizonte and the capacity of the government to work inside favelas to implement them attest to the administration's willingness to transform its own procedures and processes to meet the needs of traditionally marginalized communities.

    55. Maria Auxiliadora Gomes, coordinator of Belo Horizonte's participatory programs, interview, March 25, 2004.
    56. "Acompanhamento Financeiro Orçamento Partcipativo Regional," 2003.

Yet the administrative and financial opportunities afforded by the wealth of Belo Horizonte have not been transferred to PB delegates by the mayoral administration. The financial conditions in Belo Horizonte might have enabled the creation of a new decision-making body. Instead, the government gradually drew down existing resources, thereby limiting the potential impact that the institution might have had, if it had been fully funded.

Synthesizing the Results

In Belo Horizonte, PB has created the possibility for citizens to be directly involved in policy making. Over a ten-year span, citizens have made decisions that have affected how hundreds of million Brazilian reales, equivalent to U.S.$125 million, were spent. Projects have been implemented throughout the municipality, helping to transform the lives of citizens in favelas and other low-income areas. Although the policy impact of PB has been substantial, there are two other trends that have limited PB's effect on citizenship and accountability issues. First, PB has gradually diminished in importance as each successive administration has dedicated a lower percentage of resources to the program. Second, PB delegates and many participants have become part of a "captured audience" whose claims are increasingly being ignored by government officials. PB has not altered decision-making processes in Belo Horizonte in any substantial fashion. At best, PB has provided a forum for some citizens to make decisions about where low levels of resources will be spent. At worst, PB has allowed the PT to co-opt the most active CSOs.

From the vantage point of citizenship, Belo Horizonte's program has helped to initiate the expansion of rights. Citizens participate by the tens of thousands, learning to make decisions that have directed governmental outputs. The projects selected have become more sophisticated and expansive as PB has developed, but they have also become better planned, which increases the likelihood that they will be implemented. Citizens are making political and policy decisions that result in governmental action. And yet, even though citizenship rights have begun to be inculcated, delegates also have become dependent on government officials. PB delegates have become consumers of the materials that government officials have produced about PB rather than seeking out independent information to verify what was occurring. In interviews and focus groups, I questioned delegates about their knowledge of spending patterns and policy outcomes.

They were generally well informed about local issues—what PB projects had been built in their local communities and the status of projects that were slated to be built. Knowledge about how PB functioned in the larger municipality was absent. This took the slogan Think Globally, Act Locally to an extreme, reinforcing a politics of "neighborhoodism" (*bairrismo*), a politics of the local, at the expense of a broader political focus. And although this focus on the local may help to extend new sets of rights within some communities, it, ironically, may curtail efforts to inculcate a set of beliefs about individuals' broader political, social, and economic rights. There was no evidence collected during this research project to indicate whether participants in a neighborhood-level participatory program had a positive effect on reshaping citizens' attitudes on national or international issues. The evidence, as presented in Chapter 3, does suggest that some PB programs have the capacity to reshape citizens' attitudes and behavior. It would be fruitful for future research projects to more closely examine whether PB has the potential to change citizens' attitudes on issues unrelated to local public policies and localized political practices.

Santos classifies the extension of rights to Brazilian workers in the 1930s as "regulated citizenship," in which the state set the terms for the scope of rights. Of the eight PB programs analyzed, the extension of rights in Belo Horizonte most closely resembles regulated citizenship. Decision-making authority has been partially delegated, but the scope of authority is determined by government officials. CSOs and citizens are fragmented, precluding the possibility of their development of a unified strategy to press the government for a greater extension of rights. Contentious politics has been present, but on a case-by-case, individual-CSO basis rather than as a combined front.

As the examples of contentious politics illustrate, PB's administrators have responded to public demonstrations, thereby indicating that societal accountability is part and parcel of the process. Societal accountability is a form of pressure politics that often transpires outside formal institutional venues. Although PB was designed as an institution that would accommodate different groups and demands, the lack of governmental commitment to funding projects has helped to foster societal accountability while undermining horizontal accountability. A formalized, internal decision-making process that is transparent and adhered to by government officials has not been implemented.

Horizontal accountability has been established at the regional level in the form of the oversight committees that allow citizens to closely monitor the government's actions. Of the eight municipalities, Belo Horizonte's delegates have had the greatest role in the oversight stage of policy making. However, the lack of a centralized "PB council" has weakened the overall impact that CSOS and citizens could potentially have on governmental decision making. The lack of a PB council removes one possible base of support that CSOS and PB participants could use to pressure the municipal government.

Vertical accountability was limited in Belo Horizonte and actually decreased over time. It was limited because PB participants negotiated over increasingly smaller amounts of the budget, since PB never occupied a central role in the basic decision-making process that affects how resources and authority are distributed. Each successive mayoral administration spent lower levels of resources on PB; as a result, the ability of PB delegates to make decisions that would reshape their communities also diminished over time.

Conclusions

Recife's and Belo Horizonte's respective PB programs manage to partially delegate decision-making authority to citizens, but both programs are hampered by shifting mayoral interests. This undermined the impact of PB on political outcomes because citizens were uncertain how to best make use of PB's rules structure. Citizens are, at times, decision makers, but only when they are allowed to be so by a mayor's governing strategy. For PB participants this creates a new form of political dependence on whoever is occupying the mayor's office. Although PB was initiated to overcome clientelism and personalism, Recife's and Belo Horizonte's respective PB programs are being used to reward those groups closest to the mayor's office.

There have been noteworthy advances: the institutionalization of direct citizen participation in public policy processes and the demand by citizens that government officials comply with their commitments to PB. When PB participants now turn to public demonstrations outside PB, they do in defense of PB and decisions made within PB. When PB participants want to place claims on government officials for governmental inaction, they first do so in the context of PB. PB is now widely recognized as being a legitimate site for negotiation and decision making.

In Belo Horizonte, the PT is the predominant party that promotes participatory politics in public society, which means that participants in PB are largely a captured block of PT supporters.[57] Of course, the PB participants could exit the PT and move to another political party, but the problem for PB participants is that there are no other political parties that emphasize participatory politics. PB delegates and citizens can pressure the PT government through contentious politics to implement specific projects, but CSOs and PB delegates lack the necessary power to force the government to dedicate much higher sums of resources to PB.

In Recife, two political parties actively compete for the attention of CSOs and PB delegates. The centrist, catchall PMDB and the leftist PT each governed Recife's PB with the goal of supporting their allies and reaching out to potential supporters. The fundamental problem for PB as an institution has been that the most important decisions regarding the program were made by government officials far from view. Citizens had to change their strategies with each new administration to best secure resources. Recife's PMDB mayor, Vasconcelos, limited the number of citizens who could participate in the process, thereby making them directly dependent on his administration. Recife's PT mayor, João Paulo, radically expanded the number of people who could participate, thereby hoping to create new ties between a CSO base and the government. PB delegates, under both Vasconcelos and João Paulo, were ultimately dependent on the political interests and strategies of the mayors.

Recife's and Belo Horizonte's PB offer, at best, contradictory results. Citizens make some policy decisions in public formats. However, government officials are largely unwilling to delegate any real authority to citizens, and these same citizens have been unable to place enough pressure on the government to ensure that officials would actually delegate authority. CSOs in both Recife and Belo Horizonte are willing to engage in contentious politics against their respective governments, which helps to explain why the governments do allow citizens to engage in some decision making. Governments are threatened by individual CSOs' willingness to use public demonstrations as a means to force the government to comply with previously reached agreements. The threat of public demonstrations places sufficient strain on governments that municipal officials have been willing to implement specific projects, but the pressure has not induced them to increase the authority or resources afforded to PB.

---

57. Avritzer 2002; Wampler and Avritzer 2004.

8

Deepening Democracy Through the
Expansion of Citizenship Rights
and Accountability

> I'm uncertain if we have any power, but we do have
> rights. . . . To understand how to access and use
> power, you have to first understand the rights asso-
> ciated with PB.
>
> —PB DELEGATE IN SÃO PAULO

> We always sought out CSOs that were stronger, that
> could turn out high numbers of people. We need
> their support to have our projects approved just as
> they would need our support to have their projects
> approved.
>
> —PB DELEGATE IN BELO HORIZONTE

PB programs spread across Brazil during the 1990s, following the founding of this new decision-making institution in Porto Alegre in 1989.[1] PB's
strongest advocates sought to build on the reported successes of Porto
Alegre's program, which has deepened democracy, promoted social justice, improved how local states function, and made government officials
accountable to their constituents.[2] Expectations for PB-generated outcomes
are high, not just in Brazil, but also across the globe, as hundreds of local
governments have adopted PB on the basis of their political interests and
the encouragement of the World Bank, U.N. Habitat, and other international organizations. In this book I develop a generalizable analytical framework that accounts for the wide variation in PB programs' outcomes and
improves our understanding of how governments and citizens work within
and parallel to PB. The findings, presented in Chapters 3–7, demonstrate

---

1. More than 250 programs were adopted in Brazil between 1989 and 2004. Wampler
and Avritzer 2005.
2. Genro 1995b, 1995a; Jacobi and Teixeira 1996; Fedozzi 1998; Abers 2000.

that some PB programs can extend accountability and citizenship rights, but other PB programs produce few discernible short-term effects.

The purpose of this concluding chapter is to pull together the various threads of the argument introduced in Chapter 1 and substantiated throughout the remainder of the book. What does a comparative, mixed-method approach grounded in accountability and citizenship debates reveal about how PB programs affect citizens, states, and state-society relations? This approach demonstrates that the interaction of two factors best explains the outcomes produced by PB: mayoral willingness to delegate authority *and* the willingness of CSOs to engage in contentious politics. This book focuses on PB, but the findings are generalizable to similar institutions that directly incorporate citizens into policy-making venues.[3]

PB programs represent a new form of distributing political authority in Brazil whereby citizens organize themselves in civil society to take advantage of new political opportunities offered by PB, an institution at the intersection of political and civil societies. Organized citizens move into political society from the realm of civil society, exercising new rights in state-sanctioned policy-making institutions. Successful PB programs now allow citizens to exercise new rights, including the right to exercise *voice* and *vote* in state-sanctioned institutions to secure social programs and public policies that will directly improve the quality of their lives. Building one set of rights (political) to obtain another (social) is an arduous process, though one that has long been associated with the development of democratic regimes.[4] This book demonstrates that state actors, working in conjunction with citizens, can construct new processes that enhance state performance, promote social justice by allocating greatly needed social services, and deepen democracy.[5]

When governments are uninterested in delegating real decision-making authority or when CSOs and citizens are unwilling pressure government officials inside or outside PB, then PB's effects are far more limited. If the degree of authority delegated is limited, then it is not possible to claim that there are significant changes or "advances" (*avanços*). It is possible that unsuccessful programs will leave "residual" effects and repertoires of political action that will be picked up during future political struggles

3. Fung and Wright 2003.
4. McAdam, Tarrow, and Tilly 2001; Marshall 1950; Thompson 1966; Rueschemeyer, Stephens, and Stephens 1992.
5. Roberts 1998; Alvarez 1993; Gaventa 2002; Pateman 1970; Roussopoulos and Benello 2005.

by citizens, cso leaders, politicians, and state officials seeking solutions to seemingly intractable problems.[6] The danger, however, is that the residual effect left by poorly performing PB programs may not outweigh the cynicism and distrust that developed among civil society leaders as they discovered that their local government sought to incorporate them into a weak and emasculated political institution. This is an empirical question that requires additional investigation if we are to better understand whether failed participatory programs help set the terrain on which future political struggles are waged.

Explaining Outcomes

Figure 2 illustrates how csos' willingness to use contentious politics *interacts with* the degree of mayoral support for the direct delegation of authority to citizens to produce a wide spectrum of outcomes, ranging from the institutionalization of participatory democracy to its emasculation. The extent to which democracy will be deepened through PB depends primarily on the interactions between civil society and political society actors. As demonstrated in this book, looking exclusively at either political society actors (mayors, legislators) or civil society actors (cso leaders, PB participants) will provide a partial and uneven understanding of how democracy is transformed through participatory institutions. To analyze how new participatory democracy institutions affect democracy, it is vital that we look at the interests and interactions of citizens, csos, and government officials.

The classification of these PB programs is based on their performances during the 1997–2004 period, with the exception of São Paulo, which is based on the 2001–4 period. PB is a dynamic institution that includes formal, state-sanctioned meetings as well as hundreds of informal meetings, conversations, and negotiations that occur parallel to PB. The evidence from PB now clearly demonstrates that the most successful PB participants are being rewarded for their ability to work with their own cso and to forge alliances with other csos (see Chapter 3). This marks an important shift in Brazil's local democracy. Brazilian political

6. My thanks to Patrick Heller for emphasizing that participatory institutions leave "footprints" or "residual traces" that become part of political memory that citizens and cso leaders can use in future political struggles.

csos' Willingness to Use Contentious Politics

	High	Low
High	*Institutionalized* *Participatory Democracy* Porto Alegre Ipatinga	N/A
Medium	*Informal and Contested* *Participatory Democracy* Recife Belo Horizonte	*Co-opted* *Participatory Democracy* Santo André São Paulo
Low	N/A	*Emasculated* *Participatory Democracy* Blumenau Rio Claro

Mayoral
Support for
Delegation
of Authority
to Citizens

Fig. 2. Participatory Budgeting Outcomes

history is notable for the long-standing presence of individual-level exchanges in which government officials provide resources to private citizens (clients) or presidents of community associations in exchange for
their support during campaigns and elections.[7] Citizens who participate
in PB are being induced by a state-sanctioned institution to work together
to exercise their political rights as a means to secure new social rights. A
brief description of the outcomes in the eight municipalities will help illustrate how these two factors interact. Once again, the comparative approach,
as used in this book, advances our theoretical understanding of how
localized processes and interests explain the wide variation in outcomes.

Porto Alegre and Ipatinga

The upper-left box of figure 2, "institutionalized participatory democracy,"
captures the outcomes produced in Porto Alegre and Ipatinga as a result
of the governments' strong support for the delegation of authority and
csos' use of contentious politics as a political tool (see Chapter 4). Of the
eight cases analyzed in this book, these two were the most successful

7. Gohn 1995; Nunes 1997; Carvalho 1987; Avritzer 2002; Graham 1990.

because government officials, csos, and citizens worked together to create the political processes necessary to allow citizens to learn about, deliberate over, and vote on substantive public policies. Government officials delegated control over policies and institutionalized the processes through which demands were transformed into policy proposals and, later, into actual projects.

Inside PB meetings, direct contestation took place, as government officials allowed for and even encouraged intense debate. Government officials firmly believed that they could defend their PB-related policies and actions, which is why they encouraged citizens to play an active role in demanding their rights.[8] Within public venues, there was intense conflict as participants raised their voices as rights-bearing citizens. The intense conflict, though, had its limits because PB participants and government officials shared a common interest: strengthening PB as a means with which to achieve social justice and deepen democracy. It was conflict among friends, rather than conflict between political rivals.

Outside PB, contentious politics remained more of a reserve threat than an actively used political resource. Citizens were willing to use public venues, such as Porto Alegre's World Social Forum, to publicly air their complaints about how PB was being managed. csos, PB delegates, and citizens were more likely to use public displays of political protest against municipal legislators and local media outlets, because both were considered by PB supporters to be actively opposed to PB. The presence of contentious politics in PB participants' political toolbox drastically limited the governments' ability to co-opt citizens, since the citizens used public-meeting formats to discuss how the governments were administering each respective PB program. Individuals involved in PB programs were not mere clients of the state or simply users of a new policy-making process; they were rights-bearing citizens who demanded that their newly established political rights be respected. The increased debate, transparency, and openness present in these successful PB programs allowed PB participants to pressure their governments to increase their support of PB.

Porto Alegre's PB did not begin, obviously, as an institutionalized form of participatory democracy. During the 1989–96 period, Porto Alegre's PB is more appropriately classified in the *informal and contested* box (middle

---

8. Assis Brasil Olegário Filho, PB coordinator (1998–2004), interviews, May 22, 1999; March 27, 2000; April 20, 2004; March 28, 2006, Porto Alegre. André Passos, PB administrator (1998–2004), interviews, May 24, 1999; March 30, 2000; April 26, 2004, Porto Alegre.

left in fig. 2).[9] The cooperation and contestation exhibited by citizens during this period led the Workers' Party (PT) government to increase its commitment to the delegation of authority. The implication is that as governments' and CSOs' interests change over time, there will be movement from one classification type to another. After the PT lost the 2004 mayoral election in Porto Alegre, a new government led by the PDT was in charge of administering PB. The new government has a weaker commitment to PB than that held by the previous PT government.[10] In terms of the typology, the preliminary evidence suggests that Porto Alegre's PB is starting to slide back into the "informal and contested" category because of the PDT government's (2005–8) uneven commitment to the process. I visited Porto Alegre in March 2006 to assess how PB was functioning. Perhaps most interesting was the delegates' emphasis on their rights and PB's rules. As the new government sought to decrease the importance of PB as a policy-making institution, the delegates were using the political skills, knowledge, and language that they had gained during the previous sixteen years to directly confront the government. PB delegates were no longer simply citizens trying to get the government to listen to them; they were rights-bearing members of the polity seeking to force the government to comply with their previous commitments and the institutionalized rule structures that governed the distribution of public works projects. The sixteen-year PB experience in Porto Alegre will make it difficult for the PDT government to use an "informal" decision-making process, because many of Porto Alegre's PB delegates now have a solid understanding of their legal rights as well as the administrative, legal, and regulatory requirements the municipal government must follow. PB will likely be the site of increased political contestation as the PDT and PB delegates seek to use PB in a manner that reflects their political needs.

Blumenau and Rio Claro

The lower-right box of figure 2, *emasculated participatory democracy*, is marked by the absence of contentious politics, which occurred in the cases of Blumenau and Rio Claro. Citizens and CSOs were not willing to

---

9. My thanks to Ben Goldfrank for making this observation. See Goldfrank 2003; Abers 2000.

10. Felisberto Luisi, PB delegate, interviews, May 21, 1999, and March 26, 2006, Porto Alegre; focus group, March 28, 2006, Porto Alegre City Market, Porto Alegre; Sergio Baierle, coordinator of Cidade (NGO), interviews, March 26, 2006, Porto Alegre.

use contentious politics and were therefore left without any means to publicly pressure their elected governments. csos were unwilling to use contentious politics for two basic reasons. First, there was no tradition in either municipality of this type of political activity as a means to pressure local governments to respond to their demands. Second, the csos that were most likely to be interested in using contentious politics were allies of the government and were unwilling to engage in public acts that might potentially embarrass the government. pb in Blumenau and Rio Claro, therefore, became an institutional space of deliberation on the terms set by the government.

Government officials in both cases did not delegate authority to citizens through pb. The former did not fear a public airing of how poorly they administered their pb programs because the absence of contentious politics left csos and citizens with little way to publicly denounce and pressure their governments' weak performances. The evidence indicates a strong association between rights-bearing citizens and their willingness to directly confront government officials inside and outside participatory institutions.

"No contestation, no delegation" is the key lesson learned from Blumenau and Rio Claro. Under this scenario, pb developed into a political space that served to increase the number of contacts between csos leaders and government leaders. pb did not develop into a political space that allowed citizens to make meaningful decisions or exercise basic political rights. Another key lesson learned from these two cases is that if citizens do not demand that participatory institutions directly delegate authority and if they do not act as rights-bearing members of political society, it is unlikely that the government will delegate authority. This, in turn, suggests that implementing pb from above will not necessarily yield results similar to those of Porto Alegre, because citizens need to be active participants to expand their political space within the state. pb can help to transform basic state-society relationships, but the results from Blumenau and Rio Claro strongly suggest that a state-driven effort will not necessarily produce robust results. Blumenau and Rio Claro demonstrate that the roles of citizens and states must be analyzed simultaneously to show how civil society actors interact with political society actors to produce outcomes.

São Paulo and Santo André

The middle-right box of figure 2, *co-opted participatory democracy*, captures outcomes produced when governments impose their political agendas on the csos and citizens working within PB. In these cases, the governments do delegate some authority to citizens, but they induce the PB delegates to promote the policies and politics of incumbent politicians and to downplay their own strategic agendas. In São Paulo and Santo André, contentious politics were part of the "political toolbox" of csos, but csos were unwilling to engage in public demonstrations against the incumbent mayor for electoral reasons. In both municipalities, csos were willing to directly confront government leaders *inside* PB. But it was also clear that csos and PB delegates would not air these disputes *outside* formal PB meetings because of the possible negative political repercussions for the incumbent government. Contentious politics became an "empty threat." Since the government did not feel pressured, no additional authority was delegated. Both governments exploited this empty threat even further. Since they did not feel politically threatened as a result of their weak support for PB, government officials then used PB as a means to legitimize their own policies. PB became a "flagship" program that helped to legitimate the governments' policy agendas, thereby resulting in the participatory institutions' rubber-stamping of the governments' policy initiatives, even though the governments dedicated low levels of political and financial resources to PB.

In São Paulo and Santo André, PB was situated in a broader political environment in which electoral and party politics were deemed more important than advancing the efforts of cso leaders to carve out a participatory venue that would serve their long-term interests. The demands of representative democracy trumped efforts to extend participatory politics into the state. This helps to account for why co-optation of leadership was a significantly larger threat in São Paulo and Santo André than in other cases. Government officials worked closely with PB delegates, maintaining support from the PB delegates despite the governments' limited abilities to implement PB-related projects. PB delegates were, thereby, incorporated into a state-sanctioned participatory institution, but the governments set the agendas and dominated the institutions. The governments' agendas supplanted the PB delegates' agendas, which led to the co-optation of csos.

Belo Horizonte and Recife

The middle-left box of figure 2, *informal and contested participatory democracy*, is perhaps the most contradictory within the context of PB. In Belo Horizonte and Recife, the governments delegated moderate levels of authority and resources. PB delegates, CSOs, and citizens used contentious politics to publicly pressure their governments to increase the levels of resources, time, and energy given to PB in the hope that a greater number of PB projects would be implemented. Contentious politics were used by CSOs to embarrass their elected governments and shame officials into implementing the CSOs' preferred PB projects. When the public demonstrations were large and drew the attention of the local media, the governments were likely to respond to their demands (see Chapter 7). The governments responded to these demands to minimize the impact of the public demonstrations carried out by these elected citizen representatives.

The governments' actions were contradictory in the context of PB because the governments' quick responses to activists' demand had the effect of moving the governments further away from their own goal of standardizing implementation procedures. Contentious politics helped specific CSOs have their PB-selected projects implemented more quickly, but there was not a PB-related rational for implementing their projects rather than other projects already slated for implementation. Contentious politics was necessary to publicly pressure the governments to implement projects, but it also undermined efforts to induce the governments to adhere to PB's rules, which they had helped to initiate.

If CSOs had not used contentious politics in Recife or Belo Horizonte, it is probable that their governments would have effectively decreased the importance of PB, as occurred in São Paulo and Santo André. The governments in Recife and Belo Horizonte were more responsive to the demands of their PB delegates than was the case in São Paulo and Santo André, which helped to place PB near the center of their respective decision-making processes. But this also had the effect of encouraging informal PB processes, such as the sidestepping of PB's rules and other internal procedures.

This brief overview of the eight case studies highlights the advantages of a comparative, subnational approach, which provides us with an opportunity to more clearly identify the processes and factors that best explain the wide variation in outcomes. Large, federal countries often have significant subnational variation in how their respective local civil and political societies are structured. Researchers working with a single-case-study approach may not be able to identify the full range of factors that are needed to best account for what is driving or producing political change. Building theory through single case studies ultimately is limited because of the difficulties in identifying the causal processes that produce the resulting outcomes. This book fits within efforts to build "middle-range generalizations about the role of states . . . about the social and economic policies pursued by states, and about the effects of states on political conflicts and agendas."[11] By studying subnational governments and the civil society actors that interact within and outside participatory institutions, we gain greater analytical leverage on how democracy is being (or not being) deepened, how the state is being transformed, and how citizens are seeking out state institutions through which to channel their political and social demands.

It is only through rigorous comparison between and among cases, for example, Porto Alegre, Belo Horizonte, and Recife, and a mixed methodology that the importance of a government's adherence to PB's rules becomes apparent. The theoretical and empirical findings established through the comparative method used in this book significantly extend our understanding of how outcomes associated with PB are produced through the interactions of states and citizens. Comparisons within a single country enable researchers to hold a significant number of factors constant (constitution founding, larger historical process) that then allows for the identification of key processes that best explain the wide variation in outcomes. A subnational comparison approach offers significant analytical advantages in the process of building theoretical explanations for the vast range in outcomes produced by local participatory institutions.

Accountability and Citizenship

The extension of accountability and citizenship rights depends on the joint actions of government officials and private citizens (for an in-depth discussion, see Chapter 1). Rights cannot be firmly rooted in a polity if government officials "give" these rights to citizens.[12] Citizens cannot act as clients of government officials if they wish to secure additional social rights through PB. And citizens cannot actively exercise citizenship rights if state officials do not work to ensure that individuals' rights will be respected by private citizens or other state officials. Accountability functions in much the same way. Citizens must be willing to monitor their government, and the government officials must be willing to be monitored

11. Skocpol 1985, 29.
12. Sales 1994.

by outside parties. The extension of accountability and citizenship rights can help to deepen democracy by enhancing the responsiveness of state and government officials to citizens, by allowing citizens to be more directly involved in governmental decision-making venues, and by encouraging cooperation among citizens as they seek solutions to the intense problems faced by low-income residents in urban environments in developing countries.

Participatory institutions provide a unique institutional space in which to extend accountability and citizenship rights because of the active presence of government officials and citizens. PB in Brazil *has* successfully incorporated low-income citizens, often from communities that historically have been excluded from political society, which has made it possible for many people to activate their basic citizenship rights (see Chapter 3).[13] Participatory institutions have the potential to act as citizenship schools and as incubators of citizenship rights, especially for low-income citizens.[14] Citizens use PB not only as a means to learn about government, but also to make decisions that will directly reshape their communities and their lives.[15]

Citizenship

Returning to T. H. Marshall's classification of citizenship rights as consisting of civil, political, and social components, we can conceptualize PB as allowing interested citizens to exercise their political rights in a state-sanctioned venue in order to secure social rights.[16] Simply stated, citizens exercise new political rights to win social rights. The majority of public works projects approved in PB programs are geared toward improving the basic quality of life of residents in underserved areas. Building local health care clinics and schools, putting in sewer systems, paving roads, and building housing are the principal types of projects selected by PB delegates. Participants' *voice* and *vote* are being used to force the local state to provide the types of services that have long been provided by Brazilian governments to middle- and upper-class neighborhoods. Thus, PB is a state-sanctioned institution that gives low-income and historically marginalized

13. See also Goldfrank 2003; Nylen 2003; Avritzer 2002; Houtzager, Acharya, and Lavalle 2004.
14. Baiocchi 2005.
15. Abers 2000; Fedozzi 1998; Baiocchi 2005.
16. Marshall 1950; Somers 1993; Oxhorn 2003.

citizens the opportunity to exercise *voice* and *vote*, thereby fundamentally altering how these citizens interact with the local state. By changing the interactions between states and citizens, PB programs are altering basic state-society relations, which, in turn, contribute to the deepening of Brazilian democracy.

As has been well documented elsewhere, establishing rights is a slow, arduous process that involves citizens' placing pressures on states to recognize and protect the rights of marginalized citizens as well as the state's reaching out to new groups of potential supporters that can be incorporated into the government's ruling coalition.[17] During the 1980s and 1990s, the development of "participatory publics" and "the right to have rights" permeated Brazilian civil society, encouraging ever larger numbers of citizens to conceptualize themselves as rights-bearing members of their polity.[18]

PB is the current manifestation of efforts to institutionalize these demands. Citizens and government officials cooperate to extend rights to citizens to allow them to be more actively involved in public deliberations and decision-making venues that shape how scarce resources will be used. But PB also allows for, at times even encourages, direct confrontation among political allies as citizens pressure government officials to adhere to PB's basic rules as a means to secure additional social benefits for their communities. PB is a vehicle through which participants use deliberation to secure public policies to directly benefit their communities. PB delegates consistently told me that they are involved in PB as a means to improve their communities, to use political rights they won with the return to democracy, and to promote a greater sense of social justice. PB is a practical application of many of the values enshrined in Brazil's 1988 Constitution.[19]

Yet, as demonstrated in this book, not all PB programs delegate authority to citizens, and as a result underperforming PB programs are only partially extending citizenship rights. PB offers the potential to serve as an incubator of rights, but it relies on the coordinated actions of government officials, citizens, and CSOs to create these positive conditions. Of the eight cases analyzed in this book, it is only in Porto Alegre and Ipatinga that it is possible to confirm a sufficient convergence of political

17. Marshall 1950; Thompson 1966; McAdam, Tarrow, and Tilly 2001; Rueschemeyer, Stephens, and Stephens 1992.
18. Wampler and Avritzer 2004; Avritzer 2002; Dagnino 1998.
19. Avritzer 2002.

interests to make the extension of citizenship rights a reality. In four other cases, Recife, Belo Horizonte, São Paulo, and Santo André, there was a partial extension of citizenship rights. Citizens were able to exercise moderate degrees of *voice,* and smaller degrees of *vote,* as they sought to use these new political powers to gain access to new social rights. When there is a decrease in citizens' ability to exercise political rights, there is also a decline in their access to new social rights.

At the extreme end, citizens in Blumenau and Rio Claro were able to exercise very few political rights in PB, resulting in their inability to gain access to any new social rights. Under these circumstances, it is difficult to claim that democracy was deepened. The partial extension of political rights will allow some citizens to secure some new social benefits. These social benefits are strongly contingent on the interests of government officials, suggesting that these rights are more akin to "regulated" citizenship rights than to having a full set of rights.[20] When PB programs are unable to uphold a new set of rights, the most important contribution of actual, existing PB programs may be to help inculcate an understanding that individuals have rights. "The right to have rights" is often promoted by CSOs and some government officials in even the weakest cases.[21] For example, in Blumenau and Rio Claro, where the PB programs were weak, PB served as an institutional environment that helped provide the seeds for the "right to have rights," whereby citizens position themselves as rights-bearing members of their community. Even though citizens gained few short-term benefits, discussions about rights, democratic values, and the distribution of authority provide the building blocks from which future movements can be based.

Accountability

Vertical, horizontal, and societal variants of accountability used throughout this book demonstrate how PB programs reshaped the state and state-society relations. The weakest results were in the area of horizontal accountability, defined as the capacity of one part of the government to place a check on another part (see Chapter 1). Ironically, PB programs depend on the concentration of authority in the mayor's office, thereby limiting the legislative branch and municipal departments from having

20. Santos 1979.
21. Dagnino 1994b, 1998.

clearly defined roles in the policy-making process. There are few legal checks that legislators can use to pressure the mayor to allow them to more actively participate in policy making. PB allows citizens to make decisions, but it divorces municipal legislators from the process. Through the lens of horizontal accountability, the most significant drawback to PB is this circumvention of the municipal legislature in order to give authority directly to citizens.

Yet there is one clear process through which it is possible to confirm that horizontal accountability is being extended: adhering to the rules. Some governments closely follow the published rules. PB programs are based on a clear set of rules that citizens, PB delegates, and government officials are formally committed to following. Generally, the rules can only be changed by majority vote in the PB council. When governments follow the rules, horizontal accountability is being extended because government officials and citizens are adhering to an agreed-upon set of rules. In a political context, when there is the weak rule of law and high flexibility in the way state institutions operate, adherence to an agreed-upon rule set is a noteworthy advance. Adherence to the rules occurred most conspicuously in the cases of Porto Alegre and Ipatinga, where it is possible to argue that the rule of law is being established because the governments committed themselves to following the law they helped establish.[22] The governments elected in Porto Alegre and Ipatinga in 2004 have weaker commitments to strictly adhering to the rules, but some PB delegates are now framing their demands in terms of PB's rules.[23] Therefore, PB offers an alternative means through which reformists can promote the rule of law. Citizens and governments can both be induced to follow an agreed-upon rule set, as the new rules are in both their interests.

There are more promising results from vertical accountability, defined as the capacity of citizens to use institutional means to influence the government's actions (see Chapter 1). When mayors and governments commit themselves to delegating authority to PB, they find it necessary to provide transparent information, organize well-run meetings, meet with citizens and PB delegates outside formal meeting times, and reorganize the bureaucracy. Citizens use the information and capacity-building support provided by the government to make more reasoned choices about

22. O'Donnell 2004.
23. Felisberto Luisi, PB delegate, interview, March 26, 2006, Porto Alegre; focus group, March 28, 2006, Porto Alegre City Market, Porto Alegre.

their policy preferences. As the support from the government increases, there is a corresponding increase in the participation rates and support for PB from citizens and participants. Increases in support, in turn, encourage the government to commit further resources and time to PB because of the potential political, policy, and democratic advances. Vertical accountability through participatory institutions appears to be extended as part of a virtuous circle in which the shared interests of government officials and citizens are premised on the belief that it is mutually beneficial to promote democracy, transparency, public debate, and social justice. In the cases of Porto Alegre and Ipatinga, this has had a spillover effect into electoral politics, as evidenced by the fact that the PT was able to win three elections (1992, 1996, 2000) in which PB was at the forefront of their campaign rhetoric.

Societal accountability, defined as the use of contentious politics and extrainstitutional forms to pressure government officials to respond to citizen demands, was also present in PB (see Chapter 1). Inside PB, citizens often demanded that government officials fulfill their commitments. Citizens also used the public formats to appeal for group solidarity among citizens in order to increase pressure on government officials. The formal structure of PB allowed for networking and organizing across traditional community and policy-arena lines to flourish, which encouraged CSOs to build new alliances. Outside PB, citizens and PB delegates most notably used extrainstitutional forms of societal accountability in Belo Horizonte and Recife when they sought to publicly shame and pressure the government into implementing projects that had been previously selected in PB. Citizens used political tactics common among politically marginalized groups seeking to have their voices heard: street mobilizations, petition drives, and packing of public meetings to place favored issues on the public agenda. The use of contentious politics had a contradictory effect on PB. It had the positive effect of engendering additional support from the government for the specific policy projects. This indicates that societal accountability can be successfully used as method to pressure state actors to respond to citizens' demands. Yet it also had a negative effect on horizontal accountability. The public pressure placed on governments led them to bypass existing procedures and rules associated with PB, which had the effect of undermining the much needed emphasis on the rules of the game. The use of contentious politics to secure additional government support must therefore be considered a mixed blessing.

In sum, a disaggregated analysis of accountability provides a clearer understanding of how PB affects the actions of citizens, CSOs, and government officials. There is great potential for PB programs to induce government officials to establish more open and transparent processes, which then increases trust and encourages greater participation. PB programs demonstrate that the local state can be used by government officials to enhance accountability. Thus, establishing the basis to foster the development of accountability should not be viewed as largely the responsibility of civil society actors; rather, government officials can use the local state to establish processes that promote new state functions. However, the most significant limitation is already inscribed in PB's rules: government must follow PB's rules and respond to citizens' demands in a timely fashion. When the pressure to address the demands outweighs the pressure to abide by the rules, PB becomes an informal institution that is no different from many others in Brazil or other developing countries. When the rules outweigh the demands, the risk is that PB will turn into a bureaucratic institution in which adherence to the rules becomes more important than deliberation, negotiation, and the promotion of intergroup solidarity.

Using the concept of accountability in a disaggregated method shows the different potential advances that PB can produce. PB has the potential to deepen democracy and improve basic state-society relations, but the evidence also clearly shows that we should not expect participatory programs to be this decade's "magic bullet" that will overcome long legacies of authoritarian and exclusionary practices. Again, this finding is derived from the comparative methodology that permits the analysis of a mixed-set of results. The evidence clearly shows that PB, under some circumstances, can extend accountability. But it also shows that poorly performing PB programs will have a limited effect on efforts to extend accountability. Therefore, it is not possible to present a parsimonious conclusion that confirms or denies that PB can extend accountability. Rather, the findings indicate that specific types of localized processes and interactions among government officials and citizens best account for how and when accountability can be established.

Accountability and citizenship are intertwined in PB. Citizens must seek to activate their rights to promote accountability just as they must use their new set of rights in PB to secure social improvements for their neighborhoods. Increases in accountability allow citizens to have access to transparent information and to more closely monitor the actions of the state, which then contributes to the extension of citizenship rights, because

greater numbers of people are able to exercise their rights in a public format. When PB programs function well, they provide citizens with the
opportunity to be actively involved in carving out a new political space for
individuals from historically marginalized groups. But we should not expect accountability to be promoted unless CSO leaders and some citizens
are willing to engage in the often tedious work of holding government
officials accountable for their actions. This does not mean that all citizens
need to be engaged in this part of the process, but rather that some community and CSOs leaders must be willing to exercise their political rights
as a means of holding government officials accountable for how they
administer the new participatory institutions.

Theoretical Insights: Institutional Debates

PB is an excellent institutional venue to demonstrate how citizens, CSOs,
and government officials affect efforts to deepen democracy in Brazil. Citizens use PB to exercise their newly won political rights to secure social
rights. More important, they also use PB to express their *voice* in key public debate as well as exercise their right to *vote* on key decisions made at
the local level. Some PB programs encourage citizens to make alliances
with members of their own community, with individuals from neighbor-
ing communities, and across the entire municipality in order to induce
governments to change their behavior. PB is at the intersection of civil
society and political society, which is why this book contributes to ongoing civil society and institutional debates.

There are two theoretical findings that contribute to institutional
debates. First, PB is a state-sanctioned participatory policy-making institution thoroughly dependent on the representative democratic system in
which it is situated, so the broader institutional environment profoundly
affects how PB programs function. PB draws citizens into public decision-
making venues, but only when the broader political conditions support
the direct delegation of authority. Establishing the conditions that allow
for this broad support is something that is not built overnight, but is
based on years and decades of political organizing by CSOs and interested
political parties.[24]

In Brazil, the devolution of authority to municipalities in the late 1980s

24. Heller 2001, 2000; Baiocchi 2005; Avritzer 2002.

and early 1990s provided mayors with unprecedented access to resources as well as increased responsibilities over public policies. The concentration of authority in the mayor's office provided mayoral administrations with considerable flexibility with which to decide the level of authority that would be delegated to citizens. PB programs are structured to incorporate citizens directly into decision-making venues and to provide a direct challenge to long-standing ways of distributing resources and power, but it is the mayoral administration that must ultimately decide how much authority will be delegated. The importance of the institutional environment is confirmed by work on participatory programs conducted by Goldfrank, Heller, and Nylen.[25]

The willingness of mayors to delegate authority is driven by a combination of factors, including representative democracy's biannual campaigns and elections, intraparty support, mayoral-legislative relations, and ideology.[26] The constant contact between government officials and CSOs gives party elites numerous opportunities to identify the most active community leaders and the most pressing problems faced by the well-organized communities. PB, therefore, can be used by mayors to build a base of electoral support as well as to devise campaign strategies that will appeal to their constituents' desire to meet the latter's most pressing needs. This process has the potential to deepen democracy, since mayors can propose policy solutions to a community's most pressing problems. However, it is also quite possible that mayors may use their increased contacts for narrow partisan gain, thus subverting the ability of PB to deepen local democracy.

PB's success is not based on the government's "benevolence" or "goodwill," but instead on a common shared set of interests between elected officials, their most ardent supporters, and interested constituents.[27] When politicians believe that the delegation of authority will help their long-term political interests, they are more likely to establish a state-sanctioned political institution that is capable of promoting participatory politics. This shared set of interests, however, draws attention to the possibility of extensive co-optation of CSOs and citizens by governments, which further underscores the importance of the presence of contentious politics as a means to limit co-optation.

25. Goldfrank, 2007; Heller 2000; Nylen 2003.
26. Goldfrank, 2007; Nylen 2003.
27. Abers 2000.

PB gives citizens the authority over small projects, long the bread and butter of local legislators. When mayors have a stable voting majority in the municipal legislature, it makes it easier for them to delegate authority to citizens because the mayors don't have to engage in exorbitant side payments to legislators in order to pass the mayors' legislative agendas. As the mayor's voting block decreases, there is also a decline in the level of resources that can be dedicated to PB projects because of the resources needed to fund projects to gain the support of municipal legislators. This is in line with Nylen's findings in Belo Horizonte and Betim.[28]

As revealed by the eighteen mayors in the eight municipalities analyzed in this book, mayors with stronger ideological ties to the expanding field of "participatory publics" were more likely to be deeply committed to the direct participation of citizens in decision-making venues than mayors with more tenuous relationships to these new CSOs.[29] Mayors with closer ties to participatory CSOs were more willing to engage in extended debates, provide relevant policy information, and implement public works projects selected by citizens. Mayors with weaker ties to participatory CSOs were *unlikely* to delegate any real authority directly to citizens. These mayors paid rhetorical lip service to participatory institutions, and among the mayors are those from leftist political parties (PT and Green Party; see Chapter 5). One implication of this finding is that CSOs interested in encouraging politicians to support participatory politics must first be willing to overhaul their own internal processes to promote more democratic practices as well as be more active in advocating for the right of citizens to express their voice and vote in public venues.[30] When CSOs place participatory politics at the front of their agendas, they may be able to foster the growth of alliances with politicians who are willing to support the implementation of state-sanctioned participatory institutions.

Participatory politics, of course, can be created outside state-sanctioned institutions, but the focus of CSOs and leftist party activists during the 1980s and 1990s in Brazil was to establish state institutions that allow for direct citizen participation.[31] The current support for participatory programs by the World Bank, U.N. Habitat, and other organizations represents a broader global movement that emphasizes the direct involvement of citizens in policy-making venues. The argument and evidence presented

28. Nylen 2003, 2002.
29. Wampler and Avritzer 2004.
30. Wampler and Avritzer 2004.
31. Wampler and Avritzer 2004; Avritzer 2002; Barber 1984.

in this book suggests that CSOs, NGOs (national and international), international funding agencies, and think tanks that advocate the adoption of participatory institutions need to be more cognizant of the potential trade-offs associated with the functioning of participatory institutions. State-sanctioned participatory institutions appear to function best as political spaces in which to expand accountability and citizenship rights and deepen democracy when government officials believe that these new institutions will help them advance their own political goals. When governments are not interested in promoting these new institutional spaces, they are more likely to overlook the demands of PB participants, thereby emasculating the institution. If governments implement participatory programs at the behest of international donors and lending agencies and not because of their own strategic, long-term interests, we should expect to see results more similar to those in Blumenau and Rio Claro (see Chapter 5) than in Porto Alegre and Ipatinga (see Chapter 4).

The second institutional finding of this book is that PB's specific rules also significantly affect the outcomes produced.[32] The specific configuration of rules that allows citizens to make certain decisions (and not other decisions) and the internal organization of citizens within PB have significant effects on the outcomes. PB rules can encourage the formation of intragroup solidarity because participants know that they can make long-term deals and alliances to pursue their political and policy interests, as seen in Porto Alegre and Ipatinga. However, PB rules can also fragment participants (Belo Horizonte), neutralize them (Santo André), isolate new groups (São Paulo), or discourage debate (Rio Claro). A goal of the research project behind this book was to hold the rules of the game as constant as possible, so it is notable that when governments chose to select different rules, there was a corresponding change in the outcomes produced by PB programs. There are three different ways that the rules appear to strongly affect PB outcomes: (1) the type of decision-making authority directly delegated to citizens, (2) the internal organization of citizens, and (3) the willingness of the government to follow the rules.

With regard to the delegation of authority directly to citizens, what matters most significantly is that there is a clearly known and easy-to-understand method for allowing citizens to select specific policies. A clear and knowable format allows citizens to quickly identify whether their projects are to be included in the annual budget and, if so, when their projects

---

32. Fung and Wright 2003; Fedozzi 1998.

are likely to be implemented. A well-publicized and easy-to-understand system produces greater transparency, thereby reducing uncertainty, which helps to empower the citizens involved in the process. Although most of the PB programs analyzed in this book copied the rules of Porto Alegre's PB, what distinguishes Porto Alegre and Ipatinga from the other six cases was the establishment of a clear and knowable administrative system for selecting and implementing public works. This finding suggests that a participatory institution's rules should be structured in a straightforward manner, both to improve citizens' understanding and to diminish the government's ability to manipulate the process through which selected projects are implemented. Reorganizing the state is a first step necessary to allow PB programs to flourish.[33]

The internal organization of citizens, which distributes authority within PB, is another rule set that strongly affects outcomes. Porto Alegre's model of electing PB delegates on a sliding scale (based on mobilization) and the creation of a centralized PB council appears to strike a necessary balance between centralization/decentralization and mass mobilization/elite representation. Porto Alegre's model creates neighborhood representatives (PB delegates) and regional representatives (PB councilors; see Chapter 2). The PB delegates organize their communities, negotiate with other PB delegates, and oversee their project proposals from the initial debates through final implementation. PB councilors, two of whom are elected from each region, are the principal checks on the government. The representatives closely follow and monitor PB and the government. The PB council allows its members to build alliances that are municipal-wide. The absence of a PB council (Belo Horizonte) produces a situation in which PB delegates from far-flung regions had little to no contact with one another, thus making it difficult for them to build a broad-based coalition that might counteract the government's interests. PB delegates in Belo Horizonte were fragmented by their PB's rules.

The election of a large number of PB delegates has a detrimental effect on PB. In Recife, there were simply too many PB delegates (six thousand) to allow leaders to strike the necessary bargains that enable intergroup solidarity to be established. It was difficult for PB delegates to communicate with their region's PB delegates, to effectively represent the interests of their region, and to negotiate among themselves to decide which projects would be selected.

33. Fedozzi 1998, 2000; Abers and Keck 2006.

Santo André used a PB council but did not have PB delegates until 2003. The lack of PB delegates made it very difficult for the PB councilors to effectively represent their regions. There was no efficient way to foster dialogue and debate between the elected PB councilor and PB participants because of the limited number of PB councilors and the lack of formal meeting spaces. The implication of this finding is that participatory programs should be structured to provide a well-defined and limited number of PB delegates. Too many representatives (Recife) made negotiations and debate difficult, and too few PB delegates (Santo André and Rio Claro) made it difficult for a region's broad range of interests to be represented. The absence of a PB council (Belo Horizonte) further complicated the PB process because there was a lack of elected representatives who were responsible for oversight duties.

By having a limited number of representatives who exercise specific types of authority, it is possible to improve the quality of debates and negotiations. This implies that PB should not be conceptualized as direct democracy in which all citizens have voice and vote, but a neighborhood-level form of representative democracy in which interested citizens have the right to exercise *voice* and *vote* at different moments of the policy-making process. Citizens are engaged at the local level, and their elected representatives defend their interests within the region and at the municipal level.

The final "rules matter" factor is derived from the government's willingness to adhere to the rules established by PB.[34] At issue is whether the government creates internal, standardized processes by which bureaucrats, appointed officials, and the elected government adhere to PB's rules. Given the flexibility with which Brazilian governments have traditionally approached the enforcement of laws, adherence to PB rules by the government could mark a significant turn in how local Brazilian governmental officials interact with the law.[35] Of the eight cases, Porto Alegre and Ipatinga stand out because their local governments created standardized processes that followed and strengthened their PB programs. Quite simply, these two governments created internal processes that made implementation a standardized process that was more resistant to government manipulation. Although it would be naive to assume that Porto Alegre's and Ipatinga's governments did not engage in any rule transgressions, their publicly known internal administrative procedures made

34. Fedozzi 1998; Nylen 2003; Fung and Wright 2003.
35. O'Donnell 2004.

it more difficult for government leaders to manipulate P B and the implementation of public work projects. In the other six cases analyzed in this
book it is *not* possible to demonstrate that the government implemented
a broad range of internal reforms that would promote PB as a new policy-
making process.

Theoretical Insights: Civil Society

P B programs function better when cs os are able to cooperate with the
government while also being able to use contentious forms of politics
against government officials and P B's opponents.[36] Citizens must act—
or use P B to learn to act—as rights-bearing members of their polity in
order to use their political rights to secure social rights. Citizens must be
willing and able to work closely with government officials and their fellow citizens in order to select public policy projects that are financially,
administratively, and legally viable. Citizens rely on government officials
to provide information and general administrative support, both of which
allow individuals with low levels of education and few resources to navigate in and contribute to complex policy arenas. Citizens need to mobilize
to make their presence felt, but there also needs to be a responsive and
capable state that is able to implement the demands selected by citizens.

Citizens must also be able to convince their P B colleagues to support
their projects, which often requires building intergroup solidarity and
networks of support. Within P B, there is often intense competition among
cs os over access to scarce resources, but the process also encourages citizens to engage in negotiations and deal-making with their fellow citizens.
There is ample evidence to demonstrate that citizens will enter into long-
term negotiations with their fellow citizens, often sacrificing short-term
gains for future gain.[37] The lesson to be drawn from this finding is that
participatory institutions can induce individuals to engage in different
types of behaviors than they are accustomed to practicing under representative democracy. Citizens will forge alliances with their fellow community
members in cs os as well as with other cs os if there is the perception
that their collective organization can provide specific benefits for their
particular interests.

36. Tarrow 1998.
37. Baiocchi 2005; Abers 2000; Nylen 2003; Avritzer 2002; Heller 2000.

The evidence clearly demonstrates that intense cooperation among citizens as well as between citizens and government officials is a necessary condition for allowing PB programs to function well. This finding demonstrates that the state must be placed at the center of our analysis of participatory institutions. If we do not account for the interests of state actors, including elected officials, appointed administrators, and bureaucrats, we will have only a partial understanding of how participatory institutions function. This finding on the importance of citizen-government cooperation confirms the work on Porto Alegre conducted by Abers, Avritzer, and Baiocchi; the work on Belo Horizonte conducted by Avritzer and Nylen; and the analysis of participatory programs in Kerela, India, conducted by Heller.[38] Abers argues that a "synergy" between citizens and government officials produced Porto Alegre's strong outcomes.[39]

Yet the obvious danger for PB delegates and participants is that extensive cooperation can lead to co-optation, whereby the political and governing agenda of the government supplants the political interests and policy goals of PB participants. The antidote to co-optation appears to be the ability and willingness of PB delegates and participants to use contentious politics, both within and outside PB. Within the institutional parameters of PB, citizens need to be able to sharply criticize government officials for the government's policies and actions. For PB to function well, citizens need to be able to position themselves as rights-bearing members of their polity rather than as clients of the state who are asking the government to implement a specific public work. For example, in most meetings I attended in Porto Alegre, citizens spoke to their fellow citizens, first and foremost, and to government officials secondarily. There was a strong emphasis by speakers in Porto Alegre on how they, as citizens and participants, needed to act to improve the quality and authority of PB and increase their access to basic state services. In Belo Horizonte and Recife, there was a much greater mix because although some citizens sought to engage their fellow citizens, the majority of speakers meekly presented themselves to the government, asking it to solve problems rather than attempting to exercise the political rights that had been formally extended to them.

Citizens need to be able to act as rights-bearing members without fear of retribution from government officials. If officials are unable to accept

38. Abers 1998, 2000; Avritzer 2002; Baiocchi 2005; Nylen 2002, 2003; Heller 2000.
39. Abers 2000, 1998.

criticism and thus engage in acts of political retribution, the political space opened to citizens through PB will be quickly constricted. This implies that government officials must be willing to work with citizens in a format in which the government's authority can be challenged by citizens. This is a particularly difficult political skill for politicians to acquire, but it appears to be closely associated with PB programs' most successful outcomes.

The central importance of citizens and CSOs using contentious politics as a means to more fully exercise their newly won political rights has not received as much theoretical attention as has the need for cooperation among citizens and government officials. Baiocchi, and Avritzer and I all note that the ability of citizens to actively make claims on the state as rights-bearing citizens encourages the strengthening of PB programs.[40] However, the evidence and argument presented in this book demonstrates that PB participants need to be willing to act as rights-bearing citizens within PB in order to place sufficient pressure on the government to act in a manner that strongly supports PB.

Although it was beyond the scope of this research project to analyze how PB might encourage the growth of *trust* among participants, the preliminary evidence suggests that PB may encourage the growth of bridging and bonding forms of social capital.[41] Brazilians have notoriously low levels of trust, but a recurring theme in my ethnographic research is that PB participants describe the long-term alliances they built within their own CSOs and across community lines with other CSOs in order to secure long-term goods. The building of trust and social capital through PB is deserving of further attention from scholars.[42] Remarkably, for Brazil, building networks of solidarity and support involved the direct involvement of state actors. Government officials in Porto Alegre and Ipatinga were able to inspire sufficient confidence in their actions that citizens were willing to make political deals involving benefits that would not reach a given community for at least three years.

In sum, the strategies, choices, and decisions of CSOs and citizens regarding how they will interact with government officials *inside* and *outside* PB significantly affect PB programs' outcomes. Importantly, the capacity of PB delegates to position themselves as rights-bearing members of their polity has a significant impact on the success of PB programs. When

40. Baiocchi 2001, 2005; Avritzer 2002; Wampler and Avritzer 2004.
41. Putnam 1993, 2000.
42. Abers 2000, 160–61.

citizens demanded to be able to exercise *voice* and *vote* in a new state institution, PB participants helped to translate their newly won political rights into social gains. One of the policy implications of this finding is that PB will not likely flourish in a political environment in which participants are either unable or unwilling to act as rights-bearing citizens to confront government officials. The deepening of democracy through PB appears to function best when CSOs are able to engage in cooperative and contentious forms of political activities. Conflict among participants is common because of the competition over scarce resources, but so too is intra- and intergroup solidarity. Citizens and groups that seek to use PB to advance their particularistic goals must learn to build stable alliances with other groups. PB does not overcome a fundamental problem of representative democracy: Small minorities or disenfranchised individuals will not be able to secure public policies of their choosing. But PB does allow low-income citizens to organize themselves to participate in a state-sanctioned institution that gives them unprecedented decision-making authority. PB allows low-income and poorly educated citizens to use new political rights to secure social rights.

Conclusions

PB is now being disseminated across Brazil, elsewhere in Latin America, and the developing world. At least 250 Brazilian municipalities have adopted it.[43] Cities and municipalities in at least forty other countries have adopted participatory programs inspired by PB's rules and purported successes.[44] The analysis presented in this book suggests that we should expect a wide variation of outcomes, based primarily on institutional and civil society factors (see fig. 2, this chapter). The analysis also suggests that PB can have a broad impact that contributes to the deepening of democracy.[45] In Porto Alegre and Ipatinga, citizens are engaged in public debates after which they make specific decisions that the government then implements. The results are very encouraging in both these cities, but it also appears that these two cities are exceptional cases. In these two successful cases, democracy is being deepened; we see that citizens are actively

43. Wampler and Avritzer 2005.
44. Cabannes, n.d.
45. Roberts 1998.

involved in their local governments through the selection of specific public policies as well as through engagement in oversight activities. Citizens are producing a culture of participatory politics, which is helping to strengthen democracy.

When PB programs are implemented *without* the strong support of CSOS and the most important political officials, it is unlikely that the programs will produce outcomes that resemble those of Porto Alegre or Ipatinga. When PB programs *lack* basic support from key sectors of the government, then citizens are being invited to devote their political and social organizing efforts to a depowered political institution. When mayoral support for the delegation of authority is low, and when citizens and CSOS are unable to engage in both cooperation and contentious political behavior, then it is not likely that PB programs will make any significant contributions to the deepening of democracy. Therefore, PB's advocates—the political Left, international funding agencies, the World Bank, U.N. Habitat—should carefully chose where and when they will promote the adoption of PB and similar participatory institutions. As shown in this book, PB programs can and do fail, which obviously drastically undermines efforts to deepen democracy, promote social justice, extend accountability, and establish citizenship rights.

PB programs are not a universal, one-size-fits-all solution to improving state performance, working toward social justice, empowering citizens, or deepening democracy. As demonstrated in this book, PB programs do have the potential to promote these positive attributes, but it has also been shown here that we should not necessarily expect such positive outcomes. PB programs are helping to transform basic decision-making processes, but the evidence shows that PB can also be used as an additional decision-making venue rather than being the principal venue for making policy decisions. When governments and CSOS work together, while also allowing CSOS to actively contest the claims of government, we see the best conditions for advancing the deepening of democracy.

APPENDIX

Interviews

Andrade, Edinara, professor, January 10, 2004, Blumenau.

Agenor, Monaco, former PB administrator and municipal employee in Secretary de Subprefeituras, October 15, 2003, São Paulo.

Assis, Franciso, secretary of social policy, Recife (1997–99), September 8, 1998, Recife.

Baierle, Sergio, coordinator of Cidade (NGO), March 26, 2006, Porto Alegre.

Barbosa, Evanildo, president of FASE, December 2, 2003, Recife.

Barbosa, Guilherme, city council member, May 4, 1999, Porto Alegre.

Barrato, Gilson, city council member (1997–2004) (PSDB), April 7, 1999. São Paulo.

Burity, Joanildo, professor, August 25, 1998, Recife.

Cheiza, Rosa Angela, PB adminstrator, May 25, 1999, and June 26, 2000, Porto Alegre.

Conseulo, Maria Gloria, deputy director of finances, April 16, 1999, São Paulo.

Cordeiro, Eleine, municipal employee in health care and in charge of PB projects in health care, October 13, 2003, São Paulo.

Costa, Antonio José, advisor to city council member Zancra, April 19, 1997, São Paulo.

Costa, Fatima, PB administrator responsible for affirmative action program (Segmentos) with PB, October 22, 2003, São Paulo.

Costa, João, PB administrator, December 9, 2003, Recife.

Costa, Liberato, city council member, January 20, 1999, Recife.

Costa, Walner, PB administrator, February 26, 2004, and January 3, 2005, Blumenau.

Daniel, Bruno, professor and Fundap researcher, November 20, 2003, São Paulo.

Dimas, Alexandre, former PB administrator and municipal employee in Department of Subprefeituras, October 15, 2003, São Paulo.

Erundina, Luiza, mayor of São Paulo, May 15, 1997, São Paulo.

Fedozzi, Luciano, professor, former administrator, May 25, 1999, Porto Alegre.

Fonseco, Paulo Cesar, Brazilian Institute of Municipalities, June 22, 1999, Rio de Janeiro.

Gabriel, Celso, advisor to city council member Mohamad Said Mourad, March 25, 1997, and April 20, 1999, São Paulo.

Geddes, Odilon, PT city council member and former submayor of Jabaquara, November 18, 2003, São Paulo.

Gomes, Maria Auxiliadora, coordinator of PT in Belo Horizonte, March 18, 2004, and June 5, 2000, Belo Horizonte.

Grazia de Grazia, FASE NGO, October 24, 2003, Brasilia.

Gutz, Ricardo, city council member, May 8, 1998, Porto Alegre.

Hoflfeldt, Antonio Carlos, city council member (PSDB), May 31, 1999, Porto Alegre.

Jacobi, Pedro, professor at the University of São Paulo, September 1, 1993, São Paulo.

Jorge, Eduardo, secretary of health care under Luiza Erundina and Marta Suplicy, federal deputies, March 31, 1997, São Paulo.

Kayno, Jorge, Instituto Polis, August 19, 2003, São Paulo.

Klunderman, Jean, city council member, January 12, 2004, Blumenau.

Lima, João Paulo, mayor of Recife (2001–8), April 15, 2000, Austin, Texas.

Luisi, Felisberto, PB delegate, May 21, 1999, and March 26, 2006, Porto Alegre.

Luxembergo, Catia, professor, August 25, 1998, Recife.

Mafra, Inácio da Silva, vice mayor, January 22, 2004, Blumeneu.

Melo, Marcos, professor, September 15, 1998, Recife.

Mindrisz, Mauricio, PB planning secretary, October 14, 2003, Santo André.

Navarro, Zander, professor, April 27, 2004, Porto Alegre.

Neder, Carlos, city council member (1999–2004) and state legislator (2005–6), August 10, 1995, and April 22, 1997, São Paulo.

Olegário Filho, Assis Brasil, PB coordinator 1998–2004, May 22, 1999, March 27, 2000, April 20, 2004, March 28, 2006, Porto Alegre.

Oliveira, Ana Beatriz de, Rio Claro's secretary of planning, September 12, 2003, Rio Claro.

Oliveira, Carlos Thadeu C. De, PB administrator in São Paulo, September 4, 2003, and December 4, 2003, São Paulo.

Padre Mauro, Morro de Papagaio, March 14, 2004, and March 25, 2004, Belo Horizinte.

Paiva, Antonio, city council member, May 9, 1997, São Paulo.

Passos, André, PB administrator, 1998–2004, May 24, 1999, March 30, 2000, April 26, 2004, Porto Alegre.

Pintaude, Silviana, PB administrator, September 12, 2003, Rio Claro.

Pizzirana, Fabianne, PB administrator, November 2, 2003, Rio Claro.

Police, Jose, deputy director of finances, São Paulo municipal government, November 6, 2003, São Paulo.

Pont, Raul, Mayor of Porto Alegre, April 26, 2004, Porto Alegre.

Pontual, Pedro, coordinator, Santo André, September 3, 2003, São Paulo.

Rolim, Reidy, researcher, January 10, 2004, Blumenau.

Sanchez, Felix, coordinator of PB in São Paulo, August 15, 2003; September 17, 2003; and October 10, 2003, São Paulo.

Santos, Manualinha, PB adminstrator, April 8, 2004, Ipatinga.

Santos, Teresa, PB administrator, October 14, 2003, Santo André.

Santos, Teresinha, PT administrator, municipal legislature of São Paulo, October 22, 2003, São Paulo.

Silva, Maria Carmen, municipal employee in education department and in charge of PB projects in education, October 20, 2003, São Paulo.

Silva, Niede, ETAPAS (NGO), December 5, 2003, Recife.

Singer, Paulo, professor at USP and secretary of administration under Mayor Luiza Erundina, May 30, 1997, São Paulo.

Soler, Salvador, secretary of social policy, Recife (1993–96), October 6, 1998, Recife.

Teixeira dos Santos, Walter, Jr., secretary of planning, Prefeitura Municipal de Ipatinga, April 8, 2004, Ipatinga.

Trinidade, Isabella, PB administrator, September 4, 2003, São Paulo.

Ursla, Dias, Former PB administrator, September 5, 2003, São Paulo.

Vecina, Gonzalo, secretary of health care under PT mayor Suplicy, December 14, 2003, São Paulo.

Villas Boas, Renata, former POLIS employee and researcher, May 6, 2004, São Paulo.

Zancra, Archibald, city council member, May 7, 1997, São Paulo.

Focus Group Meetings

Alto Vera Cruz, focus group, April 13, 2004, Belo Horizonte.
Capella de Soccorro, delegate forum focus group, November 1, 2003, São Paulo.
FASE NGO, focus group, December 4, 2003, Recife.
Ipatinga City Hall, focus group, April, 8, 2004, Ipatinga.
Morro de Papagaio, focus group, April 5, 2004, Belo Horizonte.
Perus district, focus group, November 19, 2003, São Paulo.
Porto Alegre City Market, focus group, March 28, 2006, Porto Alegre.
Santa Lucia, focus group, April 7, 2004, Belo Horizonte.
Tres Carnerios, focus group, December 10, 2003, Recife.

Survey

Methodology

The survey was conducted by the Instituto Ethos de Pesquisa between November 25 and December 10, 2003, in eight municipalities. Survey methodology: This survey is a random sample of PB delegates within each municipality. There were 695 total surveys completed out of 8,000 possible participants. The distribution among the different municipalities was: Porto Alegre (60), Ipatinga (60), Belo Horizonte (60), Santo André (60), São Paulo (300), Recife (60), Blumenau (60), and Rio Claro (30). In all cities, with the exception of Santo André, the surveys were conducted via telephone. To generate an appropriate phone list of current delegates, the author contacted each municipal government to obtain the names and phone numbers of individuals who were serving as PB delegates in 2003. In the municipalities of São Paulo, Ipatinga, Blumenau, Rio Claro, and Recife, complete lists of all delegates were obtained. Individuals were then randomly selected. In Porto Alegre, we were able to obtain 50 percent of the appropriate numbers, from which we generated a random selection. In Belo Horizonte, we obtained less than 30 percent of potential names and phone numbers, from which we generated a random selection. In Santo André, surveys were conducted in-person at PB neighborhood meetings. Of all the cases, Santo André represents the most likely selection bias toward individuals who are willing to attend a neighborhood meeting during the months of October and November.

Survey Instrument

Name of the interviewer_____ Municipality:_____

First name of interviewed_____ Phone (   )-_____ Date____/____/ 2003

Questionnaire: Participatory Budgeting

1.   Are you currently a delegate or councilor in Participatory Budgeting in *(name city)*?
      1 Delegate   2 Councilor   3 No

1a   (*If no*) Were you previously a delegate or councilor in Participatory Budgeting?
      1 Previously a delegate   2 Previously a councilor   3 No (*stop interview*)

2.   How many times have you been elected delegate in Participatory Budgeting
      in (*name city*)?
      1   2   3   4   5 or more

3.   With PB, were you elected as a representative from regional, thematic, or
      segmented population?
      1 Regional   2 Thematic   3 Segments (affirmative action)   4 Other _____

4.   What is the percentage of the budget that the municipal government spends
      on investments?
      _____ (*note %*)   99. Don't know

4a   Of the total amount of investment spending that the municipal government
      will allocate this year, what is the percentage that is negotiated within PB?
      _____ (*note %*)   99. Don't know

5.   In your opinion, what was the most important factor that led to the adoption
      of PB in your city? (*Read in different order.*) And the second most important?

	Most important	Second most important
Mayor's party	1	1
Personal initiative of the mayor	2	2
Mobilization of community and social movements	3	3
Don't know	4	4
Other_____	5	5

6.   Of the following reasons, what best describes the principal reason that led you
      to participate in PB? (*Read in different order.*) And the second most important?

	Most important	Second most important
Make demands	1	1
Monitor the municipal government	2	2
Inform your community about the municipal government's action	3	3
Help set the municipal government's general priorities	4	4
Don't know	5	5
Other_____	6	6

7. In your opinion, who has the most influence in setting the agenda for the topics that will be debated within PB? *(Read in different order.)* And the second most important?

	Most important	Second most important
Mayor	1	1
PB's councilors	2	2
Government officials	3	3
Government bureaucrats	4	4
Don't know	5	5
Other_____	6	6

8. In your opinion, what is the most important activity that delegates carry out in PB? *(Read in different order.)* And the second most important?

	Most important	Second most important
Gather information	1	1
Deliberate	2	2
Represent their community	3	3
Mobilize their community	4	4
Monitor	5	5
Don't know	6	6

9. When you are negotiating with other delegates within PB, what do you think is the most important factor to convince them to support your particular demand? *(Read in different order.)* And the second most important?

	Most important	Second most important
Present technical information	1	1
Demonstrate that your demand is just	2	2
Demonstrate the mobilization of your community	3	3
Demonstrate that you have the political support of the municipal government	4	4
Don't know	5	5
Other_____	6	6

10. In the past two years, has your neighborhood secured a specific policy benefit from PB?
    1 Yes   2 No   3 Don't know

11. In the past two years, outside PB, has your neighborhood secured a specific policy benefit?
    1 Yes   2 No   3 Don't know

12. *(If yes)* How were these public benefits secured? *(Read in different order.)* And the second most important?

	Most important	Second most important
Through personal contacts with city council members	1	1
By placing pressure on the municipal government through the mobilization of the community	2	2
Through personal contacts with the mayor	3	3
Through an issue-oriented council	4	4
Through a formal public program sponsored by the municipal government	5	5
Don't know	6	6

13. To have a public work included in PB, in your opinion, the support of which of the following groups is most important? *(Read in different order.)* And the second most important?

	Most important	Second most important
Support of own CSO or community group	1	1
Support of other organized groups	2	2
Support of city council members	3	3
Support of other PB delegates	4	4
Support of the municipal government	5	5
Other_____	6	6

14.   After your public work has been formally included in the budget, the support of which of the following groups is most important to ensure that it is actually implemented? *(Read in different order.)* And the second most important?

	Most important	Second most important
Support of own cso or community group	1	1
Support of other organized groups	2	2
Support of city council members	3	3
Support of other PB delegates	4	4
Support of the municipal government	5	5
Other_____	6	6

15.   In your opinion, what is the principal problem that the municipal government faces when it tries to comply with the priorities decided in PB? *(Read in different order.)* And the second most important?

	Most important	Second most important
Lack of the mayor's political interest	1	1
Interferences by city council members	2	2
Lack of financial resources	3	3
Inability of the government to control municipal bureaucracy	4	4
Don't know	5	5

With what frequency, in your opinion, do PB delegates have authority to:

16.   Establish the rules that regulate PB?
       1 Always   2 Almost always   3 Sometimes   4 Never   5 Don't know

17.   Decide general priorities for the city?
       1 Always   2 Almost always   3 Sometimes   4 Never   5 Don't know

18.   Select specific projects?
       1 Always   2 Almost always   3 Sometimes   4 Never   5 Don't know

19.   Stop government projects?
       1 Always   2 Almost always   3 Sometimes   4 Never   5 Don't know

20.   Select projects beyond the financial levels established by the government?
       1 Always   2 Almost always   3 Sometimes   4 Never   5 Don't know

21.   Monitor the implementation of PB-selected projects?
       1 Always   2 Almost always   3 Sometimes   4 Never   5 Don't know

22.   In your opinion, does the government respect the PB process?
       1 Always   2 Almost always   3 Sometimes   4 Never   5 Don't Know

23.   In your opinion, do PB delegates respect the PB process?
    1 Always   2 Almost always   3 Sometimes   4 Never   5 Don't know

24.   Are you currently participating in a community organization or social move-ment?
    1 Yes   2 No

24a.   *(If no to question 24),* have you participated in a community organization or social movement in the past five years?
    1 Yes   2 No

25.   *(If yes to question 24 or 24a)* Are you currently in a leadership position in a community organization or social movement?
    1 Yes   2 No

26.   Have you ever been elected as a representative to a municipal issue-based council?
    1 Yes, currently a representative   2 Yes, already served   3 Never been elected

27.   Do you belong to a union?
    1 Yes   2 No

28.   Do you belong to a political party?
    1 Yes   2 No

28a   *(If yes)* Which party?_____

29.   Do you remember for whom you voted for city council member in 2000?
    1 Yes   2 No

29a   *(If yes to question 29)* If you voted for a party list, which party?_____
    If you voted for an individual candidate, who was the candidate?_____

30.   How old are you?_____

31.   *Interviewer note gender:*
    1 Male   2 Female

32.   What is your level of education
    (1) Don't know how to read or write
    (2) Some elementary school
    (3) Completed elementary school
    (4) Some high school
    (5) Complete high school
    (6) Some college
    (7) College graduate

32.   Using the categories of the IBGE, what is your race?
    1 white   2 brown   3 black   4 yellow   5 indigenous   6 other_____

33.   What was your household income last month?
    (1) 0–2 minimum monthly salaries
    (2) 2–5 minimum monthly salaries
    (3) 6–9 minimum monthly salaries
    (4) 10–20 minimum monthly salaries
    (5) More than 20 minimum monthly salaries
    (6) Don't know/Didn't respond

Data Codes

Variable	Type	Coding
Gender	Dichotomous	(1 = Male, 0 = Female)
Union	Dichotomous	
cso	Dichotomous	
Partisan party identification	Dichotomous	
Policy council participation	Dichotomous	
Times elected as delegate	Interval	
pb benefits	Dichotomous	
Income (household)	Ordinal	(1 = 0–2 minimum monthly salaries, 2 = 3–5 minimum monthly salaries, 3 = 6–9 minimum monthly salaries, 4 = 10–20 minimum monthly salaries, 5 = more than 20 minimum monthly salaries)
Human Development Index	Interval	
Population	Interval	
Total number of years	Interval	
Investment per capita	Interval	
% of mayor's election victory	Interval	
% leftist seats in legislature	Interval	

BIBLIOGRAPHY

Abers, Rebecca. 1998. "From Clientelism to Cooperation: Local Government, Participatory Policy, and Civic Organizing in Porto Alegre, Brazil." *Politics and Society* 26:511–37.

———. 2000. *Inventing Local Democracy: Grassroots Politics in Brazil.* Boulder, Colo.: Lynne Reinner.

Abers, Rebecca, and Margaret E. Keck. 2006. "Mobilizing the State: The Erratic Partner in Brazil's Participatory Water Policy. Paper presented at the annual meeting of the American Political Science Association, Philadelphia, August 31–September 3.

Abrucio, Fernando Luiz. 1998. *Os barões da federação: Os governadores e a redemocratização brasileira.* São Paulo: Hucitec.

Abrucio, Fernando Luiz, and Cláudio Gonçlaves Couto. 1996. "A Redefinição do Papel do Estado no Âmbito Local." *São Paulo em Perspectiva* 10:40–47.

Acioly, Claudio, Jr., Andre Herzog, Eduardo Sandino, and Victor Henry Andrade. 2002. "Participatory Budgeting in the Municipality of Santo André, Brazil: The Challenges in Linking Short-Term Action and Long-Term Strategic Planning." Manuscript draft.

Almeida, Carla Ceília Rodrigues. 1998. *Explorando novos caminhos para a democracia: os desafios da participação na gestão público e o movimento de alfaetização de jovens e adultos da Cidade de São Paulo (MOVA-SP), 1989–1992.* Master's thesis, State University of Campinas, São Paulo.

Alvarez, Sonia E. 1990. *Engendering Democracy in Brazil: Women in Transition Politics.* Princeton: Princeton University Press.

———. 1993. "'Deepening' Democracy: Popular Movement Networks, Constitutional Reform, and Radical Urban Regimes in Contemporary Brazil." In *Mobilizing the Community,* ed. Robert Fisher and Joseph Kling. Newbury Park, CA: Sage.

Alvarez, Sonia E., Evelina Dagnino, and Arturo Escobar. 1998. *Cultures of Politics/Politics of Cultures: Re-visioning Latin American Social Movements.* Boulder, Colo.: Westview Press.

Ames, Barry. 1994. "The Reverse Coattails Effect: Local Party Organization in the 1989 Brazilian Presidential Election." *American Political Science Review* 88:95–111.

———. 1995a. "Electoral Rules, Constituency Pressures, and Pork Barrel: Bases of Voting in the Brazilian Congress." *Journal of Politics* 57:324–43.

———. 1995b. "Electoral Strategy Under Open-List Proportional Representation." *American Journal of Political Science* 39:406–33.

———. 2002. *The Deadlock of Democracy in Brazil: Interests, Identities, and Institutions in Comparative Politics.* Ann Arbor: University of Michigan Press.

Amorim, Octavio Neto. 2002. "The Puzzle of Party Discipline in Brazil." *Latin American Politics and Society* 44:127–44.

Andrade, Edinara. 1996. "As organizações político partidárias (subdiretórios) da decade de 70 e a relação com a estrutura das atuais associações de moradores de Blumenau." Blumeanu, Brazil: Regional University of Blumenau.

————. 1999. "Orçamento Participativo de Blumenau: As mediações entre o poder publico local e a populalção." Blumeanu, Brazil: Regional University of Bluenau.

————. 2000. "Poder local, participação popular, descentralização e clientelismo: A experiênica do Orçamento Participativo de Blumenau." Blumeanu, Brazil: Regional University of Blumenau.

————. 2001. "Desafios de democracia participativo: O Orçamento Participativo de Blumenau e seu impacto sobre as associações de moradores." Blumeanu, Brazil: Regional University of Blumenau.

Araújo, Ilza Andrade. 1996. Políticas e poder: O discurso de participação. São Paulo: AD Hominem.

Araújo, Manoel Caetano, and Maria Izabel Noll. 1996. "Eleições Municipais em Porto Alegre (1947–1992)." Cadermos de Ciênica Política (Porto Alegre: UFRGS).

Armony, Ariel C. 2004. The Dubious Link: Civic Engagement and Democratization. Stanford: Stanford University Press.

Avelino, George Filho. 1994. "Clientelismo e política no Brasil: Revistando velhos problemas." Novos Estudos 38:225–40.

Avritzer, Leonardo. 2002. Democracy and the Public Space in Latin America. Princeton: Princeton University Press.

————, ed. 2004. A Participação em São Paulo. São Paulo: Editora UNESP.

Avritzer, Leonardo, Marisol Recamán, and Gustavo Venturi. 2004. "O associativismo na cidade de São Paulo." In A participação em São Paulo, ed. Leonardo Avritzer. São Paulo: Editora UNESP.

Avritzer, Leonardo, and Zander Navarro, eds. 2003. A inovação democrática no Brasil: O Orçamento Participativo. São Paulo: Cortez Editores.

Azevedo, Neimar Duarte. 2003. Orçamento Participativo de Belo Horizonte: Elementos para uma leitura institucional. PhD diss., Universidade Federal de Minas Gerais, Belo Horizonte, Brazil.

Azevedo, Sergio , and Virgínia Rennó dos Mares Guia. 2001. "O Orçamento Participativo como política pública: Reflexões sobre o caso de Belo Horizonte." Caderno CRH 35:179–97.

Baierle, Sergio. 1992. Un novo princípio etico-político: Prática social e sujeito nos movimentos populares urbanos em Porto Alegre nos anos 90. Master's thesis, Universidade de Campinas, Campinas, Brazil.

————. 1998. "The Explosion of Citizenship: The Emergence of a New Ethical-Political Principle in Popular Movements in Porto Alegre, Brazil." In Cultures of Politics/Politics of Cultures: Re-visioning Latin American Social Movements, ed. Sonia E. Alvarez, Evelina Dagnino, and Arturo Escobar. Boulder, Colo.: Westview Press.

Baiocchi, Gianpaolo. 2001. "Participation, Activism, and Politics: The Porto Alegre Experiment and Deliberative Democratic Theory." Politics and Society 29:43–72.

————, ed. 2003. Radicals in Power: The Workers' Party (PT) and Experiments in Urban Democracy in Brazil. New York: Zed Books.

————. 2005. Militants and Citizens: The Politics of Participatory Democracy in Porto Alegre. Stanford: Stanford University Press.

Balcão, Nilde, and Ana Claudia Teixeira, eds. 2003. Controle social do orçamento público, no. 44. São Paulo: Pólis Instituto.

Baquero, Marcello. 2003. "Construindo uma otra sociedade: O capital social na estruturação de uma cultura politica participativa no Brasil. *Revista de Sociologia e Politica* 21 (November): 83–108.

Barban, Vilma, ed. 2003. *Fortalecimento da sociedade civil em regiões de extrema pobreza*. São Paulo: Pólis #43.

Barber, Benjamin. 1984. *Strong Democracy: Participatory Politics for a New Age*. Berkeley and Los Angeles: University of California Press.

Barbosa, Evanildo. 2003. *Das tensões ás intenções: Gestão do planejamento urbano e Orçamento Participativo no Recife* (1997–2002). PhD diss., Universidade Federal de Pernambuco, Recife, Brazil.

Benevides, Maria Victoria, Paulo Vannuchi, and Fábio Kerche, eds. 2003. *Reforma política e cidadania*. São Paulo: Instituto Cidadania and Editora Fundação Perseu Abramo.

Berg-Schlosser, Dirk, and Norbert Kertsing. 2003. *Poverty and Democracy: Self-Help and Political Participation in Third World Cities*. New York: Zed Books.

Blair, Harry. 2000. "Participation and Accountability at the Periphery: Democratic Local Governance in Six Countries." *World Development* 28 (1): 21–39.

Boone, Catherine. 2003. *Political Topographies of the African State: Territorial Authority and Institutional Choice*. New York: Cambridge University Press.

Bryan, Frank M. 2004. *Real Democracy: The New England Town Meeting and How It Works*. Chicago: Chicago University Press.

Buarque de Holanda, Sérgio. 1936. *Raizes do Brasil*. Rio de Janeiro: J. Olympio.

Burdick, John. 1993. *Looking for God in Brazil: The Progressive Catholic Church in Urban Brazil's Religious Arena*. Berkeley and Los Angeles: University of California Press.

Cabannes, Yves. n.d. "Municipal Finance and Participatory Budgeting: Base Document." Book manuscript.

Caldeira, Teresa. 1996. "Fortified Enclaves: The New Urban Segregation." *Public Culture* 8:303–28.

Campbell, Tim. 2003. *The Quiet Revolution: Decentralization and the Rise of Political Participation in Latin American Cities*. Pittsburgh: University of Pittsburgh Press.

Carvalho, José. 1987. *Os Bestializados: O Rio de Janeiro e a República que não foi*. São Paulo: Companhia das Letras.

Carvalho, Maria do Carmo A., Ana Claudia C. Teixeira, Luciana Antonini, and E. Inês Magalhães. 2002. "Orçamento Participativo em municípios Paulistas (1997–2000)" *Dicas* 5. São Paulo: Instituto Pólis.

Carvalho, Maria do Carmo A. A., and Ana Claudia C. Teixeira, eds. 2000. *Conselhos Gestores de Políticas Públicas*, no. 37. São Paulo: Pólis.

Casteñeda, Jorge. 1993. *Utopia Unarmed*. New York: Vintage Books.

Chaui, Marilena. 1989. *Cultura e Democracia—o discurso competente e outras falas*. São Paulo: Editora Cortez.

Chavez, Daniel, and Benjamin Goldfrank. 2004. *The Left in the City: Participatory Local Governments in Latin America*. London: IAB/TNI.

Coelho, Vera Schattan P., and Marcos Nobre, eds. 2004. *Participação e Deliberação: Teoria Democrática e Experiências Institucionais no Brasil Contemporâneo*. São Paulo: Editora 34.

Cohen, Jean, and Andrew Arato. 1992. *Civil Society and Political Theory*. Cambridge: MIT Press.

Cohen, Jean, and Joel Rogers. 1995. *Associations and Democracy*. London: Verso.
Collier, David, and Steven Levitsky. 1997. "Democracy with Adjectives: Conceptual Innovation in Comparative Research." *World Politics* 49:430–51.
Couto, Cláudio Gonçalves. 1995. *O Desafio de ser governo: O PT na Prefeitura de São Paulo (1988–1992)*. Rio de Janiero: Paz e Terra.
Couto, Cláudio Gonçalves, and Fernando Luiz Abrucio. 1995. "Governando a cidade? A força e a fraqueza da Câmara Municipal." *São Paulo em Perspectiva* 9:57–65.
Crawford, Sue E. S., and Elinor Ostrom. 1995. "A Grammar of Institutions." *American Political Science Review* 89:582–600.
Cunha, Eleonora Schettni Martins. 2004. *Aprofundado a democracia: O potencial dos Conselhos de Polítícas a Orçamentos Participativos*. Ph.D. diss., Universidade Federal de Minas Gerais, Belo Horizonte, Brazil.
Dagnino, Evelina. 1994a. *Os Anos 90: Politica e sociedade no Brasil*. São Paulo: Editora Brasiliense.
———. 1994b. "Os movimentos sociais e a emergência de uma nova noção de cidadania." In *Anos 90: Política e Sociedade no Brasil*. São Paulo: Brasiliense.
———. 1998. "The Cultural Politics of Citizenship, Democracy and the State." In *Cultures of Politics/Politics of Cultures: Re-visioning Latin American Social Movements*, ed. Sonia E. Alvarez, Evelina Dagnino, and Arturo Escobar. Boulder, Colo.: Westview Press.
———. 2002. *Sociedade civil e espaços públicos no Brasil*. São Paulo: Paz e Terra.
Dagnino, Evelina, Alberto J. Olvera, and Aldo Panfichi, eds. 2006a. *A disputa pela construção democrática na América Latina*. São Paulo: Paz e Terra.
———. 2006b. "Para uma Outra Leitura da Disputa Pela Construção Democrática na América Latina." In *A disputa pela construção democrática na América Latina*, ed. Evelina Dagnino, Alberto J. Olvera, and Aldo Panfichi. São Paulo: Paz e Terra.
Dahl, Robert A. 1961. *Who Governs? Democracy and Power in an American City*. New Haven: Yale University Press.
———. 1971. *Polyarchy: Participation and Opposition*. New Haven: Yale University Press.
Daniel, Bruno. 2003. "O orçamento participativo local no seu devido lugar: Limites colocados por seu desenho institucional e pelo contexto brasileiro—reflexões sobre a experiência de Santo André nos períodos 1989–1992 e 1997–2000." Ph.D. diss., Catholic University of São Paulo.
Daniel, Celso. 1994. "Gestão local e participação da socieade." In *Participação Popular nos Governos Locais*, ed. Renata Villas Boas. São Paulo: Instituto Pólis.
Davis, Mike. 2006. *Planet of Slums*. New York: Verso.
de Souza, Marilete, 2003. *Análise sócio política do Orçamento Participativo: Município de Blumenau no período de 1997 a 2003*. Master's thesis, Universidade do Vale do Itajaí, Santa Catarina, Brazil.
Diamond, Larry, Jonathan Hartlyn, Juan J. Linz, and Seymour Martin Lipset. 1999. *Democracy in Developing Countries: Latin America*. Boulder, Colo.: Lynne Reinner.
Diamond, Larry, and Leonardo Morlino. 2004. "The Quality of Democracy: An Overview." *Journal of Democracy* 15 (4): 20–31.
Diani, Mario. 1992. "The Concept of Social Movement." *Sociological Review* 4:1–25.

Diniz, Eli. 1982. *Voto e maquina política: Patronagem e clientelismo no Rio de Janeiro*. Rio de Janeiro: Paz e Terra.

———. 1997. *Crise, reforma do estado e governabilidade: Brasil, 1985–95*. São Paulo: Fundacão Getúlio Vargas.

Diniz, Eli, and Sérgio de Azevedo, eds. 1997. *Reforma do Estado e Democracia no Brasil*. Brasília: Editora UnB and ENAP.

Dirceu, José, and Vladimir Palmeria. 1998. *Abaixa a ditadura: O movimento de 68 contado por seus líderes*. Rio de Janeiro: Garamond.

Doimo, Ana Maria. 1995. *A vez e a voz do popular movimentos sociais e participação pós-70*. Rio de Janeiro: ANPOCS.

Domínguez, Jorge I., and Michael Shifter. 2003. *Constructing Democratic Governance in Latin America*. Baltimore: Johns Hopkins University Press.

Dryzek, John S. 2000. *Deliberation Democracy and Beyond: Liberals, Critics, and Contestations*. Oxford: Oxford University Press.

Eaton, Kent. 2004a. "Designing Subnational Institutions: Regional and Municipal Reforms in Post Authoritarian Chile." *Comparative Political Studies* 37:218–44.

———. 2004b. *Politics Beyond the Capital: The Design of Subnational Institutions in South America*. Stanford: Stanford University Press.

Edwards, Bob, Michael W. Foley, and Mario Diani, eds. 2001. *Beyond Tocqueville: Civil Society and the Social Capital Debate in Comparative Politics*. Hanover: University Press of New England.

Edwards, Michael. 2004. *Civil Society*. Cambridge: Polity Press.

Erundina, Luiza. 1990. "Sem medo de ser governo." *Teoria e Debate* 11:13–15.

———. 1991. *Exercício da Paixão Política*. São Paulo: Cortez Editora.

Escobar, Arturo, and Sonia E. Alvarez. 1992. *The Making of Social Movements in Latin America*. Boulder, Colo.: Westview Press.

Escobar, Cristina. 2002. "Clientelism and Citizenship: The Limits of Democratic Reform in Sucre, Colombia." *Latin American Perspectives* 29 (5): 20–47.

Evans, Peter, Dietrich Rueschemeyer, and Theda Skocpol. 1985. *Bringing the State Back In*. New York: Cambridge University Press.

Evers, Tilman. 1985. "Identity: The Hidden Side of New Social Movements in Latin America." In *New Social Movements and the State in Latin America*, ed. David Slater. Amsterdam: CEDLA.

Farah, Marta Ferreira Santos. 1996. "Gestão pública e cidadania: Iniciativas inovadoras na administração subnacional no Brasil." *Revista da Administração Publica* 31:126–56.

Faria, Antonio, and Otávio Prado. 2002. "Orçamento Participativo Interativo." In *20 experiências de Gestão Público e Cidadania*. São Paulo: Programa Gestão Público e Cidadania and the Getulio Vargas Foundation.

Faria, Claudia Feres. 2002. "Relatorio de pesquisa: Consideracoes sobre a dinamica, a implementacão e os atores do Orcamento Participativo-RS." In *A Inovação Democratica no Brasil*, ed. Leonardo Avritzer and Zander Navarro. São Paulo: Cortez.

Fedozzi, Luciano. 1998. *Orçamento Participativo: Reflexões sobre a experiência de Porto Alegre*. Porto Alegre: Tomo Editorial.

———. 2000. *O poder da aldeia: Gênese e historia do Orçamento Participativo de Porto Alegre*. Porto Alegre: Tomo Editorial.

Felgueiras, Débora, and Maria do Carmo A. A. Carvalho. 2000. *Orçamento Participativo no ABC: Mauá, Ribeirão Pires e Santo André.* São Paulo: Instituto Pólis.
Figueiredo, Argelina Cheibub, and Fernando Limongi. 1999. *Executivo e legislativo na nova ordem constitucional.* Rio de Janeiro: Editora Fundaçao Getúlio Vargas.
———. 2000. "Presidential Power, Legislative Organization, and Party Behavior in Brazil." *Comparative Politics* 32:151–70.
Fischer, Frank. 2003. *Reframing Public Policy: Discursive Politics and Deliberative Practices.* Oxford: Oxford University Press.
Font, Mauricio A. 2003. *Transforming Brazil: A Reform Era in Perspective.* Lanham, MD: Rowman and Littlefield.
Fontes, Breno Augusto S. M. 1997. "Práticas de gestão compartildadas entre o estado e a sociedade civil: O exemplo do Projeto Parceria nos morros da Cidade do Recife." In *Política Contemporaneidade no Brasil,* ed. Marcos Aurélio Guedes de Oliveria. Recife: Bagaço.
Fox, Jonathon. 1994. "The Difficult Transition from Clientelism to Citizenship: Lessons from Mexico." *World Politics* 46:151–84.
Fraser, Nancy. 1993. "Rethinking the Public Sphere: A Contribution to the Critique of Actually Existing Democracy." In *The Phantom Sphere,* ed. Bruce Robbins. Minnesota: University of Minnesota Press.
French, John D. 1992. *The Brazilian Workers' ABC: Class Conflict and Alliances in Modern São Paulo.* Chapel Hill: University of North Carolina Press.
Friedman, Elisabeth Jay, and Kathryn Hochstetler. 2002. "Assessing the Third Transition in Latin American Democratization: Representational Regimes and Civil Society in Argentina and Brazil." *Comparative Politics* 35 (1): 21–42.
Fundação Perseu Abramo. www.fpabramo.org.br/.
Fung, Archon, and Erik Olin Wright. 2001. "Deepening Democracy: Innovations in Empowered Participatory Governance." *Politics and Society* 29:5–41.
———. 2003. *Deepening Democracy: Institutional Innovations in Empowered Participatory Governance.* New York: Verso.
Gaventa, John. 2002. "Introduction: Exploring Citizenship, Participation and Accountability." *IDS Bulletin* 33 (2): 1–11.
Gay, Robert. 1994. *Popular Organization and Democracy in Rio de Janeiro: A Tale of Two Favelas.* Philadelphia: Temple University Press.
Genro, Tarso. 1995a. "Reforma do estado e Democratização do Poder Local." In *Poder Local, Participação Popular, Construção da Cidadania,* ed. Renta Villas Boas and Vera Telles. São Paulo: Fórum Nacional de Participação Popular nas Administrações Municipais.
———. 1995b. *Utopia Possível.* 2d ed. Porto Alegre: Artes e Ofícios.
———. 1997. *Porto da Cidadania.* Porto Alegre: Artes e Ofícios.
Genro, Tarso, and Ubiratan de Souza. 1997. *Orçamento Participativo: A experiência de Porto Alegre.* São Paulo: Editora Fundação Perseu Abramo.
Gestão Público e Cidadania. www.inovando.fgvsp.br/.
Gohn, Maria da Gloria. 1995. *História dos movimentos e lutas sociais: A construção da cidadania dos Brasileiros.* São Paulo: Edições Loyola.
Goldfrank, Benjamin. 2003. "Making Participation Work in Porto Alegre." In *Radicals in Power: The Workers' Party (PT) and Experiments in Urban Democracy in Brazil,* ed. Gianpaolo Baiocchi. New York: Zed Books.
———. 2007. "The Politics of Deepening Local Democracy: Decentralization, Party

Institutionalization, and Participation." *Comparative Politics* 39 (January): 147–68.

Goldfrank, Benjamin, and Aaron Schneider. 2003. "Restraining the Revolution or Deepening Democracy? The Workers' Party in Rio Grande do Sul." In *Radicals in Power: The Workers' Party (PT) and Experiments in Urban Democracy in Brazil*, ed. Gianpaolo Baiocchi. New York: Zed Books.

Gomes, Lilian Cristina. 2004. "Entre o legal e o ilegal: Associativismo e participação em três vilas e favelas de Belo Horizonte—estudo de caso comparativo." Masters' thesis, Universidade Federal de Minas Gerais.

Graham, Richard. 1990. *Patronage and Politics in Nineteenth-Century Brazil*. Stanford: Stanford University Press.

Grau, Nuria Cunill. 1997. *Repansando o público através da sociedade: Novas formas de gestão pública e representação social*. Rio de Janeiro: ENAP and Editora Revan.

Grau, Nuria Cunill, Sonia Ospina, and Ariel Zaltsman. 2004. "Performance Evaluation, Public Management Improvement, and Democratic Accountability: Some Lessons from Latin America." *Public Management Review* 6 (2): 229–51.

Guidry, John. 2003. "Not Just Another Labor Party: The Workers' Party and Democracy in Brazil." *Labor Studies Journal* 28:83–108.

Hagopian, Frances. 1996. *Traditional Politics and Regime Change in Brazil*. New York: Cambridge University Press.

Harvard University, Graduate School of Design, Center for Urban Development Studies. 2003. "Assessment of Participatory Budgeting in Brazil." Washington D.C., Inter-American Development Bank.

Held, David. 1987. *Models of Democracy*. Stanford: Stanford University Press.

Heller, Patrick. 2000. "Degrees of Democracy: Some Comparative Lessons from India." *World Politics* 52 (4): 484–519.

———. 2001. "Moving the State: The Politics of Democratic Decentralization in Kerala, South Africa, and Porto Alegre." *Politics and Society* 29 (1): 131–64.

Hochstetler, Kathryn. 2000. "Democratizing Pressures from Below? Social Movements in the New Brazilian Democracy." In *Democratic Brazil: Actors, Institutions, and Processes*, ed. Peter R. Kingstone and Timothy J. Power. Pittsburgh: University of Pittsburgh Press.

Hollanda, Sergio. 1937. *Raizes do Brasil*. Rio de Janeiro: Jose Olympio.

Horn, Henrique Carlos. 1994. *Porto Alegre: O desafio da mudança: As políticas financeira, administrativa e de recursos humanos no Governo Olívio Dutra, 1989–1992*. Porto Alegre: Ortiz.

Houtzager, Peter B., Arnab Acharya, Adrian Gurza Lavalle. 2004. "Civil Society Representation in the Participatory Budget and Deliberative Councils of Sao Paulo, Brazil. *IDS Bulletin* 35 (2): 40–48.

Hunter, Wendy. 2004. "From Opposition Movement to Government Party: Growth and Expansion of the Workers' Party in Brazil." Paper presented at the 100th annual meeting of the American Political Science Association meeting, Chicago. September.

Instituto Brasileiro de Geografia e Estadística [Brazilian Institute for Geography and Statistics]. www.ibge.gov.br/.

Jacobi, Pedro. 1989. *Movimentos sociais e políticas públicas: Demands por saneamento básico e saúde, São Paulo, 1974–84*. São Paulo: Cortez Editora.

———. 2000. *Políticas Sociais e Amplicacao da Cidadania*. Sao Paulo: FGV Editora.

Jacobi, Pedro, and Marco Antonio Teixeira. 1996. "Orçamento Participativo: Co-responsabilidade na gestão das cidades." *São Paulo em Perspectiva* 10:119–28.

Jelin, Elizabeth, and Eric Hershberg. 1996. *Constructing Democracy: Human Rights, Citizenship, and Society in Latin America.* Boulder, Colo.: Westview Press.

Keck, Margaret E. 1992. *The Workers' Party and Democratization in Brazil.* New Haven: Yale University Press.

Kingstone, Peter R., and Timothy J. Power. 2000. *Democratic Brazil: Actors, Institutions, and Processes.* Pittsburgh: University of Pittsburgh Press.

Kleettenberg, Josiane. 2002. "Participação popular na função legislativa do município de Blumenau." Undergraduate thesis project, Regional University of Blumenau.

Koeble, Thomas A. 1995. "A Review Article: The New Institutionalism in Political Science and Sociology." *Comparative Politics* 27:231.

Koonings, Kees. 2004. "Strengthening Citizenship in Brazil's Democracy: Local Participatory Governance in Porto Alegre." *Bulletin of Latin American Research* 23 (1): 79–99.

Kowarick, Lúcio, and André Singer. 1993. "A experiência do Partido dos Trabalhadores na Prefeitura de São Paulo." *Novos Estudos CEBRAP* 35: 205–20.

Larangeira, Sônia. 1996. "Gestão e participação: A Experiência do Orçamento Participativo em Porto Alegre." *São Paulo em Perspectiva* 10:129–37.

Mahoney, James, and Dietrich Rueschemeyer. 2003. *Comparative Historical Analysis in the Social Sciences.* Cambridge: Cambridge University Press.

Mainwaring, Scott, and Timothy R. Scully. 1995. *Building Democratic Institutions: Party Systems in Latin America.* Stanford: Stanford University Press.

Marinho, Geraldo, and Milton Botler. 1998. "10 anos de PREZEIS: Uma Política de Urbanização no Recife." Recife. Mimeo.

Marquetti, Adelmir. 2003. "Democracia, equidade e effciencia, o caso do Orçamento Participativo em Porto Alegre." In *A Inovação Democrática no Brasil: O Orçamento Participativo,* ed. Leonardo Avritzer and Zander Navarro. São Paulo: Cortez Editores.

Marshall, T. H. 1950. *Citizenship and Social Class.* Cambridge: Cambridge University Press.

Martinez, Fernanda. 2003. "A democracia digital." Programa Gestão Público e Cidadania and Getulio Vargas Foundation.

Martinez, Fernanda, Jose Carlos Vaz, and Winthrop Carty. 2004. "Internet Use and Citizen Participation in Local Government: Ipatinga's Interactive Participatory Budgeting." Boston: Ash Institute, Harvard University.

McAdam, Doug. 2001. *The Dynamics of Contention.* New York: Cambridge University Press.

McAdam, Doug, John D. McCarthy, and Mayer N. Zald. 1996. *Comparative Perspectives on Social Movements: Political Opportunities, Mobilizing Structures, and Cultural Framings.* New York: Cambridge University Press.

McAdam, Doug, Sidney Tarrow, and Charles Tilly, 1996. "To Map Contentious Politics." *Mobilization* 1:14–28.

———. 2001. *Dynamics of Contention.* New York: Cambridge University Press.

Migdal, Joel S. 2001. *State in Society: Studying How States and Societies Transform and Constitute One Another.* Cambridge: Cambridge University Press.

Ministério da Fazenda. www.stn.fazenda.gov.br.

Moisés, José Alvaro. 1995. *Os Brasileiros e a democracia*. São Paulo: Atica.

Montero, Alfred P. 2000. "Devolving Democracy? Political Decentralization and the New Brazilian Federalism." In *Democratic Brasil: Actors, Institutions, and Processes*, ed. Peter R. Kingstone and Timothy J. Power. Pittsburgh: University of Pittsburgh Press.

Montero, Alfred P., and David J. Samuels. 2004. *Decentralization and Democracy in Latin America*. Notre Dame: University of Notre Dame Press.

Mouffe, Chantal. 1992. *Dimensions of Radical Democracy: Pluralism, Citizenship, Community*. New York: Verso.

Moura, Alexandra Sobreira. 1990. *Terra do Mangue: Invasões urbanas no Recife*. Recife: FUNDAJ.

Munck, Gerardo, and Jay Verkuilen. 2000. "Measuring Democracy: Evaluating Alternative Indices." Paper presented at the annual meeting of the American Political Science Association, Washington, D.C., August.

Navarro, Zander. 2003. "O 'Orçamento Participativo' de Porto Alegre (1989–2002): Um conciso comentário crítico." In *A Inovação Democratica no Brasil: O Orçamento Participativo*, ed. Leonardo Avritzer and Zander Navarro. São Paulo: Cortez.

Nunes, Victor Leal. 1997. *Coronelismo, enxada e voto: O município e o regime representativo no Brasil*, 3d ed. São Paulo: Editora Nova Fronteira.

Nylen, William R. 2002. "Testing the Empowerment Thesis: The Participatory Budget in Belo Horizonte and Betim, Brazil." *Comparative Politics* 34:127–45.

———. 2003. *Participatory Democracy Versus Elitist Democracy: Lessons from Brasil*. New York: Palgrave Macmillan.

O'Donnell, Guillermo. 1994. "The State, Democratization, and Some Conceptual Problems: A Latin American View with Glances at Some Post-Communist Countries." In *Democracy, Markets, and Structural Reform in Latin America*, ed. William C. Smith, Carlos H. Acuma, and Eduardo A Gamarra. New Brunswick, Conn.: Transaction.

———. 1998. "Horizontal Accountability in New Democracies." *Journal of Democracy* 9:112–26.

———. 2004. "Why the Rule of Law Matters." *Journal of Democracy* 15 (4): 32–46.

O'Neill, Kathleen. 2003. "Decentralization as an Electoral Strategy." *Comparative Political Studies* 36 (9): 1068–91.

Ostrom, Elinor. 1990. *Governing the Commons: The Evolution of Institutions for Collective Action*. Cambridge: Cambridge University Press.

Oxhorn, Philip. 1995. *Organizing Civil Society*. University Park: Pennsylvania State University Press.

———. 2003. "Social Inequality, Civil Society, and the Limits of Citizenship in Latin America." In *What Justice? Whose Justice? Fighting for Fairness in Latin America*, ed. Susan Eva Eckstein and Timothy P. Wickham-Crowley. Berkeley and Los Angeles: University of California Press.

Paoli, Maria Celia, and Verada Silva Telles. 1998. "Social Rights: Conflicts and Negotiations in Contemporary Brazil." In *Cultures of Politics/Politics of Cultures: Re-visioning Latin American Social Movements*, ed. Sonia E. Alvarez, Evelina Dagnino, and Arturo Escobar. Boulder, Colo.: Westview Press.

Pateman Carole. 1970. *Participation and Democratic Theory*. Cambridge: Cambridge University Press.

Pedrini, Dalila Maria, Edinara Andrade, Reidy Rolim, and Sabrina Muller. 1999. "O Orçamento Participativo de Blumenau: Processo de Implementação e Desenvolviento 1997–1998." *Dynamis* 7 (27): 96–102.

Pires, Valdemir. 2002. "Limites e pontencialidades do Orçamento Participativo." *Revista ABOP (Associação Brasileira de Orçamento Público)* 4 (43).

Pont, Raúl. 2003. *Democracia, igualdade e qualidade de vida: A experiência de Porto Alegre.* Porto Alegre: Veraz.

Pontual, Pedro de Carvalho. 2000. *O processo educativo no Orçamento Participativo: Aprendizados dos atores de sociedade civil e do estado.* PhD diss., Catholic University of São Paulo.

Power, Timothy. 2000. *The Political Right in Postauthoritarian Brazil: Elites, Institutions, and Democratization.* University Park: Penn State Press.

Przeworski, Adam, Susan C. Stokes, and Bernard Manin. 1999. *Democracy, Accountability, and Representation.* New York: Cambridge University Press.

Putnam, Robert. 1993. *Making Democracy Work: Civic Traditions in Modern Italy.* Princeton: Princeton University Press.

————. 2000. *Bowling Alone: The Collapse and Revival of American Community.* New York: Simon and Schuster.

Quem é o Público do Orçamento Participativo: Se Perfil, Porque Participa, e o Que Pensa do Processo. 1999. Porto Alegre: Cidade.

Revista de COMPOR. 1999. Prefeitura de Ipatinga, MG.

Ribeira, Frank de Paula. 2001. "Cidadania possível ou neoclientelismo urbano? Cultura e política no Orçamento Participativo de Habitação em Belo Horizonte (1995–2000)." Belo Horizonte: Escola de Governo, Fundação João Pinheiro, Governo de Minas Gerias.

Ribeiro, Ana Clara, and Grazia de Grazia. 2003. *Experiências de Orçamento Participativo no Brasil: Período de 1997 a 2000.* Petrópolis: Vozes.

Ribeiro, Darcy. 1995. *O povo Brasileiro: A formação e o sentido do Brasil.* São Paulo: Companhia Das Letras.

Ribeiro, Luiz César de Quiroz. 1994. "O municipio e a reforma urbana: Os desafios do política redistributiva." *Proposta* 62:5–13.

Ricci, Rudá. 2004. "Contradições na implementação das ações de participação." Paper presented at the workshop "Aprofundando os Aspectos da Participação," Belo Horizonte, Brazil, April 23.

Roberts, Kenneth. 1998. *Deepening Democracy? The Modern Left and Social Movements in Chile and Peru.* Stanford: Stanford University Press.

Rolim, Reidy. 2001. *Desafios da democracia participativa: O Orçamento Participativo de Blumenau e seu impacto sobre as associações de moradores.* Master's thesis, Regional University of Blumenau.

Roniger, Luis. 1994. *Democracy, Clientelism, and Civil Society.* Boulder, Colo.: Lynne Reinner.

Rother, Larry. 2004. "Corruption Accusations Arise from Brazil Mayor's Death." *New York Times,* February 1, International Sec.

Roussopoulos, Dimitrios, and C. George Benello, eds. 2005. *Participatory Democracy: Prospects of Democratizing Democracy.* Montreal: Black Rose.

Rueschemeyer, Dietrich, Evelyne Huber Stephens, and John D. Stephens. 1992. *Capitalist Development and Democracy.* Chicago: University of Chicago Press.

Rustow, Dankwart. 1970. "Transitions to Democracy." *Comparative Politics* 2:337–63.

Sales, Teresa. 1994. "Raízes da desigualdade social na cultura política Brasileira." *Revista Brasileira de Ciências Sociais* 25:26–37.

Samuels, David. 2002. "Pork Barreling Is Not Credit Claiming or Advertising: Campaign Finance and the Sources of the Personal Vote in Brazil." *Journal of Politics* 64:845–63.

Santos, Boaventura de Sousa. 1998. "Participatory Budgeting in Porto Alegre: Toward a Redistributive Democracy." *Politics and Society* 26:461–510.

————. 2002. *Democratizar a democracia—Os caminhos da democracia participativa.* Rio de Janeiro: Civilização Brasileira.

————, ed. 2005. *Democratizing Democracy: Beyond the Liberal Democratic Canon.* New York: Verso.

Santos, Orlando Alves dos, Jr., Luiz Cesar de Quieroz Ribiero, and Sergio de Azevedo, eds. 2004. *Governança Democrática e Poder Local: a Experiência dos Conselhos Municipais no Brasil.* Editora Revan and Observatório das Metrópoles.

Santos, Wanderly Guilherme. 1979. *Cidadania e justiça: A política social na ordem Brasileira.* Rio de Janeiro: Editora Campus.

Schettini, Eleonora. 2004. "Aprofundando a democracia: O potencial dos Conselhos de Políticas e Orçamentos Participativos." Master's thesis, Federal University of Minas Gerais.

Sellers, Jefferey M. 2002. *Governing from Below: Urban Regions and the Global Economy.* Cambridge: Cambridge University Press.

Silva, Evanildo Barbosa da. 2003. *Das tensões ás intenções: Gestão do planejamento urbano e Orçamento Participativo no Recife (1997–2002).* Ph.D. diss., Universidade Federal de Pernambuco, Recife.

Silva, Marcelo. 2002. "A construcao da participacao popular: Uma discussão sobre as condicões de possibilidade da experiência de democratizacão da gestão municipal em Porto Alegre." In *A Inovação Democratica no Brasil: Orçamento Participativo,* ed. Leonardo Avritzer and Zander Navarro. São Paulo: Cortez.

Silva, Neide. 2003. *Gestão participativa no Recife: Do PREZEIS ao Orçamento Participativo.* Recife: ETAPAS.

Silva, Neide Maria, Marcia Maria da Silva Amorim, and Antonio Torres Montenegro. 1988. *Movimento de bairro: Repetição/Invenção.* Recife: ETAPAS.

Singer, André. 1999. *Esquerda e Direita no Eleitorado Brasileiro: A identificação ideológica nas disputas presidenciais de 1989 e 1994.* São Paulo: EDUSP.

Singer, Paul. 1996. *Un governo de esquerda para todos: Luiza Erundina na Prefeitura de São Paulo (1989–1992).* São Paulo: Editora Brasiliense.

Skocpol, Theda. 1985. "Bringing the State Back In: Strategies of Analysis in Current Research." In *Bringing the State Back In,* ed. Peter Evans, Dietrich Rueschemeyer, and Theda Skocpol. New York: Cambridge University Press.

Smulovitz, Catalina, and Enrique Peruzzotti. 2000. "Societal Accountability in Latin America." *Journal of Democracy* 11:147–58.

Soares, José Arlindo. 1982. *A Frente do Recife e o Governo do Arraes: Nacionalismo em Crise, 1955–1964.* Rio de Janeiro: Paz e Terra.

————. 1996. *Mudanças e impasses na gestão das grandes cidades no Brasil (1986–1996).* Teses de Doutorado. Universidade de Brasília, Brasil.

————. 1998. *Os desafios de gestão municipal democrática: Recife.* Recife: Centro Josué de Castro.

Soler, Salvador. 1991. *O PREZIES: Um processo de participação popular na Formação da Cidade.* Dissertação de mestrado. Universidade Federal de Pernambuco.

Somers, Margaret R. 1993. "Citizenship and the Place of the Public Sphere: Law, Community, and Political Culture in the Transition to Democracy." *American Sociological Review* 58 (5): 587–620.

Souto, Anna Luiza Salles, Jorge Kayano, Marco Antonio de Almeida, and Victor Augusto Petrucci. 1995. *Como reconhecer um bom Governo.* São Paulo: Instituto Pólis.

Tarrow, Sidney. 1998. *Power in Movement: Social Movements and Contentious Politics.* 2d ed. New York: Cambridge University Press.

Tatagiba, Luciana. 2002. "Os conselhos gestores e a democratização das políticas públicas no Brasil." In *Sociedade Civil e Espaços Públicos no Brasil,* ed. Evalina Dagnino. São Paulo: Paz e Terra.

————. 2006. "Os desafios da articulção entre sociadade civil e sociadade política sob o marco da democracia gerencial: O caso do Projeto Rede Criança em Vitória/ES." In *A Disputa Pela Construção Democrática na América Latina,* ed. Evelina Dagnino, Alberto J. Olvera, and Aldo Panfichi. São Paulo: Paz e Terra.

Teixeira, Ana Cláudia. 2003. "Experiências de Orçamento Participativo no Brasil, 1997–2000." In *A Inovação Democrática no Brasil: O Orçamento Participativo,* ed. Leonardo Avritzer and Zander Navarro. São Paulo: Cortez Editores.

Teixeira, Ana Cláudia Chaves, and Maria do Carmo Albuquerque. 2005. *Orçamentos Participativos: Projetos politicos, partilha de poder e alcance democrático.* São Paulo: Instituto Pólis.

————. 2006. "Orçamentos Participativos: Projetos políticos, partilha de poder e alcance democrática." In *A Disputa Pela Construção Democrática na América Latina,* ed. Evelina Dagnino, Alberto J. Olvera, and Aldo Panfichi. São Paulo: Paz e Terra.

Tendler, Judith. 1997. *Good Government in the Tropics.* Baltimore: Johns Hopkins University Press.

Tersca, Laura. 2004. "Governo digital." *Cidades Vivas,* 76–77.

Thompson, E. P. 1966. *The Making of the English Working Class.* New York: Vintage Press.

Thomson, Ken. 2001. *From Neighborhood to Nation: The Democratic Foundations of Civil Society.* Hanover: University Press of New England.

Tocqueville, Alexis. 1969. *Democracy in America.* New York: Harper Perennial.

Tribunal Supremo Eleitoral de São Paulo. www.tse.gov.br/eleicoes/.

UAMPA. 1986. *A participação popular na administração municipal.* Porto Alegre: UAMPA.

Venturi, Gustavo. 1999. "Orçamento Participativo: Estudo junto aos participantes das plenárias regionais e temáticas de 99 (2^{fri} fase): Perfil e Avaliação." Mimeo.

Villas Boas, Renta. 1994. *Participação Popular nos Governos Locais.* São Paulo: Instituto Pólis.

Villas Boas, Renta, and Vera Telles. 1995. *Poder local, participação popular, construção da Cidadania*. São Paulo: Fórum Nacional de Participação Popular nas Administrações Municipais and Instituto Pólis.

Walzer, Michael. 1992. "The Civil Society Argument." In *Dimensions of Radical Democracy: Pluralism, Citizenship, Community*, ed. Chantal Mouffe. New York: Verso.

Wampler, Brian. 1997. "Popular Participation and Reform: Municipal Health Councils in São Paulo." In *Policymaking in a Redemocratized Brazil*. Vol. 1: *Decentralization and Social Policy*. LBJ School of Public Affairs, Policy Research Project Report 119.

———. 1999. "Orçamento Participativo: Os paradoxos da participação e governo no Recife." *Cadernos de Estudos Sociais* 15:343–73.

———. 2000a. "Guide to Participatory Budgeting." Available online: http://www.internationalbudget.org/cdrom/papers/home.htm#Participatory. March 8, 2007.

———. 2000b. *Private Executives, Legislative Brokers, and Participatory Publics: Building Local Democracy in Brazil*. PhD diss., University of Texas.

———. 2002. "Orçamento Participativo: Uma explicação para as amplas variações nos resultados." In *A Inovação Democratica no Brasil: O Orçamento Participativo*, ed. Leonardo Avritzer and Zander Navarro. São Paulo: Cortez.

———. 2004a. "The Diffusion of Participatory Budgeting Across Brazil." Paper prepared for the Latin America Studies Association conference, Las Vegas, Nev., October 7–9.

———. 2004b. "Expanding Accountability Through Participatory Institutions: Mayors, Citizens, and Budgeting in Three Brazilian Municipalities." *Latin American Politics and Society* 46:73–100.

———. 2004c. "Instituições, Associações e Interesses no Orçamento Participativo do São Paulo." In *Associativismo em São Paulo*, ed. Leonardo Avritzer. São Paulo: Edusp.

Wampler, Brian, and Leonardo Avritzer. 2004. "Participatory Publics: Civil Society and New Institutions in Democratic Brazil." *Comparative Politics* 36:291–312.

———. 2005. "The Spread of Participatory Democracy in Brazil: From Radical Democracy to Good Government." *Journal of Latin American Urban Studies* 7:37–51.

Weffort, Francisco. 1984. *Porque democracia?* São Paulo: Editora Brasiliense.

———. 1989. "Why Democracy?" In *Democratizing Brazil: Problems of Transition and Consolidation*, ed. Alfred Stepan. New York: Oxford University Press.

Weyland, Kurt. 1996. *Democracy Without Equity: Failures of Reform in Brazil*. Pittsburgh: University of Pittsburgh Press.

———. 2002. "Limitations of Rational-Choice Institutionalism for the Study of Latin American Politics." *Studies in Comparative International Development* 37:57–85.

Willis, Eliza, Christopher Garman, and Stephen Haggard. 2001. "Fiscal Decentralization: A Political Theory with Latin American Cases." *World Politics* 53:205–36.

Wolfe, Joel. 1993. *Working Women, Working Men: São Paulo and the Rise of Brazil's Industrial Working Class, 1900–1955*. Durham: Duke University Press.

Yashar, Deborah J. 2005. *Contesting Citizenship in Latin America: The Rise of Indigenous Movements and the Postliberal Challenge*. Cambridge: Cambridge University Press.

306   Bibliography

Government Documents

"90 dias de reconstrução." 2001. Prefeitura Municipal da Cidade de São Paulo, April.
"A população como parceira." 2003. Jornal do Orçamento Participativo. Prefeitura Municipal de Santo André.
"Acompanhamento financeiro Orçamento Participativo Regional: op 94 a 2004/ 05 Empreendimentos Concluídos." 2003. Prefeitura Municipal de Belo Horizonte.
"As prioridades para 1999." 1999. Jornal do Orçamento Participativo. Prefeitura Municipal de Santo André.
"Belo Horizonte comemora 10 anos de Orçamento Participativo." 2003. Prefeitura Municipal de Belo Horizonte.
"Distribuição do Orçamento Regionalizado." 1998. Secretaria de Políticas Sociais. Prefeitura da Municipal Cidade de Recife.
"Estrutura de Funcionamento do Programa Orçamento Participativo/ppb." 1998. *Secretaria de Políticas Sociais.* Prefeitura da Cidade de Recife.
Federal legislation 4.320. 1964, March.
"Fique de Olho: Informativo do Grupo de Articulação Cidadania Popular." 1998. Recife: gacip, no. 2:4.
"Ipatinga: Aqui você vive melhor." 2002. *Diário Oficial de Prefeitura Municipal de Ipatinga* (1994–2004). Prefeitura Municipal de Ipatinga.
"Ipatinga Hoje." 2003. Prefeitura Municipal de Ipatinga, September. Ano 2, N. 27.
"Número de participantes plenários regionais do Orçamento Participativo." 2004. Prefeitura Municipal de Porto Alegre.
"Número de reuniões da Secretaria do Orçamento Participativo e Gestão Cidadã." 2003. Prefeitura Municipal da Cidade Recife.
"op 10 Anos: Orçamento Participativo." 2003. Trabalho Pela Vida. Prefeitura Belo Horizonte.
"Orçamento Participativo." 1996. Prefeitura Municipal da Cidade de Recife. *Secretaria de Políticas Sócias.*
"Orçamento Participativo." 2003. Prefeitura Municipal da Cidade de São Paulo, December.
"Orçamento Participativo: A vontade do povo vai mostrar a sua força." 2002. Prefeitura Municipal de Blumenau.
"Orçamento Participativo: Democratizando o Dinheiro Público." 2002. Prefeitura Municipal de Rio Claro.
"Orçamento Participativo: Metodologia." 1995. Prefeitura Municipal da Cidade de Recife. *Secretaria de Políticas Sociais e Secretaria de Planjemento Urbano e Ambiental.*
"Orçamento Participativo: Plano de investimento regionalizado 1996." 1996. Prefeitura Municipal da Cidade de Recife. *Secretaria de Políticas Sociais e Secretaria de Planejamento Urbano e Ambiental.*
"Orçamento Participativo: Regimento interno, critérios gerias, técnicos e regionais." 2003. Prefeitura Municipal de Porto Alegre.
"Orçamento Participativo: 3 anos invertendo prioridades." 2003. Prefeitura Municipal de Recife.
"Orçamento Participativo 1997–2000: Rio Claro." 2001. Prefeitura de Rio Claro.

"Plano de Investimentos do Orçamento Participativo." 1998. Prefeitura Municipal de Blumenau.

"Plano de Obras e serviços do Orçamento Participativo 2003." 2003. Conselho do Orcamento Participativo. Prefeitura Municipal da Cidade de São Paulo, August.

"Plano regional de empreendimentos Orçamento Participativo 2003/2004." 2003. Prefeitura Municipal de Belo Horizonte.

"Prestação de Contas." 2003. Prefeitura Municipal de São Paulo, November.

"Prestação de contas do Orçamento Participativo." 1999. Prefeitura Municipal de Blumenau.

"Processo participativo de elaboração do Orçamento Público." 1993. Prefeitura Municipal de São José dos Campos.

"Programas de obras 2004: Ate 13° COMPOR." 2004. Prefeitura Municipal de Ipatinga. *Secretaria Municipal de Obras Publicas,* February 27.

"Quado da relação entre o previsto e o executado pela URB/PCR no Orçamento Participativo: 1996 a 1999." 2000. Prefeitura Municipal da Cidade de Recife. Secretaria de Políticas Sociais.

"Retratos da cidade: Subsídios ao Conselho Municipal do Orçamento; Santo André Orçamento Participativo—1999/2000." 2000. Prefeitura Municipal de Santo André.

"Sintese das emendas apresentadas." *Relatario da Comissão de Finanças e Orçamento, 1994–1998.* Recife: Câmara Municipal da Cidade de Recife.

"Sistema de acompanhamento do Orçamento Participativo." 1998. Secretaria de Políticas Socials. Prefeitura Municipal da Cidade de Recife.

"Venha participar do planejamento de Rio Claro." 2001. Prefeitura Municipal de Rio Claro.

"Você Participa, A Cidade Melhora." 2003. Prefeitura Municipal de Santo André.

INDEX

www.ingramcontent.com/pod-product-compliance
Lightning Source LLC
Chambersburg PA
CBHW021850020426
42334CB00013B/272